LAST TRAIN TO FREEDOM

A Young Jewish Family's
Escape from Behind
the Iron Curtain

GALINA CHERNY

LAST TRAIN TO FREEDOM: A YOUNG JEWISH FAMILY'S
ESCAPE FROM BEHIND THE IRON CURTAIN

For permission requests, write to the author,
addressed "Attention: Permissions" at

galina@galinacherny.com

Visit Galina online at www.galinacherny.com

Cover design by Alex Cherny www.alexcherny.com

Print ISBN: 978-0-578-37696-7

First Edition: November 2022
NELS Publishing

To the memory of my parents, Yoseph and Bella.
Thank you for loving me enough to let me go.

To my husband, Yan.
I would do this life with you all over again.

To our sons, Eugene and Alex.
The greatest joy of my life is to be your mother.
This story is yours.

To our beloved grandchildren, Nathan,
Ella, Liam, and Simon.
Live with gratitude. Cherish the
value of freedom. Be good.
You have my heart forever.

CONTENTS

Author's Note

For much of the twentieth century, Jews were persecuted in the Soviet Union. It would seem absurd to anyone living in a free society that, while the Jews were unwanted in their country, when they petitioned to leave, the government denied them permission to do so.

This vicious cycle pushed Soviet Jews to assimilate and become invisible, losing their Jewish identity. Until, galvanized by Israel's victory in the Six-Day War of 1967, many regained their optimism, feeling a renewed resolve to leave the USSR and move to Israel. The four thousand Jews permitted to leave the Soviet Union in the late 1960s led the Exodus during my time.

Between the years 1970 and 1979, succumbing to the international pressure and the economic sanctions imposed by the United States, the Soviet authorities granted over two hundred thousand Jews permission to leave the country with Israeli visas. Fifty-one thousand of them left in 1979. Of that number, thirty-four thousand declared their desire to come to America instead of Israel. That request was possible once they reached Vienna, Austria, the first vital stop on the long refugee route.

My husband, John, and I were among the thirty-four thousand who escaped in 1979 with a dream of finding a home in the United States.

The three most common questions I get from curious strangers are:

"Where are you from?"

"How did you come to America?"

"Why did you leave Russia?"

While the questions are common sense and straightforward, the answers are complex, conflicting, and confusing, and I've struggled with a response. *Last Train to Freedom* is my attempt to explore these topics in the hope of uncovering the answers for myself.

Many of my friends and family members are immigrants themselves or the children and grandchildren of immigrants—each with their own story of struggle, loss, perseverance, and triumph. In some ways, our stories are similar, and yet they are unique, as each one of us is. That's true even within my immediate family. My older son Eugene remembered how his schoolmates called him "Commie" and teased him as if he, single-handedly, had run the Soviet regime. His younger brother Alex, who had been born in America, revealed his awkwardness around the Russian-speaking people as a child because he didn't understand what they were saying, and their loud, no-personal-space demeanor unnerved him. Eugene and Alex have their own stories, and so will their children, whose backgrounds are rich and broad, like America herself. John and I, besides the challenges we experienced together, each confronted our individual trials, leaving the Motherland and adapting to our new home in the US. By sharing our stories we connect to one another, and with this connection we will understand ourselves and the world.

While writing, I discovered family events, including a mystery behind my first name and the tale of my uncle's family. I found profound appreciation for my parents—both their struggles and their sacrifices. I considered our relationship through their eyes, regarding them as individuals and not only as my mother and father.

Consequently, this book is about introspection and self-reflection.

I wrote about what I encountered, either from being in the situation myself or learning about an event from Mama, Papa, Uncle Vova, aunts, Cousin Sonia, my closest friends, and John. The events described in this book have all happened; however, they may lack factual precision because they are inherently a product of my interpretation. My heart and soul lived my story alongside my mind.

In the summer of 1988, nine years after our arrival in the US, John and I traveled to Europe for the first time. We flew into London's Heathrow Airport. Following the crowd from the airplane to the security area, we noticed a red carpet line for the US citizens. With slight hesitation—not sure we "belonged" there—we walked on the red carpet toward the security booth. There, a uniformed woman glanced at our passports. She read our customs forms and looked at the passports again, raising an eyebrow.

My heart dropped into my stomach—a border check sparked a frightful memory. *What's wrong?* I wondered as I watched the woman pick up a pen, cross out my answer to the "country of origin" question, and write the US instead of what I had written: USSR. "Welcome to London, Mr. and Mrs. Cherny," she said, returning our stamped passports.

A rush of tears blurred my vision, making me look ridiculous. *My country of origin is the United States of America—in the same way it is the country of origin for those who were born here.* I will never forget that moment—there isn't another country in the world that claims you as her own whether you were born there or were "adopted." And so my story is also a pledge of gratitude and a love letter to America—not a perfect country, just the best there is.

Some ninety million people living in the United States of America are immigrants themselves or children born to immigrant parents. That's ninety million stories! Thank you for reading mine.

Prologue

No Right of Return

May 15, 1979—Kiev, USSR

Click, click, bang, bang. For as long as I can remember, every morning in my parents' house began with the kitchen noises; they comforted me as a little girl. All was well in the world if Mama was in the kitchen! As a teenager, I hated the early morning kitchen noises. Even on weekends, my mother inhabited the kitchen by six, and she made sure Papa, Misha, and I appreciated her dedication in taking care of us. *Click, click, bang, bang...* As an adult, I came to admire her resilience, her ability to run the household as a well-oiled machine, and her tireless commitment to her family. She seemed invincible.

That morning, the familiar sounds consoled me for the last time. I looked down at Zhenya sleeping next to me, comforted by *Babushka's*, Grandmother's, kitchen noises. All seemed well in the world for another moment. I closed my eyes, anticipating the comfort of the familiar for a few more minutes, but I felt a tight knot in my throat and a spasm in my stomach. I had been ignoring these sensations for weeks, or maybe months, or even years, to be honest. Every moment since Yan and I met five years earlier led to this day—this final day in my home. The home my grandfather had died defending. The home my father had fought to protect. The home of my childhood dreams. The country I loved passionately for so long until I couldn't anymore.

We had prepared for this day for almost a year, and yet it snuck up, flooding me with emotions like the waters of the Dnieper River flooded the streets of Kiev in the spring. *Just start moving.* Pulling myself against the gravity of my body, I slipped out of bed and stood in the middle of what had been my room since I was nineteen. Yan moved in when we got married, and we welcomed Zhenya here nine months later. *In this room, I became a wife and a mother, with my mother and father sleeping next door.* I smiled at the memory.

If it weren't for the lucky circumstance of Yan's mother immigrating to America two years earlier, which allowed us to move into her communal apartment, we would still live with my parents like most adult children in the Soviet Union lived with theirs.

My eight-square-meter room seemed bigger before. I took a mental image of the surrounding space. A fold-out couch served as our bed, and a picture of the three of us in a simple wooden frame hung on the wall above the couch. We had taken this picture a little over a year ago, when Zhenya turned two. I glanced at the coffee table by the window and a chair on the opposite wall. *How did we ever fit a crib in here?* Tears filled my eyes, blurring my vision. A single tear slid down, followed by another and another, dripping down my face, leaving a taste of salt on my lips. *No...no...no... I can't cry. Not today. Just keep moving.*

There was nothing left to do. We'd finished packing before Yan had left two days ago for Chop—a small town in Western Ukraine bordering Czechoslovakia and Hungary made famous by the Jewish emigration of the '70s. Yan took the same train from the Kiev central train station that Zhenya and I would take that night. He should have arrived in Chop yesterday morning and would now assist emigrating Jewish families navigating the border process.

Helping the guards weigh the luggage and assisting departing Jews to repack their belongings after the guards' search were among the duties he took on, along with other men who had arrived ahead of their families. The men either rented beds from the locals or spent a few nights at the station. I hoped Yan had found a bed.

Years later, I would come to appreciate the unspoken—almost eerie—sense of camaraderie among strangers, who would most likely never thank each other for the help they had received or see one another again. Each departing family had one goal—to board the evening train from Chop to Bratislava, Czechoslovakia—the first stop of their exodus from the Soviet Union.

Even with the help from volunteers like Yan, refugees—stateless by then—often missed the train. The guards seemed to have made a game of delaying the exit process. If they suspected even a single item deemed prohibited by the latest unwritten rules, they would empty the contents of the luggage onto the platform and ravage it, pushing and shoving belongings of others with their feet and AK-47 rifles. This often caused refugees to be late for the train to Bratislava.

The "official" list of prohibited items, quantities, and weight limitations changed often; plus individual guard teams altered them without notice. At the time of our departure, each adult could take with them a few jewelry items: one gold chain, one ring in addition to a wedding band, and a pair of earrings for women; a predetermined quantity of Russian gemstones like jade, garnet, and amber; two bottles of vodka and champagne, two photo cameras, and some Russian souvenirs. The most popular among the souvenirs were *matryoshkas*—the Russian nesting dolls. Painted wooden, lacquer jewelry boxes and wooden spoons of different sizes came next.

Why the limitations and restrictions on such ordinary things? Good question. It might have had something to do with the fact that refugees sold these items in local currency, helping themselves to survive on the route to the West. What about the limitations on grocery items and food? A family could bring a loaf of bread, a few cans of meat and tuna, a small amount of deli meat and cheese, and some fruit. Another "why" for which I don't have an answer. I suppose dealing with "enemies of the state" justified any form of humiliation and insult.

In the attempt to reduce the chance of issues at the border, Yan and I adhered to the word-of-mouth list—which not a single person we met during the immigration process had seen. Still, the guards confiscated items at will and either threw them into the garbage in front of our eyes (which was often the case with food) or declared them "property of the state" and took them without explanation. Nothing was trivial.

Zhenya and I were scheduled to arrive in Chop a little after eight in the morning, and Yan would meet us at the station. *What if we don't make it onto the train to Bratislava?* The thought of being stranded at the border with a three-year-old, the luggage, no money, and no documents made me cringe.... *Don't think. Keep moving.*

I opened the window, glancing at my sleeping son. Disturbed by the commotion, Zhenya wiggled his body, pulled the blanket closer to his face, and smiled in his sleep. Fresh morning air entered the room, bringing in the sweet fragrance of lilac. Nothing says spring in Kiev like lilacs. Mama and I planted a small lilac bush outside my window seven years earlier when we first moved into this three-room apartment on the first floor of a brand new seven-story building. Papa "supervised" the project, holding a cigarette in his right hand and keeping his left hand in the pocket of his trousers—his signature pose. An eloquent speaker, self-taught caricaturist, and musician, he was charismatic and had a distinct raspy singing voice that resembled his idol, the legendary and beloved Soviet artist, Leonid Utyosov. My father's talents, however, did not include any kind of physical labor or handyman skills. He couldn't hang a picture frame on the wall if his life depended on it, although he would supervise the heck out of anyone who could with utmost confidence.

I stood by the window, inhaling the exquisite scent. The bush had grown over the years, and now its branches, heavy with blooming pale-violet and dark-mauve clusters of lilac flowers, reached inside through the open window. Yan and I had our first date in this room six years earlier. So much had happened since that night... *Click, click, bang, bang.* My daydreaming interrupted, I got dressed and walked out of the room to face what would become the toughest day of my life.

Before Yan left, we stacked our luggage in the hallway against the wall. The two brown suitcases were packed with a few changes of clothes for each of us, a small electric burner, a travel-size immersion heater, four cans of stewed meat (*tushonka*), and four cans of sardines. Wrapped in our clothing were two bottles of vodka, two bottles of Sovetskoe Shampanskoe (Soviet champagne)—a single champagne label available in the USSR—and a bottle of men's cologne. We also carried one photo camera (the second one didn't fit our budget), three sets of *matryoshkas*, and a half-dozen small wooden spoons. Along the way we would sell or exchange for food everything except the electric gadgets. I would stash some food items for the next few days in a separate bag and make it visible to the guards in hopes they wouldn't throw it away, suspecting I tried to hide it.

The previous night, I packed two of Zhenya's favorite books after reading them to him at bedtime: *Zhivaya Shlyapa* (*A Live Hat*) by Nikolai Nosov and *Zolotoy Klyuchik Ili Priklyucheniya Buratino* (*The Golden Key* or *The Adventures of Pinocchio*) by Aleksei Tolstoy. I needed to remember where they were to retrieve them on the train. *Where is Cheburashka?* An exotic creature, whose fuzzy body resembled a koala bear with large monkey-like ears, Cheburashka—a toy made after a beloved cartoon character—was coming with us.

5

It was the only toy Zhenya would bring—leaving Cheburashka behind was not an option. *There he is—hiding behind the baul, a large handmade duffle bag stuffed to the brim with three pillows, two blankets, three sets of cotton sheets with pillowcases, and a couple of towels. Baul* production became an underground industry during the '70s, when the Jewish immigration to Israel and America reached its peak. Made of waterproof canvas, *bauls* were lightweight, which made them perfect for packing bedding.

By now the kitchen noises had reached a crescendo, which was my mother's way of telling me I should've been up by now to make breakfast for Zhenya before he woke up. Since the day Zhenya was born, feeding her grandson—her Zhenechka—became Mama's primary mission in life. What he ate. How he ate. When he ate. She discussed the topics of Zhenya's food consumption with anyone who would listen, like any Jewish grandmother would. *Will she ever forgive me for depriving her of this joy?*

Click, click, bang, bang.

I know, Mama. I know. I've been married for five years and living without your supervision for the last two, taking care of my son and husband. I got this. Stop teaching me the lessons you taught me at fourteen when I looked after Papa and Misha like they were children, while you had a heart attack and stroke in the same year. Enough parenting, Mama. I am twenty-six! Just give me a hug.

The kitchen smelled heavenly. Mama was peeling and slicing potatoes, skillfully tossing them from a cracked wooden cutting board into a large frying pan sizzling with oil. They were golden brown and crispy on the outside, soft and flaky on the inside—the very best. Yan would miss his favorite breakfast.

Mama turned toward me, still holding the knife in her hand. Her eyes were red and puffy, lacking their youthful spark. Her face was pale, ridden with anguish. Her lips looked faded without her signature red lipstick. My mother was religious about putting on her lipstick as soon as she got dressed in the morning. She wouldn't even take garbage out without it! She wore an apron over a plain dress. Short, dark-brown, almost black hair framed her round face with soft curls. At fifty-seven, she had no gray hair and looked young and full of energy. But that morning, her youthfulness drowned in grave sadness. She put down the knife.

"Dochenka," she said, addressing me in one of many endearing diminutives for daughter, "promise to write four letters to us every week."

"I promise, Mama," I said, not recognizing my voice. She turned away, wiping her eyes with a kitchen towel; then she picked up her knife and tossed more potatoes on the skillet. *Why the four letters?* I didn't ask, though I wound up writing four letters a week for nine years.

Papa walked into the kitchen after his morning cigarette. He'd stopped smoking indoors after Zhenya was born, but Misha and I had grown up watching him enjoy his cigarettes inside the apartment early in the morning, before and after each meal, while he read and all the times in between. Heck, he'd been sending me to buy his cigarettes for him since I was seven years old, at an old tobacco and beer *budka*—a raggedy kiosk across the street from our apartment on Spasskaya Street. This errand became a part of my early childhood memories. The area around the *budka* was jam-packed at all hours of the day with regular patrons, our neighbors—old men, tipsy most of the time. They drank beer from dirty glass jars, swearing and spitting on the ground between sips. The men—who smelled of stale beer mixed with a musty smell of cigarette smoke—greeted me with friendly smiles and patted me on the head, stepping aside to make room for me to squeeze between them to the counter that they were otherwise blocking. I would hand the fifteen kopeks Papa had given me to the toothless man in the booth—also half-drunk—and return home with a pack of Prima and a box of matches, smelling of stale beer and cigarettes myself.

My father was a creature of habit, and he developed most of those habits during his twenty-four years of military service. Smoking unfiltered cigarettes was one of them. Obsession with immaculate appearance was another. He retired from his civilian job six years earlier at sixty. However, every morning he got dressed as he did when he worked. Today was no exception. He wore a pair of brown wool slacks and a freshly ironed white shirt with sleeves rolled up twice, hitting below his elbows. *That's the one I pressed for him last night.* Ironing my father's shirts military style was the skill I'd learned at ten. He would undoubtedly complete the look with a blazer and tie before we left for the train station.

"Handsome as always," I noted, kissing his cleanly shaven cheek and inhaling the familiar aroma of his cigarettes lingering around him. Silvery hair, combed slightly to the right and back, revealed his prominent forehead. He gave me a long hug without saying a word. I leaned forward and down a bit to reach his shoulders and hugged him back. I'd been two centimeters taller than Papa since the age of thirteen, which, to my astonishment, gave him a great deal of joy. My father was my worst critic, a very strict and impatient parent, and my best dance partner until Yan. He sensed music like it was his second skin, and I felt enchanted waltzing in his arms.

Papa sat down at the small kitchen table with a cup of burning-hot tea my mother had made for him, and I joined Mama at the stove. We had a busy day ahead. A few friends and relatives who didn't make it to our farewell gathering over the weekend would stop by. Misha was on his way to join us for breakfast. A college friend arranged for a car to pick us up at 3:30. We should be at the station with plenty of time to catch the 5:15 train to Chop.

The door into the kitchen flew open and Zhenya ran into his *deda's* arms—missing the hot cup still sitting on the table in front of my father by a hair—demanding to continue their drawing project from the day before. At three and a half, he sensed his grandfather would do anything for him. The two had shared a passion for drawing ever since Zhenya turned one. On Zhenya's first birthday, Papa bought him a set of coloring pencils and a drawing album, insisting his grandson was an extraordinary child (his exact words), ready to be introduced to the world of art. Comfortable on *Deda's* lap, Zhenya watched in awe as dogs, cats, birds, flowers, and trees appeared on a blank piece of paper as *Deda* moved a pencil across the page. There began a lifelong love of art for Zhenya, who later passed it down to his brother.

On this last day together, *Deda* and his grandson spent the morning in the living room, drawing. Mama and I listened from the kitchen as they discussed coloring strategies and where to place various objects on a page. Zhenya spoke with ease and grace, using words far beyond his age. Papa patiently listened to his suggestions and gently guided his ideas. *What happened to my strict, impatient Papa? How I would've loved to be on the receiving end of his gentle side growing up. Wonder if he would've sent Zhenya to get his cigarettes at the* budka. I chuckled at the thought and then interrupted their work to set the table for breakfast. Fried potatoes, herring, scrambled eggs, and a chopped salad of tomatoes, cucumbers, and onions mixed with sour cream. We paired it with *Ukrainski khleb*—a dark round loaf of bread with the most delicious crust—cut into generous slices, and butter, of course. The house smelled of childhood and everything so dear.

The front door burst open and a second later, Misha stormed into the room, commanding the space around him. I noticed a fresh haircut—his almost jet-black hair cut short, impeccably parted on the right side. His eyes resembled Mama's: amber brown with a mischievous sparkle. And he was tan! Most people were still wearing jackets, but Misha's skin, naturally olive, looked golden-brown from the spring sun. In another couple of weeks, he would achieve a perfect tan from head to toe without even trying.

"*Privet*" he waved to everyone, walking toward Zhenya, who leapt into his uncle's open arms for an adventure he knew would await. Misha picked him up, threw him up in the air, and caught him quickly, spinning him around the room until the two of them fell on the sofa, laughing and giggling.

"*Escho, escho*," screamed Zhenya, locking both hands around Misha's knees in a determined hold. "More" they went, again and again, until Mama demanded everyone sit down right away. She couldn't handle the chaos Misha's arrival had created. She scolded him for being late, for almost dropping Zhenya on the floor, and if he didn't join us at the table that second, she would think of something else he did wrong. Never mind that Misha was thirty-one. Mama still parented him much more than she ever did with me. Thankfully, Misha didn't defend himself as he would've done any other day, and we had a peaceful, civilized meal. None of us spoke of the fact we would most likely not sit at the same table for a very long time, if ever. It turned out to be never.

After breakfast, my parents took Zhenya to the playground. It was their last outing together. I closed the door behind them and watched Misha check our luggage, opening and closing the locks, pulling on the handles to make sure they were sturdy enough for the weight. I cleared the table and made us coffee, waiting for him to finish his task.

"Misha, we need to talk," I said when he came into the kitchen. He sat down at the small foldout table, moving a cup of hot black coffee closer, and began pouring sugar into the cup. One teaspoon, two, three, four… Considering the sugar spilled on the way from the sugar bowl to the cup, by my estimate he ended up with two and half teaspoons in his coffee. Familiar picture. I waited for him to look at me, but he kept staring at the cup, focused on stirring the sugar.

My "younger" older brother. It wasn't just our mother who hovered over him, bailing him out of any mess he made in his life; I was guilty of that, too. Almost five years my senior, with a heart of gold, Misha had been a carefree kid for much of his life.

"Misha, we submitted paperwork for Mama and Papa to follow us," I blurted.

"I know," he said, stirring his coffee.

"They could get their permission any day. You know what that means?"

He stared at his coffee. Not responding.

"They will be expelled from the Communist Party! How will they ever survive that? Please be there for them. You must help them get out of here in one piece."

He looked up at me, his eyes blurry from tears. "Don't worry..."

"What about you? Will you try to leave?" I said.

"No. Not me. I hate the Communists, but I can't imagine building my life all over again in another country. And I love Kiev. I couldn't live anywhere else."

I loved Kiev, too. The beautiful Dnieper River crashes its waves onto the streets in the spring. Chestnut trees line the boulevards like glorious soldiers. Beautiful parks adorn the hills along the riverbank. Tulips and lilacs grace the city with brilliant hues in late April and May. Snowfall in the winter. The unforgettable color palette in the autumn. Hot summer days. I could walk the entire city with my eyes closed, recounting memories in every corner.

"I love Kiev, too," I said. We drank our coffee in silence.

I didn't know it then, but I was leaving Misha not to help my parents emigrate but to help Mama take care of our father until his last breath.

A fresh spring morning turned into a sunny midday faster than I wanted. We were on a last stretch, greeting relatives and friends who stopped by to spend these last few hours with me and Zhenya.

In my mother's family, the relational lines between family members were so confusing. My "cousins" were actually my second cousins, the children of Mama's cousins, whom I called aunts and uncles. Now, my adult sons call my cousins "cousins." I don't try to explain "who is who" anymore; they were and always will be my family. Papa's side was more straightforward that way.

The front door was open and people appeared in the living room without me noticing when they entered. My cousins (second cousins) came with their parents and grandmother, Bella (Mama's aunt). My high school friend, Vera, arrived with her husband and mother. A childhood friend's mother stopped by with a coloring book for Zhenya. She said her daughter—a Jew herself—wouldn't come, afraid it might damage her reputation at work if anyone found out about her association with the Jews who were emigrating. I understood. Mama's Aunt Basya didn't want to be there for the goodbyes. She couldn't bear it. Several neighbors came, along with a few friends of Yan's who didn't see him off.

Bella asked me to step outside with her.

"Galochka, *ne zabud nus*...don't forget us...don't forget my children...help them...don't forget them...," she begged, her voice trembling.

"*Horosho,* Bella, all right. I won't forget." I hugged her tightly, not wanting to let her go. My dear Bella... She didn't get to see her family making it to America years later. She would've been so happy.

Mama and I were clearing the table, bringing food out, and clearing the table again to make room for more food. Misha opened bottle after bottle of vodka, making sure everyone had their glass full. Papa looked after Zhenya, who desperately and often unsuccessfully tried to dodge kisses and hugs from the adults he didn't recognize. People quietly chatted in the living room, hung out in the hallway,

12

and once in a while peeked into the kitchen to see if we needed help. Just like at our farewell a few days earlier, the gathering resembled a funeral more than a celebration of our future and new beginnings.

At some point, my father invited everyone to a "concert." He set a "stage" for Zhenya in the middle of the room by using two dining room chairs. Everyone found a spot to sit down or stand nearby and cheered my little artist, who enthusiastically climbed onto the stage. He had no fear of public appearances—another trait passed on from grandfather to his grandson. For the next forty minutes, Zhenya gave the last performance in his grandparents' house. From popular children's rhymes to *Deda's* favorite World War II songs to popular Russian pop star Alla Pugacheva, he delighted his fans, who clapped while wiping their tears as Zhenya poured his heart out, having a blast.

He didn't know that in another hour he would leave this home, these people, this city, this country to never return. He didn't know he was no longer a citizen of the land, where his roots traced generations back. He didn't know his parents were called traitors because they wanted a chance for a better life for him and themselves. Letting a three-year-old in on our plan ahead of time could have had severe repercussions: If the word got out to his teachers at *sadik, daycare*, he could have been mistreated without us knowing.

A little after 3:00 in the afternoon, a friend announced that the car waited outside. It was almost time.

"Let's sit down," Papa said, "*na dorogy.*" It is an old Russian tradition to sit quietly for a few minutes before a long journey. Papa, Mama, Misha, and I sat next to each other on the sofa. Zhenya crawled into his uncle's lap and cloaked his arms around Misha's neck, holding on for dear life. Others settled around us wherever they could find a spot. As if by command, everyone lowered their gaze into the stillness of the moment.

13

"It's time." Papa broke the silence.

"We are going on the train to meet with Papa in another city," I said to Zhenya, peeling him from Misha.

"Where is Papa? In Moscow?" Zhenya asked.

"Yes, in Moscow." Even at the last hour, I was nervous to say out loud that we were leaving for good and we would meet Papa at the border city of Chop. Zhenya clapped his hands, smiling, then looked at me with concern.

"Are *Babulya* and *Dedulya* coming with us?" he said.

"No, my dear love, not today. They will come soon," I said, hoping I spoke the truth. We climbed into a Chaika, a Russian luxury automobile arranged by a college friend as a goodbye gift. Distracted by the fancy car, Zhenya accepted my answer for a little while.

Misha sat in the front seat with the driver. My parents joined us in the back. The car moved, and I gave one last look at the lilac bush. Mama touched my hand, and I squeezed hers. Papa sat erect, looking straight in front of him, twirling an unlit cigarette between his thumb and index finger. We sat in silence, listening to Zhenya's chatter.

"Look at this car, Mama!" he exclaimed. "What does it say?" he asked, pointing at street signs. "Misha, Misha, are you coming with us to meet with Papa?"

The Kiev Vokzal (train station) was a twenty-minute drive from my parents' apartment in one of the oldest neighborhoods, Podol. I had lived in this part of town my entire life and recognized every street, every corner, and every back alley. As if giving me a chance to say goodbye, the driver took us through familiar streets, by the riverbank, through the city center, Khreshchatyk Street, Besarabsky market, Kiev University, and toward the main entrance to the *vokzal*, the Central Vokzal building. The building was an impressive structure with simple, elegant lines highlighting the Ukrainian

Baroque style of the seventeenth and eighteenth centuries found in other buildings around the 1,400-year-old city.

I loved Kiev Vokzal, and I loved the trains. My most fun childhood memories are of traveling by train with my parents when Papa moved from one military assignment to another. There was nothing more adventurous than being in a small cabin of a sleeping car. Our parents slept on the two bottom beds. Misha and I took the top ones. I spent hours looking out the window, pretending to live in the places we passed while being rocked by the rhythmical motion of a moving train. The hypnotic *clickety-clack* made for a perfect lullaby at night. During the day, we drank tea from tall glasses in a *podstakannik,* a glass holder. I dipped a hard sugar cube into my steaming hot tea long enough for the cube to get softer on the outside and remain hard in the middle, and bit into it as it fell apart in my mouth, exploding with sweetness. Such a Russian way to drink tea! Boiled eggs, chicken cutlets, and *Ukrainski khleb*—I still remember the smell of this bread—with butter were our breakfast, lunch, and dinner. Mama always made enough food to feed an army, and she shared with fellow travelers, making instant connections with people. Her ability to build relationships so effortlessly was a marvel to me.

"Zhenya will enjoy drinking tea on the train. He loves tea," I reflected. Minutes later, our car approached the Central Station building, gracefully heading up the Kiev Vokzal.

As a kid, I loved walking through the Central Station building to the train tracks. The hustle and bustle, the constant announcements over the loudspeaker, the rush on the platform by people trying to get down from the train or to board a train—it all gave me a sense of adventure, and I rushed with everyone else to be a part of it, skipping and hopping all the way.

That day, however, my legs wobbled with every step. My mouth was dry and my heart pounded in my throat. I was freezing, even though I had on a warm knitted cardigan and a pair of pants. My hands were cold and clammy. *Where is Zhenya?* I held his hand a second ago. Raw panic surged through my body... I looked around. Misha walked a few steps in front of me, carrying Zhenya on his shoulders while Zhenya swung Cheburashka, his toy, in the air. I saw my parents out of the corner of my eye, walking to my left. A friend and my cousins were carrying our luggage, placing each piece next to one another on the platform, where the last car of our train should stop. The authorities (whomever they were) had allocated the last car to the departing Jews.

Dozens of people crowded the Jewish section of the platform. They huddled in groups, standing shoulder to shoulder around their luggage, protecting their suitcases, bags, boxes, musical instruments, baby strollers, and their last minutes together. Many wore winter coats despite the pleasant spring afternoon. Those were the émigrés—wearing their heaviest clothing to lighten their luggage. Yan and I had left our winter clothes behind, banking on being accepted in Los Angeles, where we were told "summer was the only season."

The atmosphere would have seemed eerie to an observer, something out of a grim movie. Small children ran around, jumping over the luggage, laughing, eager to turn the platform into a playground, while their parents attempted to shush them. Older children—more conscious of what was happening—hung near the adults, who looked ghastly. The laughter of the little kids was often drowned in bursts of sobs and moans from the adults. Like others, we stood around the luggage, murmuring. No crying or sobbing in this group. *I am freezing.* My body seemed to be dislocated from my head. I answered questions without hearing myself. Every muscle gave in to gravity. I noticed my father standing away from the group, holding Zhenya's hand. This was not his scene. Mama stood next to me, saying something, but I couldn't hear her voice.

Two men, dressed in dark civilian suits, walked back and forth. They seemed to engage in brief exchanges while scanning the platform. Others warned us to expect an undercover KGB presence and suggested that the best way to not call their attention was to avoid eye contact. As if by command, we all looked down when they walked by us.

Every five minutes, the buzzing stopped and the crowd froze while train arrival and departure announcements came over the loudspeaker. We listened, breathing a sigh of relief: not us yet.

"You didn't forget Zhenya's books and snacks?" Not waiting for my reply, Mama continued: "He doesn't look well. He's catching a cold. Make sure he wears his hat on the train, and please keep him away from the window, or he may get another ear infection." I nodded.

"Do you have all the documents?" Papa asked for the tenth time. I didn't notice him coming closer. "Keep them on you at all times," he ordered.

"*Respected passengers, may I have your attention, please.… Kiev-Chop-Uzhgorod train will arrive on platform number 3 in five minutes.*" The voice over the loudspeaker sent chills down my spine. I turned toward the direction of the train, every nerve electrified. My body wanted to run, but I remained still. The rumbling sound of the approaching train grew louder and louder.

I grabbed Zhenya. Together, we watched the locomotive pulling the train toward the station while chugging engines and screaming steam cut through the peaceful afternoon sky with a vengeance. As the steel giant slowed, screeching loudly, panic erupted around us. The crying crescendoed and people moved like bees in a hive, pulling their bags closer to the edge of the platform, yelling at the kids, giving each other last-minute instructions while crying, hugging, and kissing, all at the same time.

The train came to a full stop, and we realized the last car had ended up outside the length of the platform, making boarding much more difficult, especially for those with small children. Misha exploded with anger, cursing like the drunks at the *budka*, threatening to escalate the unfairness of the situation. *To whom, though?* I begged him to calm down. The doors of the train opened for boarding. I watched my friends drag our luggage across the tracks. Other families were doing the same. There were no porters to be found in the Jewish area, of course; we were on our own.

Misha took Zhenya from my arms to settle him in our sleeper cabin and look after our luggage, leaving me to say my goodbyes to friends and relatives, most of whom I knew I would never see again. Mama and Papa stood shoulder to shoulder, looking toward the last car. Mama rested her wrist on Papa's forearm—*pod-ruchku*.

"Do you have all your documents?" Papa said.

"I think Zhenechka is catching a cold," Mama said. That was our goodbye. My mother and father were part of the *steel* generation who had endured, stood tall, and didn't complain. And I was their daughter. There were no tears. None that we would show each other.

"*Poka. Poka. Do vstrechi!* Bye… See you soon!" I said, hugging Mama, then Papa, giving each a quick peck on the cheek. I stepped off the platform, waved to the group, and walked across the train tracks to climb into the car.

Stripped of our citizenship and our livelihood, denounced by the government and ostracized by neighbors and some friends, we were leaving our home under the law of "no right of return."

Write four letters a week… Tell us everything… Don't let Zhenechka forget us… Do vstrechi… Don't forget us… Write… Udachi… Good luck… Proschai… Farewell…

1

Worlds Apart

A Boy from Podol

Hunching over a stack of papers left by his father on the dining table, a ten-year-old Yan was reading "The Secret Speech," delivered by Soviet leader Nikita Khrushchev in February 1956 at a closed session of the Twentieth Communist Party Congress, denouncing Joseph Stalin. The text of the speech found its way to many homes in the months after the congress, even though it wouldn't be published in the press for decades. I doubt Efim meant for his young son to get his hands and eyes on the speech, exposing the atrocities Stalin had committed against millions of Soviet citizens, but it was too late.

Yan pored over the forbidden text. He didn't notice when the light from the afternoon sun rays turned into the moonlight, beaming through the window onto the pages as he wiped his tears with the back of his hand, trying to understand the complex and cruel world around him. Years later Yan would tell me about this night, and by then I would know him so well it would feel almost like a memory of my own. This night in 1956 began his journey to seek freedom.

By the time Yan was twelve, his dream of escaping the Soviet Union was vivid. It almost came to fruition when his mother tried to send him to America to live with her eldest brother, who had left Russia in the early 1900s and settled in New York. Her plan didn't work—it was unfathomable financially and logistically.

Yan's dream only got stronger with time. It was no surprise that he refused to join Komsomol, the last of the three Soviet Communist youth organizations.

The Soviet government devised a simple but brilliant strategy for indoctrinating generations of its citizens with Communist ideas. The conditioning began at seven—when children started their school years. Each first-grader became *Oktyabryonok,* a Young Octobrist who wore a red five-pointed badge with a picture of Vladimir Lenin as a child. Children wore this badge to school every day, on their uniform near their heart. At nine, Young Octobrists pledged to love the Motherland and the Communist Party leaders when they became *Pionery* and joined the All-Union Lenin Pioneer Organization. There, they would proudly wear its symbol—the red silk necktie—and solemnly salute, during formal school events, with the right hand half-raised toward their forehead. At fourteen, most students transitioned from *Pionery* to *Komsomol,* where they remained until the age of twenty-eight. *Komsomol* was not mandatory, but it was highly encouraged by Soviet culture as an honor.

Yan's refusal to join *Komsomol* caused quite a commotion among the school officials. He received a strong warning that his future career might be in jeopardy. Given that he had no plans to build his career in the Soviet Union, Yan ignored the admonition; it was only a matter of time before he escaped.

Yan grew up in Podol, the oldest neighborhood of Kiev—capital of the Soviet state Ukraine—a city whose existence dates back to the sixth century. *Podol* in Russian language means "lower part," and true to its name, the district stretches along the lower terrace of the Dnieper River's right bank and is the birthplace of the city's trade. With its rectangular sections created by the long, straight streets, *Podol* may seem easy to navigate, though only if you keep to the major streets. Growing up in this neighborhood meant knowing every pathway hidden between the old buildings and behind rectangular blocks, and finding a new way to get home every night. Being *Podolyanyn*—native of Podol—meant being one with the old buildings, streets, parks, alleys, and the Dnieper River.

The family lived in one of these old buildings, occupying two rooms in a communal apartment that they shared with Yan's uncle and aunt. A squeaky wooden staircase with a flimsy handrail on the outer side led to a poorly structured addition at the top of a four-story building. The front door opened into a narrow hallway about fifteen feet long that led into a common living space. The hallway also accommodated a kitchen and bathroom for the two families. Lined up against the wall on the left was a sink, a four-burner gas stove, and a bathtub behind a thin plywood divider, all visible from the front door. The wall on the right featured a toilet hidden in the enclosure and two small kitchen tables separated by a narrow window. Walking through the hallway required significant maneuvering to avoid bumping into objects and people. Imagine making this journey in winter clothing with bags of groceries. The common living room presented three doors, which led into private rooms. Yan, his parents, and sister Sofia occupied two rooms, and his aunt and uncle lived in the third room, between the other two. This apartment is so much a part of our story. It was our first family home.

Yan's father, an accountant by trade, was a wise and distinguished man known for his quiet, soft-spoken demeanor. He was tall and wore thin, round glasses that made him look like a professor. Yan does not recall many specific conversations with his father, but he remembers being loved unconditionally, and that feeling stayed with him for his entire life.

When Yan was around eight, he and his father developed an unspoken tradition. Every day on his way home from work, Efim would walk by a bench in the courtyard of their apartment complex. There were two other entrances, yet he always walked through the courtyard by the bench. The bench was the spot where Yan and his friends hung out every afternoon until the sun set and, one by one, their mothers called them home for supper. Every night, the boys clustered on and around the bench telling jokes, making fun of one another, and pushing each other to the dusty ground. Yan played with his friends, monitoring the gate out of the corner of his eye.

As soon as he saw Efim, he ran to him with a huge, clumsy hug, burying his head under his father's arm. Efim kissed his son on the forehead and patted him on the head, before Yan ran back to find his space taken by one of the other boys. At first, kids made fun of Yan for "running to Papa" every day. But he didn't care, and eventually they stopped. Instead, they became a part of the tradition by creating a competition of who would spot Efim first, and who would grab Yan's seat when he ran to embrace his father.

Every night after dinner, Efim would remain at the table reading while Yan practiced playing *bayan*, a chromatic button accordion. He sat there reading and listening for as long as his son practiced. Once in a while, Yan would catch him smiling.

Sunday, June 28, 1959, began like any other day. The school year had ended, and Yan was spending the summer vacation with his mother in a village on the left bank of the Dnieper, where they rented a rundown hut with no running water, gas, or electricity. They ate fruit grown by the locals and drank fresh cow's milk. Yan spent his days playing by the river or reading in a hammock outside. His family wasn't big on birthday celebrations, so he figured this year's birthday—his thirteenth—would be the same.

To his delight, Efim surprised them with a visit and stunned Yan with a gift of a brand-new bike. He couldn't believe his eyes! He never had a bike before and certainly never asked for one. They didn't have money for things like that, a fact Yan had understood since early childhood. Efim arrived on a passenger barge that ran every hour, transporting people from one side of the river to another. How he carried the bike across town and onto the barge remains a mystery. Yan was happy beyond words and spent the entire day on the bike. His father watched him ride through the countryside, a wide smile on his face.

Efim took the last barge home. He and Yan's mother, Rita, walked from the house to the dock, talking as Yan rode his bike back and forth, making figure eights around them. Efim gave his son a hug before getting on the barge. Rita and Yan stood on the sand watching the barge undock and turn toward the city at a slow pace.

Efim died at work that Monday morning from a heart attack, at the age of fifty-nine. Life changed after that. Yan's mother had to work. Sofia was sixteen and had her own life. So Yan became in charge of himself.

Yan's mother was famous for her cooking and baking of traditional Jewish dishes and pastries. I remain grateful to have enjoyed her creations for years after Yan and I got married—especially her famous *hamantaschen*, mouthwatering triangle pastries filled to the brim with a mixture of poppy seeds and sugar. Made once a year on Purim, they will always remind me of her.

Some might call Rita "a simple woman." I saw her differently. Not educated by any societal standards, she was immeasurably wise and incredibly strong. Rita gave birth to five children and lost three of them. Sofia and Yan were her only surviving babies. She shared with me the heart-wrenching story of trying to save her newborn baby girl, running from the hospital to the bomb shelter under the Nazi bombing of Kiev in the summer of 1941. Her newborn daughter died in her arms inside the bomb shelter. By then, she'd lost her first baby, also a girl, at birth, and had three-year-old Anya at home. In 1943, Anya died, a few months after Sofia was born. Neither Yan nor Sofia was aware of their siblings until Rita told me the story. And once she did, she never talked about it again. She said that she remembered nothing else.

From a young age, Yan had a tender affection for his mother. He understood her hardships and wanted to help. After Efim, Rita relied on her son for everything. Yan took on many day-to-day household chores of their laborious life. In the winter, he chopped wood and brought it up to the apartment to run the furnace. He carried sacks of potatoes and onions from the market to store for use during the cold winter months. He woke up at the crack of dawn to stand in line for milk, bread, and other produce. Food shortages were a way of life, and standing in lines was the only way to get the most necessary items.

Yan continued his music studies at Kiev Music School, a rarity for a Jewish kid. The infamous Jewish quota allowed only a few to be admitted each year. Undergraduate and graduate educational institutions had a set percentage of Jewish students accepted—a reverse of the Affirmative Action in the US. Here, the Soviet government aimed to limit young Jews from getting a higher education, but if anyone dared to speak up about this out loud, that truth would be denied. I haven't heard of anyone who did and lived to tell the story; nevertheless, it was public knowledge and a fact of life for the Jews.

Five years after graduating from the Kiev Music School, Yan attended Music Academy 850 miles away from home in Astrakhan, a city in southern Russia that lies on the Volga River. Such an

opportunity was beyond his reach in Kiev for one simple reason—
he was a Jew. But first, at nineteen, Yan was drafted for a mandatory
three-year service in the Army. His service neared completion
when the Soviet invasion of Czechoslovakia took place on August
21, 1968. Yan remembers his battalion, dressed in full fight gear,
waiting in the woods near the border for the order to proceed.
The invasion was imminent, but a few hours before it began, Yan's
battalion received a command to withdraw from their position
and return to their home base. The end of his service came two
months later.

After serving in the Soviet Army, Yan became more certain than
ever of his desire to escape. He now listened to the Voice of America
and learned about the United States from any source he could find,
which remained almost impossible, as no information came in
from the West, or anywhere else. As the Jewish emigration from the
USSR gained more attention and powerful support from the US in
the early 1970s, Yan began planning his emigration. A few months
before his twenty-eighth birthday, he had most of the paperwork
ready to apply. He was making final arrangements when we met.

A Girl from Podol

After a tube pregnancy, the doctor told my mother she couldn't
have children, so technically I wasn't supposed to be born. However,
as I learned early in life, no one told Mama what she could and
couldn't do.

"Papa and I wanted to have kids," she once told me. "When we
heard the doctor's diagnosis, we decided to adopt a baby girl from
an orphanage in Moscow. We would name her Galina after our
friend's daughter, whom we adored."

She and Papa took a one-month leave from his service duty,

and they told everyone they would spend this month in Moscow with Papa's sister, Maya. People did not discuss adoptions in those days, so they didn't want to say anything to the family until after the fact. When they didn't get a baby by the end of the month, they returned home upset and disappointed, and agreed to go back next year. Mama was twenty-six and Papa was thirty-four. They expected people would soon comment that they were getting too old to have children.

Fortunately, their disappointment was short-lived: a month after the trip to Moscow, my mother got pregnant. They welcomed my brother on September 8, 1948, and in another five years, I came along. They named him Misha after Mama's father, my *dedushka*, and for me, they had a name already picked out.

I liked my name growing up, but it wasn't until I moved to America that I realized—or acknowledged—why. My name wasn't a typical giveaway of my Jewishness. It has been my shelter.

"What's in a name?" you ask. For a Soviet Jew, a name meant the difference between being accepted into a group of peers or not, getting a job or not, being harassed and abused by your comrades while serving in the Soviet Army or not.... The list goes on. All this is because your name sounded "too Jewish" or you "looked Jewish." Your facial features, posture, mannerisms, expressions were a giveaway as well. No wonder Jews came up with this saying: *"B'yut ne po passportu, a po morde."* My best translation of this self-deprecating statement is: "It's your face that gets punched, not your passport."

The Jewish experience varied from city to city and state to state, and it may have been better in some places, especially small cities in the middle of the country where people could go their whole lives without ever once coming in contact with a Jew. People don't just leave their home for no reason. And yet, two million Soviet Jews fled in the '70s, '80s, and '90s—and that's after the two million who abandoned the Motherland, in fear of persecution and pogroms, at the turn of the twentieth century. This doesn't include the six million who perished during the Holocaust because they didn't or couldn't flee.

So, what names were a giveaway? For girls: Sonia, Rita, Alla, Rachel, Bella, Beyla, Sara, Hannah, Rivka, Ada, Sofia, Dina, Basya, Fanya, Genya. For boys: Abrasha, Aaron, Yoseph, Mark, Boris, Semion, Natan, Froim, Efim, Hanon, Isaak. I am illustrating this point using the names of people I know. The names didn't have to be "technically" Jewish—it was enough to be suspected as such. Remember, "*B'yut ne po passportu...*"

My name, Galina or Galya, Galochka, or Galka, as friends called me—along with others like Olga, Katerina, Natalia, Svetlana, Irina, Vera, Ludmila, and Alexandra—were among Russian names popular across the land and a good first-impression "protection" for the Jewish girls. I had a lucky name.

Yan had a story behind his name beyond its transition from Yan to John in the US. His birth name was Hanon. His father's "real" name was Efroim. He was Efim to the family; to his co-workers he was Fedor.

Fedor is a common Russian name—you couldn't find another Jew named Fedor if you tried. Efroim's last name was Roizenblit. Consequently, Yan's full name should've been Hanon Efroimovich (patronymic) Roizenblit—maybe the most Jewish name in all the Soviet Union. However, Rita used her maiden name (which she kept) for her newborn son. With the last name Chernyansky on his birth certificate, Yan took the first step in making his identity non-Jewish.

When he applied for his passport at sixteen, Yan petitioned to change his first name from Hanon to Yan, and his patronymic name from Efroimovich to Fedorovich. His plea worked, and the man I met was Yan Fedorovich Chernyansky.

In America, Yan changed his name to John because he invariably corrected people who mispronounced it. Although for me, he remains Yan.

Our last name also received an American makeover. After Zhenya memorized almost half the alphabet while learning to spell his last name, Chernyansky, in preschool, we shortened it from eleven letters to six. This last change made our name easier to spell and pronounce for Americans but untraceable to its origin. What's in a Jewish name? Centuries of struggle to fit in and survive.

When we came to the US, I was grateful to have a name that people pronounced more or less accurately, and one that I didn't need to go through the hassle of changing. I was grateful for that minor blessing because everything else in my life was up for major transformation; more on that later.

I was born on February 17, 1953, in Kiev, Podol, eight street blocks from where Yan lived. My parents, Misha, and I lived in a twenty-three-square-meter (250-square-foot) two-room apartment featuring no hot water, moldy walls, and an old-fashioned *pechka*, furnace, our only source of heating. During the winter months, I slept fully clothed because the old *pechka* did not do the job. A tiny kitchen off the entrance door also served as a mudroom, a hallway to the living space, and a spot where the toilet found its home next to the stove. The toilet, installed a year before I was born, saved me from having to use the outhouse shared by all the neighbors.

A large rat lived underneath the kitchen floor and often visited the kitchen at night, providing an enormous source of entertainment for Misha and terrorizing me with every hissing and scratching sound it made. Going to the bathroom, I saw the rat once, and the huge brown thing looked scarier in person than I imagined it to be from the sounds it made. To Misha's great disappointment and my gigantic relief, the rat stopped showing up after a while. I assume my parents or the neighbor's cat had something to do with its disappearance.

Beginning when I was about eight, my responsibilities included washing the dishes after family meals. The thought of sticking my hands in a large *tazik*, a bowl with hot, soapy water (Mama heated the water on the stove) gave me stomachaches before the end of each meal. The water would turn greasy with the first plate I dipped in it, and my stomach would turn over on itself as I scrubbed the dirt off the plates, pots, and pans with an old and equally greasy sponge. It is unlikely that these stomachaches were real—I don't remember being in pain—but my face grimaced in agony as if I were about to collapse, giving my father an opportunity to outstrip my yet unspoken plea with: "Don't even think about it; you are washing the dishes." To this day, washing the dishes is my most unpleasant chore.

Not having hot water in the apartment also meant weekly family trips to *banya*—a public bathhouse, a block away from where we lived. Every Sunday after breakfast, the four of us walked to *banya*, each carrying a bag with a change of clothes, a *mochalka* (rough, scratchy sponge), a bar of soap (soap I shared with Mama, and Misha with Papa), and a towel. Sometimes it took an hour or longer to wait in line. Men and women stood in separate lines (on the same staircase) and entered different sections of the facility. The inside of each section comprised two large rooms: the front room had rows of lockers with no locks and doors that half-closed; once you took off your clothes near others—who were undressing to go in, smelling of sweat, or getting dressed to go out, still red and sticky after their bath—you walked through a heavy door into a hot, foggy, steamy room with open shower stalls along the walls and long, communal benches in the center.

There were dozens of wet, soapy bodies everywhere, but Mama never seemed flustered about being naked in a wide-open space.

She scrubbed every inch of my body and I scrubbed her back, holding the sponge with both hands. Inevitably, Mama would spot someone she recognized, despite the steam, and stop to chat while I stood next to her looking at my feet, pretending to be invisible underneath all that soap and my long hair. The bright spot of the *banya* ritual was when, after we bathed, Mama gave me two kopeks to weigh myself on an old, squeaky scale. I still remember the joy of moving the level back and forth to get the exact measurement. And if the stars aligned, Misha and I got four kopeks each to buy soda water when the four of us met downstairs, washed, and cleaned.

Mama lived in the apartment on Spasskaya Street, across banya, since she and my grandmother returned to Kiev in the spring of 1944 from their refuge in the Ural Mountains during the Nazi occupation. At the beginning of September 1941, they fled Kiev on a freight train, escaping the Babi Yar massacre by a few weeks. Nearly sixty thousand Ukrainian Jews remained in Kiev when it fell to the German Army in the First Battle of Kiev on September 26. Some Jews stayed, hoping that life under Nazi rule would be better than the one under the Soviet regime; others were perhaps too old or weak to travel. On September 29 and 30 in the largest single Nazi massacre of Jews during World War II, 33,771 were slaughtered at Babi Yar. Thousands more were murdered in the ravine during the three-year German occupation of Kiev.

Long before the Soviet authorities acknowledged the horrors of Babi Yar, Jews returning to Kiev after the war heard about the bloodshed from the non-Jews who had lived through the occupation. I learned the story from my mother.

On September 28, the occupiers plastered the following announcement in Russian, Ukrainian, and German all over the city:

All Zhidi of the city of Kiev and its vicinity must appear on Monday, 29th of September 1941 by 8 in the morning at the corner of Melnikova and Dokhterivskaya streets (near the cemetery). Bring documents, money and valuables, and also warm clothing, linens, etc. Zhidi who do not follow this order and are found elsewhere will be shot. Any civilians who enter the apartments left by Zhidi and appropriate the things in them will be shot.

"Zhid" is a derogatory Russian slur for "Jew," similar to the American "Kike." The respectful Russian word is "*Yevryei.*" *Yevryei* could be called Zhid by a neighbor, a stranger in a grocery store or at a bus stop, or by the kids at school. Especially by the kids at school.

In the early hours of a chilly autumn morning, shielding from a biting wind by wrapping drab wool shawls around their shoulders and over their heads, thousands filled the streets of my future neighborhood, Podol, which had the largest Jewish population in Kiev.

What was it like for the children, elderly, and the sick to walk these three and a half miles? Sleepy boys and girls who were dressed in winter coats, wearing hats and scarves, trekked alongside the adults. Older siblings carried babies and toddlers, while their mothers and able grandparents hauled ancient pieces of luggage and satchels packed to the brim with items they would never use. Some used baby carriages to move their possessions; a few got hold of old carts. Adult children hoisted their ailing parents or pulled them in limping carriages. Pregnant women, and those who recently gave birth—what was it like for them? Men and women, leaning on one another, stumbling through the cobblestone streets of their beloved city. Some paralyzed with fear; others stoic and solemn. What went through their minds? Russian husbands accompanied their Jewish

31

wives and their Jewish children. Russian wives walked alongside their Jewish husbands. What did they say to one another, passing by the occasional dead body on the side of the road and hearing gunshots as they came closer to the gathering site?

Thousands slowly advanced in a death convoy, while non-Jewish neighbors, schoolmates, teachers, and colleagues looked on, peeking from open windows or standing outside. Some gazed away in disbelief; many watched the procession with glee, yelling profanities and spitting in the Jewish faces. All the while, young Jewish men—husbands, fathers, and brothers of those marching toward their fate—fought for their Motherland on the Western Front.

The Jews of Kiev, like the Jews across the Soviet Union, were uninformed about Adolf Hitler's vow to annihilate the Jews of Europe. Trudging through the streets of Podol, they knew nothing about the "Final Solution." Many thought they were being relocated outside the Soviet Union and considered that a welcome alternative.

Eyewitness accounts describing what happened in Babi Yar on that fatal Monday and Tuesday may differ in some detail, but the story is profoundly and agonizingly the same. At the ravine, the Jews—divided into groups of ten—were directed to place their belongings in the designated piles. Jewelry in this pile. Watches go here. Musical instruments there. Books off to the side. Shoes here. Coats there. Shabbat candles over there. Silverware over here. Who issued these instructions? It had to be the locals. They spoke the same language and knew many whose lives were about to be ripped out of them in the most vicious way.

As the Jews saw what was happening around them, panic erupted. Hysterical laughter by people losing their minds and inhuman screams echoed through the area as the soldiers forced them to strip naked. The real horror was now seconds away. The Nazis ordered the first group to lie down at the bottom of the ditch facing the ground and gunned them down one by one.... They shot in place those who hesitated, then commanded the next group to lie on top of the dead or wounded and went on with the shooting. Rows and rows of Jews fell to their deaths on top of one another. The soldiers ripped screaming babies out of their mothers' arms and threw them against the side of the ravine like wooden logs. This continued all day. In the evening, German soldiers and their Ukrainian supporters covered the ravine with dirt and rocks. They repeated the atrocity on Tuesday. For days, cries and moans came from the ground as the earth in the steep-sided valley shifted ever so slightly to carry the final breaths of those beneath it.

Over the next two years, prisoners of war and local gypsies were among the others who were murdered in Babi Yar. The exact number of people who perished in the ravine may remain unknown forever. Some sources believe it to be one hundred thousand, of which the majority were Jews.

Babi Yar is often described to be "outside of central Kiev" or "near Kiev." Both descriptions may be geographically valid, although for a Kiev native, Babi Yar was not "outside" by any means. Located only a twenty-minute tram ride from Podol and a ten-minute taxi ride from Kiev's major street, Kreschatik, Babi Yar was in the heart of Kiev. The evil of Babi Yar took place in broad daylight in the heart of the capital of the USSR's Ukrainian state.

"No monument stands over Babi Yar. A drop sheer as a crude gravestone, the wild grasses rustle over Babi Yar," wrote Yevgeny Yevtushenko in his poem "Babi Yar," published in 1961, after he visited the area and saw trucks dumping garbage into the ravine. In 1976, a monument to "Soviet citizens shot by the Nazi occupiers at Babi Yar" opened at the site, with no mention of the Jews. It wasn't until 1991 that a menorah-shaped monument dedicated to the Jews murdered in Babi Yar was erected.

I had been to the ravine many times growing up, when visiting family friends who lived nearby. Babi Yar looked dismal for as long as I remembered. Local children played in and around the ravine, throwing stones and dirt at each other and jumping inside a dusty ditch, with no knowledge of the lives ended ruthlessly—those beneath them, and those that never came after. As my mother and I stood on the balcony overlooking the ravine, I shivered while listening to her and imagining my family perishing there with the others. My family's escape was a miracle. And I grew up acutely aware that if it wasn't for this miracle, my brother and I would not exist; and all the future generations of our family would not exist, like they don't exist for the Jews of Babi Yar. This understanding still overcomes me.

I was a teenager when Mama admitted that some Ukrainians participated in the massacre. They helped round up the Jews, pointed out to the Nazis those who attempted to hide, and escorted them to their deaths. I shivered imagining that neighbors who used to stop by to borrow a pinch of salt or a couple of carrots were a part of this evil. But before I questioned the dignity of the entire human race, Mama revealed that there were also those who hid the Jews during the occupation, and she pointed at our next-door neighbor, Baba Dusia. *Baba Dusia? I never saw the old woman sober in my life! And the word "Zhid" has never left her lips! How is that possible?* I tried to envision the courage some people forged to risk their own lives and save others.

I didn't learn about the Holocaust and the Babi Yar at school. This part of World War II "escaped" our history books. We learned about the heroism of Soviet soldiers and generals, but not about the slaughter of six million Jews by Hitler, with help from local authorities across Europe. My high school teacher of Ukrainian language and literature was a known Nazi collaborator. After the war, he returned to teaching, where he treated several generations of Jewish kids, including me, with utmost disdain.

People shared war stories, and the stories of human sacrifice

34

and survival, behind closed doors. Mama told me her story many times: "We were lucky to be allowed to come back to Kiev after it was liberated, and get an apartment. Ours had been destroyed during the bombings. Many people struggled to receive permission to return. Through a good friend, I got a job at City Hall and helped hundreds of families come home and find a place to live. We all lost so much. None of the men in our family came back from the war. My father—your *dedushka*, Misha—joined the underground resistance during the occupation. In one battle, the Germans captured his unit in the woods outside of Kiev. They identified Jews among the captured and shot them, taking the non-Jewish soldiers as prisoners. We waited for your grandfather to return for several years until an eyewitness told us what happened. My brother, Abrasha, died in Ural from meningitis. He was only sixteen. So after the war it was just my mother and me."

Mama would pause here to show me a picture of *dedushka*, looking from the photo at me with a gentle, loving smile. It was a picture of her and Abrasha—two young children wearing matching sailor outfits. I loved looking through her old photo album while listening to her talk. There were also half a dozen pictures of young men—boys really—that she kept in an envelope, which had turned yellow by the time I saw it. I looked through these pictures so many times, reading handwritten inscriptions on the back. Each note started with a version of "Dear Bellochka" (Bella, Beba, Bebochka)... and ended with, "Wait for me. I will come back." None of these boys came back.

"We cried for those we lost and we cried for our beloved Kiev," Mama continued. "The city had been demolished. Only one building was left standing on Khreshchatyk Street. Podol was unrecognizable too—ruins everywhere. For months I spent all my free time cleaning the streets with others, mostly women. We worked with our bare hands, moving bricks, broken glass, and debris into piles on the side of the street, clearing a path for trucks and other machinery that came through to begin reconstruction. Gradually, we saw our city return to life, and by the time you were born, Kiev became beautiful once again."

A few weeks after I was born, on March 5, Joseph Stalin, the leader of the Soviet Union, died. A dictator of thirty years, whose regime murdered tens of millions, was gone. Several members of my father's family were among Stalin's victims.

My father was the youngest of thirteen children born to Fira and Yakov Kugel. I imagine the family, like most Jewish families of that time, moved to Kiev in the mid-1920s from one of the nearby *shtetls*. My grandfather died when Papa was two years old, but my grandmother lived until the late 1950s—she must've been in her early eighties when she passed away. A single image comes to mind every time I try to remember her: *Babushka* is sitting on a bed by the window in a small room of her communal apartment, where she lives with her daughter Hinya. Two large, square pillows support her back, and her legs hang off the bed but don't touch the floor. She seems miniature even to a five-year-old child. Her thin snow-white hair is loosely tied back in a low bun. She gives me a cautious, toothless smile when I touch her hand, but her eyes don't move, and her still gaze glides above my head toward the corner of the room.

"Babushka Fira is blind," Mama explains later. As far as Papa's siblings, his sisters Hinya, Ronia, and Maya were the only ones alive in my lifetime. My father told me his brother's story, but nothing about the other eight siblings. Were they even alive by the time he was born? If some of them were alive, what happened to them during World War II? Were they too victims of Stalin's persecution? This I don't know.

In early 1937, my father's brother, a prominent government official in Kiev, was dragged out of his home in the middle of the night. During the same time, in Moscow, Aunt Maya's husband, who also held an important government post, was charged with treason. He left his house in handcuffs, after being beaten by KGB operatives in front of his wife and two-year-old daughter, Zoya. Both men vanished into the abyss known as The Great Terror.

Later that year, Aunt Ronia and Babushka Fira "disappeared" from their home to one of the Gulag labor camps. "I watched, hiding behind a tree outside of our apartment building on Shevchenko Boulevard," Papa recounted, "as Mama and Ronia were pushed into an unmarked car which sped into the night. We didn't hear from them for two years until one day they came back, both sick and frail." Papa blew a cloud of cigarette smoke into the air between us as his words settled. The picture of a fragile Babushka Fira on her bed, meekly responding to my touch, is etched in my memory.

The exact motives for the Great Terror are debated by historians to this day. Was it Stalin's attempt to gain power as a dictator after stepping into Lenin's shoes? Was it an attempt to unify the Soviet Communist Party, or to prepare for the threat of rising Nazi influence in Europe? That's up to the scholars. The undisputed fact remains that Stalin established the use of "Fifth Paragraph" for tagging "criminal elements," primarily Jews, but also prominent Party officials and high-ranking military personnel. The decree he implemented made families responsible for the "crimes" committed by other family members, which included children twelve years and older. They, too, were subject to an arrest, a labor camp in Siberia, and execution. Because hundreds of thousands vanished and thousands more died of starvation in camps, historians still question the exact death toll of that period; many believe it to be over two million. The total number of people killed by Stalin's regime goes up to tens of millions.

I once overheard my father's Army colleague and a lifelong friend, Uncle Petya, telling Papa: "Yoseph, you have no idea what gang we belong to." By "gang" he meant the Communist Party. That statement by a decorated colonel of the Soviet Army shocked me, and I think this conversation with Uncle Petya influenced my father to reconsider his stance on our emigration. But not until much later.

Now, the tyrant—Comrade Stalin—was dead. The news came on the radio the morning after. Why was my mother crying? Tears of joy? No. She was devastated. In a panic, she grabbed a two-week-old me from the crib, frantically wrapping me in a wool blanket. Then she pulled a winter coat, hat, and gloves on a four-and-half-year-old Misha, threw her own coat on, and ran out to the street into the freezing winter air, holding me in one arm and dragging Misha by the hand with her other arm. People flooded the streets. They raced toward Kiev's Red Square, in the center of Podol. Hundreds, maybe thousands were devastated and heartbroken, like Mama. Those who rejoiced did so quietly in their homes, Yan's family among them.

Reflecting on this day years later, Mama said: "I didn't think the sun would come up the next day without our *Vozhd*, Leader."

"Why, Mama? He murdered so many people!" I wanted to understand.

"Not him. He didn't have any knowledge of what went on. Bad, unpatriotic people in his cabinet acted behind his back." My father, an officer of the Soviet Army, believed the same story. So did I for many years.

My parents, Yoseph and Bella, began their life together with a sense of glamour and adventure. Papa, a proud decorated Army major. Mama, a beautiful military wife who followed her husband to the end of earth, making lifelong friends along the way, and creating a loving home for the family no matter the environment. The two got married in November 1945 when my father returned from the

Great Patriotic War (which the rest of the world called World War II) for a brief vacation. Their first military assignment as a couple took them to Dresden, Germany. Three years later, military orders brought them to Vladivostok, a city in Siberia, near the borders of China and North Korea, followed by an assignment in Leningrad (renamed to St. Petersburg in 1991 after the collapse of the Soviet Union) and Stalingrad (renamed to Volgograd after Khrushchev exposed Stalin in 1961). During brief visits to Kiev between assignments, they showered family and friends with souvenirs and stories of their adventures. Papa was a brilliant storyteller. He could captivate an audience of one or one thousand with his wit and dry sense of humor, delivered in a deep, raspy voice.

Their life of enchantment and romance ended abruptly when, after twenty-four years of service, the Army pushed my father into an early retirement, one year before his long-expected promotion to lieutenant colonel and a full military pension were due. He fell victim to another wave of anti-Semitism in the Soviet Army, this time directed toward high-ranking Jewish officers.

At first, Papa was optimistic, expecting to be picked up by a regional Communist Party office for a leadership position or a military school to teach history or political science. When every door shut in his face, he began looking for any job, landing a role as a purchasing manager at a production plant. He was emotionally crippled, yet unable to comprehend—or didn't want to believe—the simple truth. The reason for his rejections was the fact that he was a Jew. Nothing shook his patriotic loyalty to the utopian cause of Soviet doctrine.

Mama, too, didn't admit that it was pure and obvious anti-Semitism that brought her husband to his knees at fifty-three. The vibrant and exciting man she had married vanished. The father I grew up with was often harsh, critical, and abrasive.

My parents were wounded financially, emotionally, and in every other way that two people who love each other could find themselves losing ground. It was my job to help. I did what I thought would make their lives easier—I became an obedient child. I did what I was told. I never argued. I didn't lie. And I believed what they believed—that our Motherland was the best in the world. Together with my schoolmates, I sang the Soviet National Anthem, trusting every word with all my heart, believing we lived in freedom and would soon know the triumph of Communism.

Like my parents, I longed for a world where "from each according to his ability, to each according to his needs." Little did we know that this world would collapse after seventy-four years and several generations of indoctrinated people. But in the meantime, my family was Soviet from head to toe.

With all that our family and the Jews around us lived through, we never spoke of anti-Semitism or what it meant to be Jewish, or even that we were Jewish. Deep awareness of this existed, with no one talking about it. We lived in Ukraine, a Soviet state, among Russians and Ukrainians, yet we were different; we were neither. We had to come to America to be called Russians. I am still struggling with how to best respond to an assumption Americans make: you were born in Russia—you are Russian; you were born in Ukraine—you are Ukrainian. This logic didn't work for the Soviet Jews, though most of them assimilated to the point of rejecting being Jewish. If they were lucky, they changed their names, too.

The word *Yevryei* had never been uttered out loud. People said it in a whisper, the kind of whisper you would use to talk about something embarrassing or wrong. "He is a good person, even though he is a Jew" was a phrase often used by Russians and Ukrainians to describe someone "suspected" to be *Yevryei*. I'd heard this phrase from neighbors and strangers since early childhood, so it's not surprising I felt uneasy walking into Kiev synagogue with my mother, for the first and last time, at five years of age. What happened there validated my growing suspicion there was something wrong with being Jewish.

Even today, six decades later, when I think about this visit, I can recreate in my mind the sensation of Mama's firm grip on my hand walking down the stairs into a *podval* leading to the synagogue's main hall. *Why do I remember the entrance being in a basement?* Maybe we walked through a side door or maybe the only synagogue in the capital of Ukraine was, in fact, located in a *podval*.

The large room we found ourselves in was dreadful, with its dim lighting and dark plain walls. Rows of brown wooden chairs faced the front of the room, where a small light dangled from the ceiling above a raised platform. Nothing around me looked familiar or inviting. I stood as close to my mother as I could without making my fear obvious. I was afraid of the gloomy room and the old man she spoke with. He had a long white beard and was dressed in black from head to toe. Never had I seen a man dressed like this. They talked quietly in a language I didn't understand, which scared me even more. However, the sound and rhythm of the language were vaguely familiar. *Did Mama speak it to her uncle in the past? Or to Papa?*

My parents exchanged a few words in Yiddish on rare occasions when they didn't want Misha and me to understand what they talked about. Standing next to Mama in Kiev synagogue, I couldn't have possibly understood that Mama talked to the rabbi in Yiddish to arrange a funeral for a relative. In the dread of this place, I was a lifetime away from the day I would sit in a synagogue in Los Angeles at a Rosh Hashanah service, overwhelmed with emotions, thinking of the scared little girl all those years ago. But that wouldn't happen for a very long time.

I tried to distract myself by looking around, without an iota of success. I began pulling the edge of Mama's coat sleeve to beg her to leave. She gave me a stern look and continued her conversation for what seemed like an eternity. Finally, she was done. Without saying a word, she took my hand, and we began walking toward the door. I wondered why Mama had said nothing to me, and I didn't ask. I knew better. Even at five I realized she, too, wanted to leave this *podval*.

We almost reached the stairs leading outside, when I heard, "Hello, my name is Sara." *Oh no,* I thought, *we'll never get out of here. Mama talks to everyone she meets for hours!* I looked up at the woman, who now stood next to Mama.

"Hello," she repeated with a friendly smile. She spoke Russian, but the words sounded strange, kind of harsh. "I am visiting from Israel," she said. Mama squeezed my hand and pulled me closer to her, as if to protect me from an evil stranger who just uttered a forbidden word. *What's wrong with Mama?* I wondered. *Why isn't she saying "hello" to the woman?* My mother, the friendliest person you'd ever meet, didn't respond to the simple "hello" and acted like she had just seen a ghost. The woman seemed nice. She had the friendliest face I'd seen in this *podval* so far!

"Hello," I said.

"*Zdravstvu,*" she responded and looked at Mama.

"Your daughter reminds me of Jewish girls in Israel. May I please give her a Magen David, and a book with pictures of Israel?" Sara asked, smiling, ignoring my mother's stern posture.

The beautiful and sparkly Star of David hung on a pretty gold chain, and the tiny book looked like a miniature accordion, with pages folded into one another. The woman picked up the book by one end, and it magically dropped the pages, revealing a mysterious faraway world. Mesmerized and excited, I extended my free hand to accept the gifts, but Mama pulled me away and mumbled, "*Nyet* No. We can't accept this," before we rushed up the stairs and out the door.

I didn't understand what had just happened, but I knew not to ask questions or mention the "incident" to anyone, let alone to speak of Israel or the Star of David. It was this encounter that convinced me there was definitely something wrong with being Jewish.

At nine, I became a member of the Soviet Pioneers organization, and like all my friends, proudly wore my red silk neckerchief tied around my neck as part of the school uniform. At fourteen, I entered the ranks of the Komsomol, which was when my teacher—a former Nazi collaborator—said to me in front of the entire class, "You don't need an 'A' because you won't get into any university, anyway." I confronted him after catching him "fixing" my grades in the class journal. Instead of entering the 5 (A equivalent) that he told me I earned, he recorded a 4 (B). He didn't seem embarrassed to be discovered and repeated his statement as a commonsense conclusion. I, on the other hand, was devastated by his words. The class of thirty-five of my peers listened to him in silence. My friends didn't stand up for me. They said nothing. I was on my own. "Watch me," I muttered, intuitively knowing I would have to fight hard to prove him wrong.

And I did! I had been accepted into the only university in Kiev with fewer restrictions for admitting Jewish students, but not before I failed the entrance exam to the National Kiev University, named after Ukrainian poet Taras Shevchenko. The college admissions process comprised a written and an oral exam. The written math exam presented results objectively—you either solved the problems correctly or you didn't. I received a 5 and proceeded to the oral part. This is where the Jewish kids were weeded out. During the oral math exam, I solved the problem correctly, but one professor from the panel insisted I wrote the wrong answer. The conversation sounded something like this:

"Galina, I see your answer…. However, what if the answer was…"

"That would be wrong. The answer can only be…"

"Are you sure about that?"

"Yes."

"Why don't you write it down and we can discuss?"

I was seventeen. An obedient Soviet child. I did what he asked.

"See…that's wrong! Wrong answer. You failed." He pulled the paper out of my hand, signed it, and told me to leave.

I remember getting lost in the narrow halls of the university building, looking for an exit. I ran up and down the stairs, trapped, panicking that I would never get out. My mother said later she didn't recognize me when she finally saw me outside. She never explained why. I must've looked the way I felt. We walked home while I told her what had happened. She listened and said nothing. There were no tears. No drama. No blaming the system, and no words of sympathy for me. By the time we got home, I decided on my next move—I would apply to a university more lenient to Jewish kids. One such place existed in all of Kiev—not the school of my dreams, but by then I'd learned that life was about doing your best with what you had, not reaching for your dreams.

Finding a job was another triumph against all odds. An engineering position opened up in a new department whose company was looking for "someone exactly like me," until my passport revealed to the Human Resources manager that I was a Jew. The job offer came off the table in an instant, with a lame excuse: "we had unexpected budget cuts." *In the time it took me to walk two doors down the hall?* No matter—it was just one more disappointment that I brushed off as "that's life." I kept on pushing and landed what we would now call an internship role. I worked without pay for six months until I finally squeezed myself into a paying job.

There I was, studying shipbuilding at night and assisting a chemistry and physics lab teacher at a two-year technical college during the day—a far cry from my dream of becoming a journalist.

When the stories of the first immigrants to America and Israel began spreading, in the early '70s, and some of our extended family members began talking about leaving, my parents not only disapproved, they denounced them. In her extreme reaction, Mama stopped speaking with her cousin Vova, whom she adored and grew up with, when he became vocal about his plans to emigrate and even more vocal about his disdain for the Soviet government. Uncle Vova was my dearest, favorite relative on the planet, and while I didn't understand his views (in fact, they scared me) I continued to be close with him and his family. Emigration remained a taboo topic at our house. At twenty-one, in spite of my firsthand experience with anti-Semitism, I stood proudly as a Soviet girl, believing there was no place like the Motherland.

2

Family Quilt

"In all of us there is a hunger, marrow-deep, to know our heritage, to know who we are and where we came from." —Alex Haley, American novelist

By the age of eight, I often walked by myself from our apartment on Spasskaya Street to Uncle Vova's on Yurkovskaya. The eight street blocks along Mezhygorskaya were a mega-adventure compared to walking to and from school or making runs to the market for Mama. I suspect my mother's generosity toward my freedom didn't thrill my father, but she ignored him. Mama said she trusted me as long as I followed the rules: take the Mezhygorskaya route and not the side streets; don't stop anywhere along the way; walk, don't run. Even though I had been dying to explore the alleys and was eager to run in the chilly air, I followed the rules because it was a given. I would have to look Papa in the eye and answer his question: "Did you follow the rules?" and my father didn't tolerate lying. He had a "one strike and you are in big trouble" policy—no exceptions. That is why, if I wanted a little freedom, I had to follow the rules.

Uncle Vova, Aunt Lillia, and their daughter Sonia, three years younger than me, lived in a neglected old building (though it would take years before I understood it as neglected; then it was a building like any other building in Podol). Yet they had hot water in their apartment, a luxury I only dreamed of. The toilet and a bathtub graced the kitchen, alongside the stove and the kitchen table. The bathtub and the toilet were in plain sight when you walked through the front door.

Visiting Uncle Vova's home was wondrous every time. I remember this to be the only place I could be a carefree child. There were no expectations, responsibilities, or obligations; no judgment, only acceptance and love. And his famous multilayered sponge cake. And laughter. And Aunt Lillia's singing in Yiddish. The melody is sad and sweet at the same time. When she finishes, Mama says softly: "We can all use a little luck. A little mazel."

Over the years, this and other Yiddish melodies deeply touched my soul, even though I didn't understand a single word. As she got older, Sonia sang with her mother, while Uncle Vova looked at both of them with tenderness and adoration. My parents enjoyed spending time with the Giverts family, and we frequently had dinners together, mostly prepared by Aunt Lillia's mother. Aunt Lillia had many talents, but cooking wasn't one of them; it was a relief to all when her mother was around to help Uncle Vova, whose specialties were salads and cakes.

During one of those delightful evenings, Uncle Vova raised a glass to toast Israel's victory in the Six-Day War of 1967. At fourteen, I had no idea what he was talking about. Any mention of the name "Israel" was still unnerving to me. Watching my parents' reaction to his toast showed me once again the need to hide my Jewishness. Papa left the table and walked outside, lighting a cigarette on the way. Mama escorted her younger cousin to the kitchen and scolded him for bringing up "such a topic in front of children."

I was an adult when I learned that in six days, from the fifth through the tenth of June, Israel seized the Sinai Peninsula and the Gaza Strip from Egypt, the West Bank from Jordan, and the Golan Heights from Syria. In the same period, Israel captured East Jerusalem from Jordan, including the Old City and the Western Wall. In this bloody conflict, a young Jewish state changed the map of the Middle East.

Decades later, I would visit Israel, walk the cobblestone streets of the Old City, and pray at the Western Wall, and to my astonishment, I would have a sense of being home. I would also discover that Israel's victory in the Six-Day War energized and expanded the Human Rights movement to allow Soviet Jews to repatriate to Israel. If someone suggested there was a worldwide Human Rights movement to free Soviet Jews, I would have reacted like my parents did to Uncle Vova's toast, because I believed with all my heart that "from Moscow to the borders, from the southern mountains to the northern sea, a man stands as a master over his vast Motherland." However, the words of this beautiful song weren't true for the Jews. Now I understand.

Sonia and I are second cousins, but because of our family dynamic, we grew up like sisters: Her father and my mother were as close as any brother and sister. Through the years, we've collected bits and pieces of their life stories and woven them together into a story quilt. Just as in a quilt, the pieces don't match flawlessly and the colors don't always go with one another, and there may be gaps with no color at all. But isn't that true of life, too?

Uncle Vova

Velvel was born on September 14, 1926, in Kiev on Yurkovskaya Street, in the very apartment I loved visiting growing up.

His mother, Sourita, helped her husband, Haim Giverts, run a bakery—a family business that Haim was very proud of. And for a good reason. The Giverts's bread had the finest reputation across town, and every morning, dozens lined up to buy the savory bread and delicate pastries. With his mother spending much of her time at the bakery, Velvel practically lived there from an early age. It was then he must have developed his love for baking. But the family's prosperity did not last. After a brief period of a *freer* economy, introduced in 1921 as New Economic Policy—*Novaya Ekonomicheskaya Politika* (NEP), the Great Break began Stalin's era in the history of the USSR.

Velikiy Perelom ended a Soviet version of free enterprise and forced millions of Soviets into nationalization and collectivization, creating a man-made catastrophe unknown in peacetime, the Great Famine of 1932-33. Five million people were starved and killed across the Soviet land, four million of them in the Ukraine.

The day a six-year-old Velvel watched his father and grandfather beaten and tortured by Bolsheviks outside their bakery—until the two men gave up everything they owned: their property, their money, and all their valuables—was the day Velvel began forming his views of the Soviet regime.

He hardly spoke of his childhood. Must be because what he witnessed interrupted it so brutally.

And just as hastily, Velvel became an adult at fifteen, when his father got killed in the first year of World War II. His sister Anya was seven years old.

From here on, Sourita's family story interlaced with that of my mother's even more than before.

Sourita was *Babushka* Genya's younger sister. The two had a brother, Misha, and three other sisters: Basya, Bella, and Manya. I vaguely remember *Babushka*, or maybe what I recall is a black-and-white photograph of her holding baby-me in her arms with a smile that melts my heart. I was three when she died. I know of Manya from the stories my parents told me. My father adored Manya for her devious sense of humor, resembling his own.

"Osya, do you like a day-old *borscht*?" she would greet my father at the door. *Borscht* is one of those soups that actually tastes better a few days after it's cooked. All the flavors blend together in perfect harmony of beets, tomatoes, cabbage, and potatoes. A Ukrainian staple.

"Of course, Aunt Manya! I love your *borscht*!"

"Well…come back tomorrow. This one is fresh—I just made it!" Her roaring laughter could wake up the dead.

Papa told this and similar anecdotes of Aunt Manya many times over the years, and, as a kid, I created my own dialogues, improvising on the ideas. How clever was I to replace *borscht* with *kotleta* and repeat the conversation verbatim to anyone who would listen? I had to be very young for my rendition to be remotely funny or cute.

I remember Uncle Misha visiting us on Spasskaya every week on his way to Banya, quietly chatting with Mama in the kitchen. At some point he stopped coming. Aunts Basya and Bella were in my life for what seemed like always, until we left. All those years later, the ache is still in my heart.

The five sisters and Uncle Misha were the children of Godl and Aaron Khatutsky, my great-grandparents. Godl was born in 1867 and Aaron in 1856. Since the family moved to Kiev, they all lived on Podol. Sourita and Genya, with their families, lived in the buildings next to each other, just a few blocks from their parents. Their two sons, Velvel and Abrasha, were the same age; they grew up as brothers and best friends. Although five years older, my mother was close to both of them. The two boys adored her. Anya was the youngest, treated as a baby doll by her brother and cousins.

To blend into Soviet life, Sourita changed her name to Sonia, and Velvel (Yiddish for Wolf) became Vova, short for Vladimir.

Years later, when Vova would arrive in the United States, a social worker—assigned to help the family settle in the new country—would tell Vova that his name, Vladimir, was too Russian, and he should choose an American name. Reluctantly, he decided on William, though he would later regret that "hasty decision."

You can't win as a Russian Jew: If your name is not too Jewish, it's too Russian. Or as I will learn later, it's a secret.

Arise, You Mighty Motherland, Arise for Sacred War

Sunday, June 22, 1941—Kiev, USSR

"*Vnimanie! Govorit Moskva. Govorit Moskva.* Attention! Moscow speaking. Moscow speaking. We are transmitting the announcement from the Soviet Government. Citizens of the Soviet Union, today, 22nd of June 1941, at four o'clock in the morning, with no declaration of war, German armed forces attacked our country. They attacked our borders in many places and bombed several cities, Zshitomer, Kiev, Sevastopol, and others. A Great Patriotic War of the Soviet Nation against German fascist aggressors has begun. Ours is the righteous cause. The enemy shall be defeated. Victory will be ours."

Yuri Levitan's voice, the most recognizable in the USSR, came over the radio waves into every home as two hundred million people listened with a collective gasp.

In early June 1941, Godl took her grandchildren to

Chernobyl—an annual vacation destination for the family. This year, she brought with her Aaron and Olya—Misha's children—and a seven-year-old Anya, Vova's little sister. Godl was seventy-four, and I will make assumptions about Aaron's and Olya's ages. I based these assumptions on a paragraph from Olya's letter: "Anechka and Aronchik are studying, but I cannot find work. They don't have anything for me, so I am helping *Babushka*." Aronchik, Aaron, must've been under ten, because he left with his grandmother while the older children took school year-end exams. Olya was nineteen or twenty; she must've had a job in Kiev by that time. She may have taken a vacation to help Godl with the kids in Chernobyl. Anechka's age is accurate. Uncle Vova repeated it every time he recounted the story I am about to tell you.

Many Kiev Jewish families spent their summers in Chernobyl; they had roots in this area and loved coming back despite the history of anti-Semitism and pogroms over the years, decades, and centuries. The village was a Jewish grandmother's paradise with fresh local fruits and vegetables, cow's milk, chicken, and eggs delivered to a rented hut by the locals. Located on Pripyat River, about sixty miles north of Kiev and twelve miles south of Belarus, Chernobyl gave children the freedom to swim in the blue waters of Pripyat, run in the woods, and play with the local kids.

My mother, the eldest of the eleven cousins—Godl's grand-children—told stories about the mischief the sisters and cousins engaged in during their summers in Chernobyl. I laughed when she told me about her aunts' annual competition of "who gained the most weight."

"In those days," Mama explained, "one sign of a wealthy life was a person's weight. '*A graube a shayne*' (from Yiddish: the bigger the better) meant you and your family were well off." Sonia, Genya, Basya, Bella, and Manya became quite competitive in this contest and their children cheered them on.

The summer of 1941 promised to be delightful once everyone joined Godl, Aaron, Olya, and Anechka. The men would stay in Kiev and come on weekends, as they had done in years past. Everyone looked forward to a happy summer. The war in Europe seemed far away.

Even though the tensions between Japan and China escalated into full-scale war by 1937, and World War II had been raging in Europe since 1939, Hitler's attack caught the Soviet citizens by surprise, presumably because of a pact, signed by Hitler in 1939, pledging not to attack the Soviet Union. The civilians weren't the only ones surprised; it appeared the military had been unprepared.

Like thousands around them, the men in Godl's family received draft notices. Sonia's husband, Haim Giverts. Bella's husband, Boris Golubchik. Manya's husband, Michail Soroka. However, Godl's son, Misha, wasn't drafted. And because he didn't join the Civil Defense either, he may have been older than *Dedushka* Misha—Mordechai Volkovitsky—who was forty-five. *Dedushka* joined a Civil Defense battalion stationed in the woods outside of Kiev. In August 1941, during an encounter with the Germans, they captured his battalion. Germans singled the Jews out from the group, shot them in place, and took other prisoners. *Babushka* Genya waited for her husband to return for several years after the war until one day, a man who survived the prison camp came by and told her what had happened. *Dedushka's* body remained missing. A letter from the government stated that my grandfather *"pogib bez vesti."* Perished without a trace.

Mama often spoke of her father, remembering his tender love and deep devotion to her mother, and his endless love for his children. One such memory struck me deeply, maybe because I wished my father would express his love to me similarly. At ten, Mama took part in the May Day parade as part of her school's girls gymnastics team. Her father met her after the parade and carried her home across the city on his shoulders. I tried to envision Papa attempting to do something like this, but there would not be a chance. *Dedushka* Misha was tall, slender, and fit. Papa was short and not athletic at all.

Inspired by her father's heroic gesture, my mother wanted to join the military herself; by the grace of G-d and her mother's immediate and forceful intervention, she didn't. Instead, she joined a Defense Youth group with a mission to prevent bombs from exploding on rooftops. Mama explained: "We threw sand on the bombs and pushed them off the roof with a broom before they exploded." I imagine that the speed and accuracy with which each interaction with a bomb had to happen would have been a matter of life and death, for those who lived in the buildings and for the members of the Youth group. For her heroic effort, Mama received a medal, *Za Oborony Kieva*, for the Defense of Kiev. I was in second grade at the time. I remember the excitement of the family and our celebration of Mama's heroism with the famous *Kievskiy tort*, Kiev cake. This is my favorite story about Mama. If I close my eyes, I can still imagine *Babushka* chasing her out of *Podol Voenkomat*, Military Committee, as she turns around to throw bombs off buildings, and lives to tell the story. That was my mama.

On June 22, Chernobyl family vacation planning turned into a nightmare. Rumors of the treatment of Jews in the Nazi-occupied territories suddenly created a genuine panic among the Soviet Jews. It became apparent that fleeing Kiev toward central Russia—the opposite direction from Chernobyl—gave a chance of survival from a lethal fate to the Jewish women and children. The farther from the Western border, the better. Sonia sent letter after letter to her mother, begging her to return home. In the meantime—scared, confused, and shocked under the relentless barrage of bomb fury—the family prepared for evacuation.

Yaroslavl, Gorky, Ufa, Sverdlovsk, Chelyabinsk, and Zlatoust were among the cities identified to admit and house evacuees. Once everyone received government permission to evacuate to one of these cities, they had to leave immediately. Trains departed from Kiev Vokzal under a flurry of bombings. More and more people piled into trains, attempting to escape to safety. Time was running out, and there was no sign of Godl and the kids. Were they still in Chernobyl? Maybe they evacuated from there? No one had answers to these questions. Vova remembered his mother's agony: "Mama became paralyzed with fear for her mother and her daughter." Uncle Misha insisted Godl and the children were safe. He said he would stay in Kiev and wait for them to return—two of his kids, Aaron and Olya, were with Godl, and his eldest son Boris had been away too. He refused to leave without them. He wanted Sonia and Vova to go with the others and promised he would take care of little Anya like his own daughter. He promised to get them all to safety and reunite as soon as possible. Reluctantly, his sister agreed. *A mother's choice.* If Sonia had made a different decision and sent Vova with the family, remaining in Kiev herself, she most likely would've never seen her son again. *An impossible choice.* With a bleeding heart, she boarded a freight train to Zlatoust with Vova and the others. Terrified by the whooshing sound of the flying bombs, they fled their home on one of the last trains, speeding through massive explosions toward safety.

The world around them crumbled and burned. After an excruciating three-day journey, frightened and starving, the eleven members of Godl's family arrived in Zlatoust, each adult carrying one piece of luggage weighing the allowable forty kilograms, eighty-eight pounds. Located 2,309 kilometers, or 1,400 miles, northwest from Kiev, in the Chelyabinsk region, Zlatoust is a large metallurgical city set in the Ural Mountains of central-western Russia between Europe and Asia. As much of the war-related industry moved to that area, evacuated Jews joined the workforce to support war efforts.

Godl and the children returned to Kiev a week after the family had left. Uncle Misha came through on his promise to his sister and organized their evacuation, but unfortunately, they went to Krasnodar Krai (in the North Caucasus region in southern Russia) and not to Ural, where the rest of the family settled. This is where the story breaks. Why didn't Uncle Misha request for them to evacuate to Zlatoust? I imagine he took the only destination offered and left Kiev with his mother, Anya, Aaron, and Olya, escaping days before the fall of Kiev and the horrors of Babi Yar took place. I learned of his son Boris's whereabouts from Olya's letter, and it turned out he too was in Chernobyl.

With hundreds of other evacuees, the five began their voyage on a cargo barge, downstream from the Dnieper River to the Black Sea. After covering 1,200 kilometers or 754 miles, over seven days, they arrived in Novorossiysk. From there, they moved to Krasnodar (most likely on a train), another 150 kilometers or 93 miles away. Zlataust, where the rest of the family had settled, was over two thousand kilometers away.

7 October 1941

Hello my dear aunts, brothers, and sisters. First, I want to tell you we are all alive and well; wishing you the same. Today, we received your letter. I can't express our happiness. We read your letter two or three times.

I will begin writing to you about our life. We came here without Boris. He was drafted from Chernobyl, and we didn't know where. You can imagine our worries, but Boris somehow was transferred here, and he's been with us for a month. He wrote to you about it himself—it's a fairytale.

Papa and Boris work on a collective farm, and we are

being rationed flour and other produce. Flour is very good so we have bread.

Anechka and Aronchik are studying, but I cannot find work. They have nothing for me, so I am helping Babushka. Our apartment is very nice and warm, and the climate here is warm. Life here is not expensive. They have grapes, watermelon, and honeydew, so it's not bad for us here. But we hear we will be sent away from here, but I don't know when and where. We will write to you before we depart.

Dear Aunt Sonia, if we knew we would stay here, we would demand that you be allowed to come to us, but we don't know if we will stay here, so we can't demand that you come. Perhaps it was destined, and nothing could be done. As long as everyone is alive and healthy. The bad times will pass, and we will see each other again soon. I hope we will celebrate together Victory over the enemy...

Dear Aunt, I want to tell you not to worry about Anechka. She is a very good girl, and we take care of her. She is in first grade, and she writes well. She gained some weight. She listens to Babushka, and she eats well.

Babushka asks Abrasha and Bebochka to write to her. I will end here. Be well, your niece, who wants to see you soon,
Olya.

Babushka, Papa, and Boris say hello.
Kisses from Aronchik and Anechka.
Sending all of you kisses 100 times.

Olya's letter from Krasnodar Krai has been in the family for over seventy years. Uncle Vova kept it among the old photos of his family. The last time he told Sonia and me this story was two years before he died. His voice trembled and deep sorrow covered his face as he told me this was the only letter they'd ever received from Olya. It arrived in Zlatoust in early 1943, over two years after she sent it.

"By the time the letter from Olya arrived, we knew they were gone," Uncle Vova explained. "Murdered by the Nazis. A relative from my father's side, who served near Krasnodar Krai, told us what happened to them. We suspected the worst when we learned Krasnodar fell, but we didn't want to believe that something horrible would happen to our loved ones. To my little sister."

Vova later learned that neither Boris nor Misha were with Godl. They survived, but only by chance. Boris had been drafted a second time, from Krasnodar, and Misha had received a transfer order to work far from where Godl and the children lived. When the Germans moved closer to the region, local officials offered Godl a relocation in the Ural area. By then, she was too weak to travel. Godl begged Olya to leave with Anya and Aron, but Olya insisted they should stay together. She was an optimist and believed nothing bad would happen to them as long as they were together.

As Uncle Vova told me this story, he let great big tears drip down his face. Shuffling through a pile of old pictures on the bed where we sat, he picked up a photo of a little girl, about six years of age. She had short, dark, almost black hair. Her big, beautiful eyes shone from the black-and-white photo with the multiple shades of amber. "Anechka...," Uncle Vova whispered, moving his fingers across the face in the photo. Anechka looked back at him with a gentle smile resembling his own.

In August 1942, the *Wehrmacht* occupied Rostov-on-Don, claiming victory over the Caucasus region, southern Soviet Union, and the oil fields beyond. In every occupied Soviet territory, including Caucasus, special German action squads, *Einsatzgruppen*— made up of Nazi (SS) units—moved in rapidly on the heels of the advancing German Army with a mission to establish German order and exterminate the Jews. It was a mission the Nazis executed flawlessly and repeatedly. Of the six million Holocaust victims, nearly one and a half million perished within the borders of the Nazi-occupied Soviet Union. Godl, Anechka, Aronchik, and Olya were among them. Nazi soldiers slaughtered them after forcing them to dig their own graves.

When the news found its way to Zlatoust, where Vova and the rest of the family lived in the cold basement of a decrepit building, they were still grieving my mother's brother, Abrasha, who had died on March 18, 1942, of kidney disease. His death devastated Vova. The two had grown up like brothers. Vova remembered his cousin as a kind and smart boy who deeply loved his family. To help the family survive, Abrasha lied about his age and took a night shift at a metallurgical plant, where he worked in a cold, damp environment, often standing in freezing water for hours. Each night he walked home in the frigid cold of Zlatoust's long, snowy winter, with the temperatures dropping to minus ten degrees Celsius, around fourteen Fahrenheit. The family believed Abrasha got sick from working and living in such dreadful conditions. His death shattered both *Babushka* and Mama. Neither one of them fully recovered from this loss. Mama spoke of Abrashenka so often that I grew up feeling like I knew him.

Shortly after Abrasha's death and the news about Godl and the children, Sonia learned that her husband, Hiam, was killed in action in 1941. In the fall of 1942, Vova contracted tuberculosis, and his mother caught the disease soon after him. Vova recovered after months of struggle; Sonia didn't. Uncle Vova often said she couldn't live after losing her beloved Anechka, Haim, and her mother. Sonia died at thirty-seven in the beginning of 1943, making her last plea to her sister Genya, my *babushka*: "be a mother to Vova in this world, and I will be a mother to Abrasha in the other." These were her words, repeated by *Babushka* to my mother and Vova, and from them to me.

GALINA CHERNY

The Bad Times Will Pass

May 9, 1945—Kiev

"*Vnimanie! Govorit Moskva. Govorit Moskva.* Attention! Moscow speaking. Moscow speaking."

This time the voice of Yuri Levitan blaring through radio speakers across the country was the voice of victory.

"Order of the Supreme High Command of the Red Army and the Navy. On the 8th of May, 1945 *(the 9th of May Moscow time)* in Berlin, the representatives of German High Command signed the Act of Unequivocal Surrender of the German armed forces. The Great Patriotic War by the Soviet nation against the Fascist invaders victoriously ended. Germany is completely defeated. Eternal glory to the heroes who fell in the battles for the freedom and independence of our Motherland. Long live the victorious Red Army and Navy! General Secretary Deputy of the Soviet Union, Stalin."

Victory found Godl's family back in Kiev, huddling together in the apartment on 25 Spasskaya Street. *Babushka* insisted everyone live with her until they were assigned their own apartments and found jobs. So *Babushka*, her three sisters with their children, Mama, and Vova—a total of nine people—all lived in a 250-square-foot apartment with no running water or indoor toilet. It was the very apartment I had lived in since birth. Together they rejoiced, celebrating the Victory, and they wept for the eleven members of Godl's family who were among the thirty million soldiers and civilians who perished in the Great Patriotic War. An entire generation of men had been decimated during this time. Godl's widowed daughters never remarried.

By the end of the war, Vova had earned his high school diploma and studied civil engineering at a local university. After graduation, he began his mandatory service as a Navy officer in the Far East on the Pacific Coast, Khabarov Region, in a port called *Sovetskaya Gavan*, Soviet Harbor. There, Vova befriended a Jewish doctor who helped to discharge him early, after learning that Vova had tuberculosis. Uncle Vova returned to Kiev in 1953.

My grandmother took her promise to her sister to heart and loved Vova like her own son. And like any Jewish mother would, she found a perfect girl for him. When Lillia—*Babushka's* distant relative from her late husband's side—came to Kiev for a summer break from her first teaching assignment on Sakhalin (an island at the far east end of Russia), Genya concluded she was the one for Vova. After dating Lillia for two weeks, so did Vova.

"I won't let you go back," he told Lillia.

"I don't want to go back," she said to him.

They married on August 20, 1955, and lived in love and harmony for fifty-eight years, thirty-four of them in America.

The Secret Name

I've always known that my great-grandmother's name was Godl. So imagine my surprise when I didn't find any reference to the name while researching for my book. There is Golda, Hodel, and other similar-sounding names, but no Godl. Her granddaughter, Beba, reassured me again recently that everyone called her grandmother Godl. "That's what we called her, Godl," she said. She pronounced the "G" with a typical Ukrainian sound, somewhere between "H" and "G."

With more research, I found out that it's quite possible that the name Hodel was pronounced as Godl in Chernobyl, her hometown. I can see how the letter "H" could've been transposed into "G" in writing. Ukrainian "G" is a letter from the Cyrillic script; that's where a combination of "H" and "G" pronunciation comes from.

The "e" in Hodel may have been dropped altogether over the years. If a Ukrainian speaker says my name, Galina, the "G" would sound exactly the way Beba pronounced it in Godl.

Be that as it may, she was Godl. Even more peculiar than her name is the fact that no one in the family was named after her. Or were they?

Naming babies after deceased relatives is a big deal for the Jews. Everyone is named after someone dear. My cousin Sonia was named after Vova's mother. My brother was named Misha after our grandfather. With the next generation of children, more family names were honored. Generation after generation of Godl's family followed the Jewish baby-naming tradition of honoring those who passed. *Has Godl's name not been commemorated?* This question haunted me as I put together Godl's family tree with the help of Beba, and my cousin, Sonia, who, like me, is Godl's great-granddaughter. I kept going back to the chart until it hit me: her name had been honored. Right there, in black and white, I saw a clear trace from Godl to Galina. Same first letter, sounding between "G" and "H" in Ukrainian. I was named after my great-grandmother.

It's inconceivable that my mother would give me a name beginning with the first letter of her grandmother's and not do it in her honor. Her mother wouldn't allow it. *But why not tell me? And why did it take me so long to figure this out?* I suspect the answer to the first question is simple: Mama did what every Jewish mother living in the Soviet Union would've done in her place—protected her child from growing up ridiculed and humiliated because of an association with a name that was too Jewish. The story my parents told about naming me after a girl they adored was much more appealing and safer in the environment we lived in. And the second question has an answer too—I must've known all along but never asked, for the same reason my mother never told me. *I am named after my great-grandmother, Godl. No need to protect me anymore, Mama.*

3

A Matchless Match

Spring 1974—Kiev

The April air was crisp. While the temperature still dropped to ten degrees Celsius at night, the days were getting warmer, and it smelled like spring—deliciously fresh air mixed with the earthy odor of damp ground. Gray winter clouds gave way to puffy white clouds, which dashed across the bright blue sky. I inhaled the freshness of the air, took off my knitted hat, and unbuttoned my coat to let the warmth of the spring sun touch my skin. I left work early to walk to the university instead of taking a tram. A brisk thirty-minute stroll would be perfect for clearing my head while enjoying this glorious day.

"Galochka, is that you?" A woman I vaguely recognized stood in front of me. "Remember me? I've known you since you were a little girl. Look at you now! All grown up. I know your mother well."

"Hello," I replied, not remembering her name or who she was. *This is awkward.* The woman didn't seem to notice my clumsiness.

"*Galochka*, are you married?"

"No." *What a curious woman!*

"Have a fiancé?"

"No." *Why is she asking?*

"Dating anyone?"

"No." *What a crazy woman!*

"How old are you?"

"Twenty-one."

"Not dating anyone?" *Didn't I just answer this question?*

She carried on: "Why aren't you dating anyone?"

Instead of responding, I smiled politely. After all, she knew my mother! But all I could think was, *what a nightmare of a Yente.* If you've ever watched *Fiddler on the Roof*, you know the type.

What happened here? A few minutes ago, I felt like a normal twenty-one-year-old, and now I was embarrassed because I wasn't married, didn't have a fiancé, and wasn't dating anyone, without an obvious reason. *I had my heart broken recently—does that count as a valid reason?*

I waited for her to pause for a second so I could say goodbye. This conversation needed to end now. There it came…a pause… She took a breath and blurted out, "I have a perfect young man for you. He is tall, handsome, and makes good money. He is a musician. You'll get married and he will take you to *Amerika*. I'll talk to your mother and introduce you two!" She paused.

What? Is she kidding me? She's crazy! And she said she knows my mother?! How well can she know her if she thinks she can introduce me to a musician who wants to go to Amerika? This conversation is over.

However, I couldn't say any of this out loud. Instead, I smiled and said, "I am not looking to get married anytime soon, and I am not going to America, so there is no point, but thank you anyway." She laughed, a sneering laugh, and pulled me into a tight hug—more like a squeeze—which scared me as much as her offer. I wiggled out of her arms and said goodbye.

I can't believe this! Who does this woman think she is? This is not a Chernobyl shtetl, this is Kiev, 1974! My face flushed. I crossed the street, walking the opposite direction from where I needed to go, just to get away.

Over the days that followed, I kept thinking about the crazy woman and what she said. "He will take you to America!" She had said it with ease and a smile. Why did my stomach churn and my hands go clammy every time that phrase popped into my head? I wanted to forget the whole incident, except that the image of a "tall, handsome musician" had not left my imagination.

Turned out, the woman didn't lack determination. Soon after our meeting, she spoke with my mother to broker the introduction, and I still suspect that given the turn of events, the crazy *yente* didn't mention one minor detail: the one where this young man would take me to *Amerika*. Because if she did, there would be no introduction and no story. Be that as it may, Mama was in! How could a Jewish mother resist?

I did not know of the plot, so when Mama asked me to stay home one night and have dinner with her instead of going out with my friends, I agreed. Her request seemed a little unusual, but my father had been out of town all week and I assumed she wanted some company.

The doorbell rang as we were finishing dinner in the kitchen. Mama followed me to the front door. I opened it and froze. I think I froze, or maybe I melted…something happened. Through the open door entered a tall, handsome man—the one I had been envisioning in my dreams for several weeks now. His eyes—a thousand hues of blue—smiled mischievously as though to say, "You and I realize this is a setup—let's play along."

He wore gray slacks and a blue button-down shirt that highlight- ed the warmth in his eyes. The soft curls of his short wheat-blond hair looked messy from the spring wind and the rain. He held a briefcase in one hand and a raincoat in the other, looking distinguished and charming. Did I mention he was tall and handsome? And he had the most beautiful name, Yan.

The rest of the night was a blur. We lost track of time and talked for hours, sitting on the sofa in my room, ignoring my mother in the next room, literally behind the wall. Yan's soft voice did not carry, and I mimicked his tone, without thinking about it, so poor Mama was "left out" of our conversation. A tough position to be in for any Jewish mother!

At some point Yan realized it was beyond late, and I walked him to the door. We made plans to meet the next day. Neither one of us brought up America.

When my father learned about our introduction, he became furious with Mama for bringing a stranger into our house and leaving their daughter alone in the room with him for the entire evening. *What was she thinking? How careless she was! Too trusting! Anything could've happened!* Never mind that I was twenty-one. Never mind that Mama sat in the next room for the entire evening. Never mind that I had a brain. Papa was not happy. A retired Soviet Army officer, he was strict when it came to my social life, and he had a history of chasing away boys who attempted to give me any romantic attention. To be perfectly honest, he was strict—period. This date would not have happened were he not away. Guaranteed! Would that have ended our story before it began?

4

Proposal

Summer 1974—Kiev

Our courtship started with Yan leaving town for three weeks of mandatory farming work. That's right! Every company sent their employees to work on a farm in the summer. Who else would dig potatoes out of the ground if not people who lived their entire lives in a city and had no interest and no skills in farming?

In a world where rotary phones wouldn't reach places outside of large cities for years to come, we resorted to the only method of communication available—letters. Every week I received two letters from Yan and wrote two letters to him, or maybe I wrote three or four because I wanted to talk to him every minute of every day. I did not keep score.

And for the first time, I kept my mother out of my personal life. I checked the mailbox several times a day to make sure I got the mail before she did, to avoid any chance of her reading Yan's letters. If you think she wouldn't, you've never met a Jewish mother, and you certainly haven't met mine. Of course, I realized my furtive behavior hurt her. She never said anything, but she didn't have to.

I knew. How? Ever met a disapproving Jewish mother? You'd know if you did.

By the time Yan came back, our closeness was real, and our bond had grown strong. Let me rephrase that. I was completely and totally in love.

We saw each other almost every evening during the week and all day on weekends. It turned out Yan lived across the street from the infamous synagogue, and a few blocks from me, which made our weeknight dating very doable. But this intensity in our relationship made my parents nervous.

"Too much too soon," said Papa.

"It doesn't look good for a respectable girl to spend so much time with a young man she hardly knows," echoed Mama one night as she greeted me at the door.

"It actually looks really good." I laughed and gave her a quick hug before marching into my room, astonished at my reaction. The words came out with ease and confidence. For the first time in my life, I pushed the limits and, according to my father, "played with fire."

Misha enthusiastically joined these exchanges whenever he was around, sarcastically pointing out that, finally, he wasn't the only "problem" child. I yelled at him for stirring up trouble, but his wink and a smile gave away his joy for me.

As my parents continued to disapprove of my "frivolous" behavior, they also began bonding with Yan. Mama loved him because he ate everything she prepared and in large quantities. He loved to eat, Mama loved to cook—the two of them were a match made in heaven! Aside from that, Yan listened to my mother's opinions and suggestions on every topic under the sun, with genuine interest and respect. Where I would jump out of my skin to prove my point, he smiled and nodded. No wonder she adored him. Papa respected Yan for being independent and responsible and half-jokingly he suggested Yan was too quiet. "Does he talk?" Papa would ask with a smirk.

"He does to me," I'd say.

I should mention my family was loud, often resolving disagreements with yelling first, talking later. Yan's quiet demeanor and soft voice brought the atmosphere in the house down two octaves, which took my parents by surprise. By being quiet and thoughtful when he spoke, Yan almost dictated a new tone for everyone. I loved it.

We dated for three months before it happened. One sultry July evening, after a long walk in the park along the riverbank, we sat down on a bench under an old chestnut tree—our favorite spot to watch the sunset. We watched the magnificent gold disk begin its graceful descent, coloring the sky in various shades of bright orange and red, illuminating a silver path across the deep, dark waters of the Dnieper. Another summer day came to an end. I rested my head on Yan's shoulder.

This is heaven. I never want to move, I thought. It was the quiet moment you want to last forever...but it didn't.

Yan gently pulled away and said, "I need to talk to you about something important." This was it. The "America" conversation. I slowly sat up.

"Since fourteen years of age, I have dreamed of escaping to America." He took my hand in his, looked into my eyes, and continued with a slight crack in his voice. "This dream got stronger with time, and I was ready to leave when I met you. I should've told you when we first met, except that I didn't think our blind date would turn into this. And now, I don't want to leave without you. I love you. Will you come with me?" His question hung in the warm summer air, swaying in the dark sky over the now black waters of the river.

Will you come with me?

So, the crazy woman told the truth! My heart sank, my head

began to spin, I felt my stomach churn, and for the next few seconds—which seemed like eternity—my life played in front of me like a silent movie in slow motion: my family, my friends, my home, theaters, movies, books, chestnut and birch trees, lilacs, Kiev, Dnieper—everything looked blurry, disappearing gradually into the darkness of the night. America would be forever; there was no coming back. I would be declared a traitor and stripped of my citizenship. My parents would be shamed and expelled from the Communist Party, but first, they would kill me. *They would kill me! But he said he loved me. The man I adored from the moment I saw him just told me he loved me.*

The word "yes" came out of my mouth, making me dizzy, cold, and shaky. I said yes to marrying this man and going to America with him. To the unknown that awaited. To our love. And, of course, there was a kiss—the kind you remember for the rest of your life. The kiss that makes the world melt away. In that moment in his love, I had all the bravery and strength I needed.

We walked the familiar streets under a gentle summer drizzle, talking about our future, and stopping once in a while to wipe the warm mist off of each other's faces. And yes, to kiss. And to make promises to one another. He promised to take care of me for the rest of my life, and I promised to iron his shirts and cook his favorite fried potatoes for him for the rest of mine. As we approached my parents' house to share the news, it hit me: *Amerika!*

"We can't mention America to them," I said. "Not right away. Please don't say anything! I need time to prepare them."

But I had no idea how to prepare them for something they rejected in their soul, something I barely understood myself. One aspect remained certain: They would stop us from getting married if they knew of our plans. This would definitely end our story.

Yan did not like my request. He did not want to start our life together with a lie. It was wrong. Yes, completely and utterly wrong, and yet, I had no choice, not if I wanted to marry him. It took major persuasion to convince Yan to let me handle the conversation with my parents at another time. When? That question I couldn't answer. For just this one moment, I didn't want to think about it. I just wanted to feel what I was feeling: that my life had finally begun.

My parents were ecstatic about the engagement. We caught them right before they went to bed, but they didn't mind the disruption. It seemed Mama had prepared for the occasion with a bottle of Soviet champagne and a box of chocolates in hand—a Jewish mother's intuition.

After the initial hugs and congratulations, Mama asked me to get champagne glasses from the kitchen.

"So Yan, do you love my daughter?"

Papa's question startled me. *Why ask this question?*

"Yes, Yoseph, I do," said Yan without hesitation. "And I promise you I will do everything in my power to make her happy."

I paused behind the door, clutching four champagne glasses in my hands, relishing his beautiful answer, though terrified by what my father might ask next. Papa was a smart man. He must have noticed the trend. But *that* question didn't come. Not until the night before the wedding.

On the celebratory night of our engagement, Papa made a toast to our happy life together and raised his glass. "*L'chaim!*" He startled me, using a Yiddish toast "To Life!" Mama cried and kept hugging Yan. I think I got a hug, too.

Three months later, we were married. I did not tell my parents about our plans and they didn't press the topic with me. The night before the wedding, however, Papa and Yan had an exchange I didn't know about for many years.

The two men were on the balcony off my parents' bedroom.

Papa enjoyed his evening cigarette, and Yan came out to keep him company. Papa inhaled and blew out a cloud of smoke before saying: "Many young people (he couldn't bring himself to say "Jewish young people") these days have ideas about leaving the country..." He inhaled again, and continued after releasing another gray cloud into the cold November air. "I want you to know, Galina is not going anywhere. Her mother and I won't allow it, and she will not go against our will." He put his hand on Yan's shoulder. "You understand, son."

Papa didn't wait for the response, and Yan said nothing.

5

Wedding Rings

October 1974—Kiev

To appreciate the potential impact the event of purchasing wedding rings could've had on our lives, I should first explain what it was like to buy wedding rings in the USSR.

After registering at the Central Marriage Registration Hall, known as Newlyweds Palace, the bride and groom received a voucher to purchase their wedding bands at a specific store on a certain date. Like many other aspects of our lives, the state controlled this process. You couldn't purchase wedding rings outside of the "system"—not legally, anyway. Besides the voucher, future newlyweds had to bring their passports to prove they were who they said they were. So we needed the voucher, passports, scheduled date, and a specific store. *Got it.*

Now, back to the story. When our scheduled day came, we rushed to the store near Victory Square. Happy couples packed the single-story space—although by their behavior, you wouldn't conclude they were happy. Scarcity, a common state of existence in the USSR, brought out the worst in people, and a hunt for wedding jewelry fell into the category of scarcity. People in the store were practically piled on top of one another, shouting, pushing, and shoving each other to move closer to the only counter displaying the wedding bands. The choices were limited to a few size and width options, and yet everyone wanted to get a glimpse of the gold bands under the glass top of the counter, hoping to see something no one else would.

The salesperson looked like she sold coffins instead of wedding rings. She scolded those who got too close to the counter and became irritated when people took too long to make a choice or wanted to try another ring that looked exactly like the one they had already tried on. We made our way to the end of the line to wait for our turn.

Hours later, we had two shiny, beautiful rose gold bands in our hands. Yan bought the thinnest one possible for himself and a wider ring for me. That's all he could afford, but it didn't matter. I loved both rings. After admiring them for a few minutes, I put the rings, the passports, and the registration into a pouch I'd brought for this purpose and placed it inside my purse, which hung on my shoulder.

Excited and relieved, we made our way out of the store and walked across town to show off our purchase to my parents, who rushed us into the living room when we walked through the door-way. Yan and I sat down next to each other on the sofa, and he handed me my purse that I left next to him.

"You show them," he said with a proud smile. I took the purse and looked inside. *Where is the pouch?* I thought Yan was playing with me and laughed, asking him to give me the pouch. He thought I was joking and laughed in return. Neither one of us was joking. We looked at each other in horror, checking the empty bag again and again. No pouch. Everything had vanished. The rings. Our passports. Newlyweds Palace registration. Gone.

In the next fifteen minutes, our emotions jumped from disbelief to anger to mourning to a realization that we might not be able to get married on our scheduled wedding day. In order to get married, we needed the three items we no longer had. It would take two months to replace the passports alone, and to replace everything else we would need passports. With the wedding date two weeks away, what were the chances of us making it?

Could our story have ended right there if we'd delayed the wedding? It didn't—thanks to Misha. He connected Yan with a clerk at the passport office. Yan bribed the clerk, and we had our new passports one week later. We purchased new bands two days before the wedding. They were narrower than the original ones, and we paid for them with the money borrowed against our wedding money gifts—wedding money is a Russian thing. To avoid any comments of "this is bad luck" that would inevitably come from family and friends (you know the kind), we did not tell anyone else about what happened. Until now.

6

Stalling

Like any story, the story about the crazy woman and our introduction had two sides. One was mine and the other—Yan's. You already listened to mine. This is Yan's. As he made his plans to leave the Soviet Union, Yan wanted to remain single, which would expedite his departure and make travel easier. Yan's mother and his Aunt Clara—his late father's sister—whom Yan regarded as his second mother, had a different opinion; they wanted him to get married before he left. The women insisted that embarking on this journey with a wife would be better in the long run, as long as he waited to have a baby until he was in America. Yan and his mother-aunt team were both right, but I am happy (an understatement) Rita and Aunt Clara won. After enduring their nagging for almost a year, Yan agreed to a blind date with a girl who lived two streets from his house and had an excellent reputation.

As far as my reputation was concerned, the crazy woman must've been their trusted source. She also must've reassured them that this girl was ready to go to *Amerika* at the drop of a hat. What did the crazy woman gain from introducing us, and what happened to her afterward? I don't have answers to these questions. We lost track of her and never asked. No one has seen her since we began dating. When we tried to invite her to the wedding as a thank you for introducing us, we couldn't find any trace of her. The crazy woman had vanished. She must've been our matchmaker from heaven.

The next five years tested—to the very core—our love for each other and our willingness to fight for our family.

We got married on November 5, 1974, six months after we met. I had every intention of discussing our America plan with my parents, giving myself a deadline for when we returned from our honeymoon in Leningrad. I believed in my intention and yet, when I found out I was pregnant—which incidentally happened fifteen minutes after we got married, despite our plans to wait—subconsciously, I welcomed a reprieve. I figured, our emigration efforts had to slow down now—we couldn't possibly embark on a voyage to the other side of the world during my pregnancy and surely not with a newborn. Excuse number one sounded defensible. Second was my schooling. I had two more years of college, and it seemed reasonable to finish it before we left. *How valuable a degree in shipbuilding would be in America!* With these big events ahead, postponing the conversation with my parents for at least a year seemed logical.

Here is the truth as I understand it now. I was scared, and I was stalling—something I couldn't admit to Yan or myself. I was scared of the unknown and terrified to leave everything and everyone behind forever. My biggest fear, however, was the need to confront my parents. What was I afraid of? That I would no longer be the "good" daughter my parents had relied on since I was a kid. The one who made their lives easier. The peacemaker. The pleaser. The fixer. The one who, unlike her brother, always did what she was supposed to do. And how would they live without Zhenya? Their Zhenechka, Zhenura.

Yan accepted my reasoning with patience and understanding,

but with each passing day, month, and year, he grew more and more concerned that we would never leave. He didn't trust the Soviet government to keep the Jewish refugee door open for much longer. We were playing with fire. *I* was playing with fire.

By the end of 1976, I had my diploma in my hands and Zhenya had just turned one. I attempted a meek conversation with Mama one day as the two of us walked home from a movie theater. I told her that Sofia and her family were getting ready to emigrate, and Rita would leave with them. As if suspecting where this conversation might go, Mama was short: "That's them. You are not going anywhere. Papa would not allow it."

"What if Yan wants to leave?" I said, looking down at my shoes. I couldn't bring my eyes to meet Mama's.

She answered right away, as though having already given it much thought. "He would never leave you and Zhenya behind—Yan is a good man."

I didn't go any further with this conversation, and Mama didn't bring the topic up again.

While I continued to delay the actual conversation with my parents, Yan began preparing for our future. He became an apprentice to a car mechanic and learned the trade as an option for a profession in America. He now worked two jobs: a music teacher by day and a car mechanic by night. Working with cars left his hands covered in grease, and he spent endless time every night scrubbing them back to pristine cleanliness so as not to alarm his students the following day.

As another year was going by, I began noticing deep sadness in Yan's eyes. Often he would lie awake at night, staring at the ceiling. I would lie next to him pretending to be asleep, afraid to ask what he was thinking about. We were less connected, avoiding the only topic that mattered; living in parallel worlds, going through the motion of day-to-day tasks, and drifting apart. We no longer pursued the same dream, and I realized we could lose each other forever if this continued much longer. The thought made me ill. The possibility of losing our family scared me more than all the repercussions from confronting my parents. I was ready to stand by Yan's side. Our story had to go on.

In the meantime, Sofia and her family left. Uncle Vova announced his plans to emigrate, infuriating my mother and Aunt Basya. It seemed all Soviet Jews were packing their bags.

Some information from "the other side" began slipping inside the Iron Curtain, with more letters reaching their destination. Mail from abroad was strictly monitored, and not all letters made it. Those that did were treasures. We passed them from family to family and read behind closed doors, often in the dark of night. Acutely aware that the government monitored all mail from abroad, people came up with code words and phrases to share their new-immigrant experiences. They provided tips on how to pass through the Soviet border. How to board the train to Bratislava. How to reduce the chances of a strip search. More and more, the stories of women being humiliated and downright abused while searched by female security guards came to us through the grapevine. I was numb to these stories. They seemed unreal, far away, and paled in comparison to the fear of talking to Mama and Papa.

From these letters, we learned what to say and what not to say during the border check-in. We learned to keep our heads down, make no eye contact with the guards, not to argue, and to make sure our luggage wasn't a single gram heavier than allowed, to reduce the chance of our belongings being thrown out onto the platform in front of a moving train.

We began receiving letters from Sofia and Rita. Sometimes later letters came first, and earlier ones showed up weeks later. Often the stories in them seemed incomplete, indicating some letters were missing. Once the four of them made it through the refugee route and settled in Miami Beach, their letters included photos of the beautiful Florida coast, the palm trees, and the ocean as blue as the sky. Color photos were still a rarity for us, so these looked unreal. Vivid colors. Beautiful scenery. And there was something different in the familiar faces. Were they smiling? Who smiled looking into the camera? It was different. There was a picture of their new car, but Sofia said in the letter that it was old. They paid four hundred dollars for it with the money they had made selling photo cameras, *matryoshkas*, and linen sheets in Italy. *Imagine, a car!*

We shared the letters and the photographs with my parents, hoping to trigger their interest so we could begin discussing our plans. Pleased to get the updates, as they cared about Yan's family, they dismissed our attempts to discuss the forbidden topic. There was no easy way to give them the news.

By then, we began hearing about *refuseniks*, those whose petitions to emigrate were declined by the government. *Otkazniki.* The authorities refused emigration for a multitude of reasons and also without any. These stories, besides Yan's growing fear of the borders being closed at any minute, made both of us eager to begin the process. The pressure was on.

7

The Night Everything Changed

December 1977—Kiev

How could I tell my parents we would never see each other again? How could I ask them not to worry? How could I tell them that I would try to call, but that it might not even be possible? That I would write letters, but they might not be delivered? That as they got older, I wouldn't be around to take care of them?

How?

One word after another. That was how.

Mama sank into the couch, sobbing before all the words had even left my mouth.

The chill and darkness of the December evening crept inside. Frigid street light filtered through the—sealed for the winter—living room window, spotlighting four motionless figures, which would be changed forever by this moment. My body trembled and my teeth chattered.

Mama was gasping for air as she put a nitroglycerin tablet under her tongue; then she clasped both hands to her chest, looking at me with a blank stare. I don't think she saw me. Without conscious thought, I helped her lift her feet to the couch and propped a pillow under her head. This was what I always did when she wasn't feeling well. Mama had a heart condition, so this reaction was not a good sign. Papa was now pacing in a small space between the couch and the dining table, inhaling cigarette smoke faster and deeper than I'd ever seen him do, breaking the rule of not smoking in the house that he had upheld since Zhenya was born. Yan stood next to me, his left arm firmly wrapped around my shoulder. I was grateful we'd left Zhenya at our apartment with the neighbor.

Papa stopped facing Yan and me, and looked only at me. I was taller than Papa, but he appeared gigantic. Under his harsh stare, I was a five-year-old about to receive a punishment for leaving my clothes lying around. When he finally spoke, his rough, gravelly voice cut the thick air like a knife.

"So, you will become a traitor and leave the Motherland for a promise of material things and better food? A piece of sausage is more valuable to you than the ideals of your country and your family? What happened to you? I don't know who you are anymore."

His words physically hurt, like a punch in the gut. I fought the urge to double over in pain. I screamed inside my head: "I hate you! I want to do better with my life than you have! And I will—you can't stop me! You can not stop me!"

"Papa, please understand…" I heard myself whimper. I was five, making a plea to a giant that was my father.

Mama sat up. Her right hand was now on her chest, as if protecting her heart from exploding.

"If you don't want to think of your parents, think of your son," she said. "Think of Zhenya! How will he grow up in a foreign land, not knowing his grandparents, not speaking the language of his family?"

"That's just it, Mama." I made a step toward the couch, taking a deep breath to stop a tremble in my voice. It didn't work. "I want Zhenya to grow up in a place...where he will be free to live, study, travel, and work wherever he chooses without being limited because he is a Jew." I stopped to catch my breath before blurting, "And I don't want him to serve in the Soviet Army. Not Zhenya! Mama, please understand...you must understand!" I blew my nose into the sleeve of my sweater and remained standing, instead of sitting down next to her, as I would normally do.

"We should've talked to you sooner. This is my fault." Yan made an attempt, but Papa stopped him with a hand gesture.

"This is not about you. This is about *my* daughter!"

Another punch to my stomach. I hunched over to loosen up what felt like a million knots inside. I was in pain. I was furious. But I was no longer afraid. I knew my family came first, and this was our only chance for a future.

"You can't pretend you haven't been living with anti-Semitism your whole life, Papa," I said, raising my voice. "I remember the stories you told me about your family. You never said who was at fault, but you knew who. Stalin. The government. The system."

Papa did not respond.

"What about you being cheated out of a well-deserved military title and your pension with no prospects of finding a job?" I continued. "I saw your struggles even though I was a little kid." *Should I take Papa's silence as a good sign?* "And what about my teacher telling me I wouldn't get into a university because I am a Jew? What about Yan's student telling him he liked him even though Yan is a Jew? I don't want Zhenya to live with this, like the rest of us! It isn't just for material things, Papa!"

The air was heavy with silence for what seemed like hours.

"I will never allow you to leave. Never." Papa sounded grim and firm. I knew this voice. He meant it with every fiber of his body.

"Papa...please!" I made my last appeal to the giant.

He extended his right arm—palm up—toward me. "You will leave when the hair grows here." He tapped the index finger of his left hand in the center of his right palm.

Papa's threat was real. Among the documents required to submit the emigration petition was a written affidavit from parents that sounded something like this:

"We, Yoseph Yakovlevich (*patronymic*) Kugel and Bella Mikhailovna Volkovitskaya (Mama kept her maiden name to commemorate her father), the parents of Galina Yosephovna Chernyanskaya, reconfirm that Galina is not in any financial debt to us. This letter is provided to the OVIR office because Galina is petitioning to emigrate to Israel." Israel was our official destination until we reached Vienna.

The adult children staying behind had to write a similar letter for their parents who were leaving, and the same was true for divorced spouses. Of course, financial debt had nothing to do with this requirement. After writing such letters, parents, children, and ex-spouses were "on the hook." They often lost their jobs, were expelled from Communist organizations in a public forum, and experienced harassment and humiliation. It wasn't surprising that, knowing these consequences, many were afraid to provide the letters. And that was exactly what the government was after: to humiliate, discourage, scare. Oh, the mastery of degrading people by the Communist regime—there was nothing like it!

I expected my parents to react exactly the way they did. And when they did as I expected, I was enraged. Why weren't they like all the other parents who understood? They were both retired, and I wished this would ease the stress of their decision. When it didn't, I interpreted their reaction to mean they were unwilling to be ridiculed on my behalf. I was wrong. They weren't afraid to face humiliation. They had all the courage in the world to deal with what was to come, but not that night.

That night was endless. We said terrible things to each other. I was angry at my parents for putting their feelings above the welfare of my family. Their point of view became irrelevant to me. I stopped considering what it must have been like for them to face our separation. I wanted to save my family, and I was ready to go to war to accomplish that. In fact, that's exactly what I did. The silent battle lasted three days and three nights. We lived across the street from my parents and saw them every day. They picked up Zhenya from preschool and played with him until we came home from work. Not seeing their grandson was inconceivable to them, and I knew that. He became my weapon. No grandson. No phone calls. No visits.

I don't know if I would have had the courage to wage this battle if it weren't for Aunt Katya. She wasn't really my aunt, but that was what Misha and I called her. Aunt Katya was my parents' best friend, the non-Jewish Jewish friend who understood everything. She didn't have children of her own, and she adored Misha and me.

"Yoseph is reading and smoking in the house all day. Bella is taking valerian drops and slams pots in the kitchen, but they are fine. Hang in there," she reported. If it weren't for Aunt Katya calling me every day to tell me that my parents were all right—that they were still alive—I would have run back to their house the next day to check on them.

Even now, do I fully comprehend my parents' struggle as they came to terms with what was inevitable? We were leaving them for a life they didn't understand, with no right to return, and ripping their only grandson out of their arms forever. Yet, with their eyes wide open, they put the welfare of my family above their own at an enormous cost to them.

At the end of day three, Papa called and asked us to come for dinner. He made one request: "Please bring Zhenya."

Mama opened the door, greeting her *vnuk* with endless hugs and kisses, telling him she made his favorite *blinchiki*, blintzes, for dinner. Papa picked him up and squeezed him tight, making Zhenya laugh out loud as he threw his arms around *Deda's* neck, asking for more. This image would live with me for the rest of my life.

Papa told us to sit down, and we pulled two dining chairs closer to the couch where he was sitting, holding Zhenya on his knee. Mama sat by his side, next to Zhenya.

"Kids, we will write you the letter and support your decision to leave," Papa said. I held my breath. I didn't know what to say. "Thank you" didn't seem enough or appropriate.

"Thank you," I said anyway.

"What about you?" Yan said. "Come with us. We want you to come. Please, Papa, think about it."

Papa let out a long sigh. "How can we? This is home…we could never…but if we decide to leave, we will take the last train." I looked at Papa in disbelief. *Was he considering what seemed unconscionable just three days ago?*

"The way things are right now, I am afraid *we* may very well be leaving on the last train. Please, Papa, Mama. Let's go together," Yan said. None of us suspected Yan was right.

"I'll tell you what. Mama and I will talk about it, but you must apply as soon as possible, and don't wait."

It never occurred to me to ask them to come with us. I was grateful Yan did so without discussing it with me first. I would not have agreed for fear of making things between us worse.

Dinner was on the table. To an outsider it looked like any other meal at my parents' house. Mama made short trips to the kitchen—bringing something out and taking something else away, never sitting down for more than a minute. But when she sat, her face lit with joy as she watched Zhenya devour *blinchiki* one after another while sipping warm milk from his personal porcelain cup.

"Where in America are you planning to settle?" Papa pulled out a map and put it on the table between himself and Yan. *Where did that map come from?*

"California. Los Angeles." Yan pointed to a strip of land that bordered the Pacific Ocean.

Papa nodded. "That's good. I like California. You will do well there. I am glad you are not going to Florida. It's a place for old people. All they have are hotels and banks. You need to be in a more industrial area with more options for work." Yan nodded in agreement.

How long had he been researching all this? I wondered. *And where did he find this information?* We had already spoken with Yan's family in Florida. They had decided to move to California, too, once we arrived. Rita would move sooner. The Florida climate didn't agree with her, but more importantly, by settling in Los Angeles first, she would make it easier for us to be permitted to settle there. Having family members live in a certain city gave immigrants more certainty for a residency in that city.

"Where will you work?" Papa leaned closer to Yan.

"I could begin as a car mechanic. I've been working as one for a while now, and I know cars. I hope Galya can take English classes right away. But we will have to figure things out once we get there."

"All of you must learn to speak English without an accent. Language is the most important. People judge you by the way you speak." If only I had a penny for every time that phrase had come out from my father's mouth into my ears: "People judge you by the way you speak." It's not surprising that for the longest time, I was petrified to speak English, fearful of exposing my accent. To this day, the worst question anyone could ask me is: "Where are you from, originally?" Instead of hearing someone's curiosity in such a question, I hear: "People judge you by the way you speak, and you speak with an accent!"

"Yes, Papa. We agree."

8

How to Leave the Motherland

If you thought the bureaucracy around buying wedding rings was bad, listen to this. The list of required documents to include with the emigration petition was long. Ironically, there was no physical *list*, nor documented procedures. The "hunt" for rules and instructions was like the hunt for everything else: food, clothing, theater tickets, etc. It involved finding someone who knew someone who had already gone through the process and would share what they'd learned. You would do the same for someone else at some point.

Before anything else, an invitation from a relative in Israel—delivered via the Foreign Ministry of Israel—asking the Soviet authorities to allow the recipient to reunite with family in Israel had to be provided. One might ask, how would anyone living in a country that kept its citizens locked inside its borders for decades have relatives in Israel, or anywhere else outside the USSR? This was rare, and yet thousands received *priglashenie*. Invitations came from fake relatives to those who smuggled their names with departing friends, relatives, and, very often, complete strangers.

Smuggling names was an elaborate operation, and nobody knew if their information made it to the "free world"—in this case, Hebrew Immigrant Aid Society (HIAS)—until they either received an invitation within an uncertain timeframe or they didn't. Jews went to great length to take names across the Soviet border. Some wrote them in address books under the tags "uncle" or "cousin," but this method proved to be risky since an item as obvious as an address book was an easy target for confiscation at the border. Others wrote the information on small pieces of paper that they sewed inside clothing or hid in the least likely personal items to be subjected to a search. We hid the names and addresses of six people given to us by a friend of a friend inside Yan's pants cuff. Once in Vienna, we passed those names to a representative from HIAS. Founded in New York in 1881 and headquartered in the United States, HIAS helped over four and a half million people escape oppression and immigrate to the United States and other countries for safety. We were among them.

So, the process began with getting your information beyond the Soviet border by any means imaginable, and if that step succeeded, you had a chance to be free.

After making it out of Chop and stopping in Bratislava to switch trains, Jews arrived in Vienna, the first refuge base. In Vienna, they were met by representatives of the Jewish Agency of Israel (JAFI) and HIAS. This is where the refugees requested their ultimate destination. JAFI assisted those who headed to Israel; HIAS guided those who wanted to go to the United States, Canada, Australia, or New Zealand.

Following a short stay in Vienna, the émigrés moved to Rome, Italy, where the US Immigration and Naturalization Service (INS) processed the requests of those who sought residency in the US.

If the names of people wishing to receive invitations from fake

Israeli relatives made it to Vienna, they would most likely result in invitations for some lucky Soviet Jews.

Miraculously, our names reached JAFI. To this day I am still astonished that neither the government, the post office, nor the mailman intercepted the invitation. In fact, our mailman was looking out for a "very important envelope" every day, receiving a few *kopeks* with a promise of a larger payout on the day he delivered the letter.

The wait seemed endless, but in early March 1978—a little over four months since we had given our names to a stranger—the mailman brought us a thick envelope from the Foreign Ministry of Israel. The ministry asked the Soviet Government to allow us to reunite with Yan's "aunt," a woman we had never met and knew nothing about, who gifted us our first triumph on a long journey to freedom.

With the invitation in hand, it all became real. Yan spoke of freedom on our horizon, and my emotions threw a wild party in my mind and body. The envelope postmarked with an Israeli address burned my hands. Here it was, the forbidden word. Israel. A Star of David on the stamp. I was five again, grabbing my mother's hand in the Kiev Synagogue. *Is this envelope our ticket to a strange, new world?*

I wanted to enter this new world, and yet I was terrified of what lay ahead. While still in Kiev, I had a recurring dream about not being able to speak English. I would open my mouth, but nothing came out. No sound, just air. People laughed and pointed their fingers at me. One of them would say repeatedly: "People judge you by the way you speak." I would wake up in a cold sweat, shaking off the dread, but the dream kept coming back as soon as I closed my eyes again. When we arrived in America, another dream haunted me. It sent shivers up and down my spine and made sweat drip from the top of my head to the tip of my toes. In this dream, three KGB men dressed in dark suits stopped me in Chop and put me on the train back to Kiev. I was alone. Yan and Zhenya were not with me. When did this dream stop? I think it was when I began dreaming in English, years later.

And so, March 1978—when we received our invitation—marked the beginning of a five-month quest to collect the rest of the documents. A letter from the university came next. Compared to everything else, this task seemed straightforward, and by then, the "diploma tax" was no longer strictly enforced. In 1972, the government first imposed the "diploma tax" on those with undergraduate and postgraduate degrees to "repay expenses for public education." Sometimes, this tax amounted to more than a decade of annual salaries, making it impossible for many professionals to leave. It was an unimaginable amount of money for anyone in the Soviet Union. Fortunately, we were permitted to pay a much more "reasonable" fee and got the letter in return. But what about our diplomas? Apparently, the diplomas were no longer ours. They became state property and had to remain inside the country.

When I wrote my resume for the first time in America, I had been worried no one would believe my education without a document to prove it. It still amazes me that no one asked me for proof. Not once! One of many marvelous things I love about America: innocent until proven guilty. Yan, too, had the same experience, but by then he realized that having his College of Music diploma in his possession wouldn't do him any good. He predicted his career as a musician was over.

Unlike Yan, who never joined Komsomol, I now needed to be expelled from the organization and receive a letter from the Komsomol District Committee office stating that they expelled me from its ranks because of my desire to emigrate to Israel. The

Komsomol office leaders conducted the expulsion, and from what I'd gathered from others, the experience was bound to be humiliating. The degree of humiliation varied from district to district, but most stories suggested that I should be prepared for several hours of degrading, shaming, and name-calling. To reduce the amount of ammunition the Komsomol leaders would use to attack me, Yan and I came up with a bulletproof answer to the inevitable question, "Why do you want to leave the Motherland?" We agreed I would blame him for wanting to emigrate, giving me no choice but to follow because we had a child. As it happened, the story wasn't too far from the truth.

Located on Kiev's Red Square, the Podol Komsomol District Committee building was familiar. Until the age of nineteen, I lived a short walk from here, on Spasskaya Street, and attended school on the same block as our house. I was an active *komsomolka*, and as a well-regarded Komsomol member, I had the privilege and honor of attending a couple of regional meetings in this very building. That day, I came to turn in my *Komsomolski bilet,* a small two-sided booklet with Lenin's profile embossed on the outer side of the red hard cover. That day, like many of that period, faded into my unconscious mind, only to resurface with clarity and raw emotions forty years later, as I write my story.

Yan insisted on coming with me. He always wanted to take the burden off my shoulders, or at least share it. He still does. We dropped Zhenya off at daycare and walked to the Red Square—the same Red Square Mama had run to with me and Misha when Stalin died. A long walk on a cool spring morning was much more pleasant than fighting crowds on a tram. We spoke more freely, walking outside, rehearsing my storyline one more time as we reached the park near the Komsomol Committee building. I left Yan waiting on a park bench and waved a quick *poka,* rushing to cross the street before he noticed how nervous I was.

As I approached the building, silently reciting my legend, the dreaded stomach spasms slowed me down. My mother's voice sounded clear in my head: "If you think you are old enough to decide to leave, you should be old enough to handle the process." I was twenty-five. I was old enough. I walked up to a massive front door and took a deep breath before pulling it open with both hands. The foyer walls were a dull shade of gray, the same color as most office buildings, shops, and schools. Dull gray was the color of our lives.

In the hallway in front of me, a small crystal chandelier hung off the high ceiling above the portraits of the three Communist leaders: Karl Marx, Friedrich Engels, Vladimir Ilyich Lenin. The men terrified me, as if they could punish me for my unpatriotic deed, even though I was well aware that they had all been dead for a very long time.

I checked in with the receptionist, who greeted me with a smirk and a look of disgust. Without saying a word, she stood up from her desk and walked toward the hallway. I followed. She stopped at the first door on her left, pointed at the doorknob, and walked away. This must be it. I hesitated for a second, but Mama's voice pushed me forward. I was old enough to handle this. I opened the door and walked into a conference room.

"*Zdravstvuite* (hello)," I said to a group of ten men, all sitting along one side of a rectangular conference table facing me. Most of them seemed to be around my age. The same three portraits I saw in the hallway also hung on the wall above the table, peering directly at me. The fourth portrait of the current Soviet *vozhd*, Leonid Ilyich Brezhnev, hung to the right of Lenin.

No one responded to my greeting, and there were no introductions. A man sitting in the middle of the group pointed at the only chair on my side of the room, which was placed a meter away from the table. I said *spasibo* into a dead silence and sat down. The setup reminded me of an interrogation scene in spy movies. The man who pointed to the chair leaned forward, placing his forearms on the table, his hands stacked one on top of the other. He looked straight at me.

"Why are you here today, Comrade Chernyanskaya?" he said.

Good, I thought. *A question I prepared to answer.*

I told the story I'd rehearsed with Yan as ten pairs of emotionless eyes (not counting the portraits) stared at me.

"...and so, because of my decision to emigrate with my husband, I ask to be expelled from Komsomol," I concluded, pulling my membership card out of my purse, ready to turn it in.

"You see, Comrade Chernyanskaya..." The man was now leaning back in his chair, clasping his hands together behind his head, "I don't believe your story. Your husband may have decided to leave, but you don't have to follow him. Just like many Soviet women before you—especially our widows after the war (referring to World War II)—with the help of the Union, you, too, can raise your son to be a proud Soviet citizen. This is a duty of every patriotic woman."

"My son needs his father...I can't raise him alone." I kept my answers as short as possible.

"Is your husband threatening you?"

"No, I want to follow him..."

"Tell us the truth, and we can help you. I promise, nothing will happen to your husband."

"No, he doesn't threaten me. I want to follow him."

Silence.

"What about your parents? Do they want you to leave?"

"No. My parents are very much against my decision. They will never leave." *Another rehearsed answer.*

"So, you are ready to betray your parents?"

"I have no choice. I am a mother...what can I do?"

"Well, in this case, you are embarrassing your parents and our

Motherland. Does this mean anything to you?" Another man jumped in.

"I understand, but I have no choice," I said, repeating the lines like a robot.

"I offer you, once again, a chance to reconsider. We will help you separate from your husband, and we will take care of you and your son. I make this promise on behalf of the Kiev Komsomol Committee."

This must have been the head. The guy who had "offered" me a chair.

"No." I no longer wanted to be polite. I was no longer afraid or intimidated. I was done. But I had to maintain my composure for this nightmare to end.

"This is treason, and you will have to live with it for the rest of your life. You are a traitor; you are unworthy of the Soviet Union, Comrade Chernyanskaya..."

Surprised at myself, I looked straight into his cold eyes and said nothing. He wore a clean white shirt, and a pack of Marlboros stuck out of his shirt pocket. I almost laughed. *Seriously? How did he get his hands on American cigarettes? Wasn't everything American poisoned by capitalism? A bunch of hypocrites!*

"Comrades, let's take a vote. Those who agree to expel Galina Yosephovna Chernyanskaya from Komsomol for betraying the Union of Soviet Socialist Republic, raise your hand."

One by one, ten hands went up in unison. Decision made.

I stood up, afraid I would fall—my legs flimsy and light, like cotton. I handed the membership card to the man with the Marlboro, and in exchange, he handed me the letter he had just signed.

"*Spasibo. Do svidaniya.*" I walked out of the conference room, not waiting for a "thank you" or "goodbye" in return.

Expelled. Another document in hand.

Finally, all we needed was a letter from our last place of work, confirming dates of employment. The letter also had to include the following statement: "This letter is given to so-and-so because he/she is immigrating to Israel." Sounds simple enough? Not so fast. I still look back on this event in disbelief. Where did we get the *chutzpah* to do what we did? Did desperation fuel our audacity? You be the judge.

It was common knowledge that many employers behaved similarly to the Komsomol officials when asked for employment verification letters, and usually an employee received the letter after resigning. Yan worked for a music school and received his letter with no issues. In fact, his boss and colleagues wished him luck. His consequence was resignation—a fair exchange, so to speak.

I worked at a city college teaching bookkeeping. I began there as a chemistry and physics lab teacher until my manager, a beautiful, intelligent, and kind woman, Nonna Grigorievna, recommended me for a paid teacher's role. For a year, she pushed hard until the dean awarded me five hours a week to teach evening classes. Bookkeeping wasn't my dream subject, and neither was chemistry nor physics, but I loved teaching, and I dove into it with all my heart. My students gave me rave reviews. I made friends with other teachers, and the dean respected me—until I came to him for the letter. He refused to give it to me, saying "no" to my request, but took me up on my offer to resign.

It was the end of May 1978. We'd spent the last couple of months collecting the other required documents, leaving letters from work to the end, to continue working for as long as possible. Now, all we had to do was figure out how to get the damn letter!

But by August we were no closer to procuring it. For the whole summer, Yan and I had taken turns showing up at the dean's office at nine in the morning, "stalking" him and asking for the letter. For the first couple of weeks, he stopped to hear our plea, but repeated his answer. Now, he ignored us, even though we spent most of the day sitting outside his office. Thankfully, most staff and students were on summer break. But those who happened to be around walked by, staring at me as if I had three heads. No one said hello except for the dean's secretary, who showed some sympathy by allowing us to sit in the waiting room. Yan often took extra turns to protect me from this humiliation. He tried talking to the dean, appealing to his humane side, but nothing worked.

We were three months out of work and still unable to apply. If this continued much longer, we might get in trouble with the government for not working. To be discovered as *parasites* would mean fines as a best-case scenario or jail time, depending on how badly they would want to hurt us. A Jew applying to emigrate, who is a deadbeat—a lethal combination.

One afternoon, after another day of defeat, Yan left the waiting room, angry and frustrated. As he turned the corner away from the building, someone called his name. It was the dean's secretary standing at the door, signaling him to come closer. She had a piece of paper in her hand. Yan's heart skipped a beat... *Is this the letter? The dean must've gotten tired of watching us outside his office day after day.* The woman handed him a blank letterhead with the dean's official stamp and said, "Here. Do what you want with it." For a second, Yan stood there processing what had just happened, then uttered a thank you, hurrying away as she disappeared into the building.

Before I continue, I need to tell you we are forever grateful to this woman. She risked a lot by doing this for us, and we never forgot it. I hope we expressed our gratitude on some level by sending her (through my parents) money and presents of makeup and jeans—some of the most precious items from the West.

So we had a blank letterhead. Now what? It was clear we were about to forge a letter from my work, but how? We needed a typewriter and an expert typist. Yan remembered that his cousin worked as a secretary and called to find out if she would help. Turned out, she had a typewriter at home, and she agreed to type the letter. This was no minor act of bravery. All typewriters were registered with the local government, and if OVIR caught us with a forged letter, it would lead to her.

Late that evening, we took a bus partway to her apartment, and rushed through the dark city, looking over our shoulders like criminals the rest of the way there. I feared we were being followed, and that at any moment we might be arrested and thrown into prison. The fear of being exposed stayed with me throughout our journey and for years after, in America. It turned into another repeated nightmare: we were stopped at the border in Chop and transported to a labor camp in Siberia for forging this document; the same labor camp my aunt and my grandmother were sent to in 1937. But that night in Kiev, I leaned on Yan, who was strong and confident, and we did what we had to do. I drafted the letter. Yan's cousin typed it, navigating the formatted page. Yan signed with the dean's name.

It was dawn by the time we left his cousin's apartment. The sun was touching the horizon, coloring the sky on the left bank of the Dnieper orange and yellow. That morning, Yan and I said goodbye to Kiev as we watched the awakening city. We were ready to take the next step.

9

Life in the USSR

I write this part of my story in my cozy living room of our Los Angeles home, a large cup of steaming hot tea on a side table next to me. I stop to enjoy the beautiful California morning. The warm sun rays stroke my face, entering the room from the open patio door. My thoughts travel through time, and I marvel in awe at the wonder of life. How much has changed! Our lives have transformed, we speak a different language (literally and figuratively), and the lives of our children are so different from ours at their age. Immense gratitude for the life we have overwhelms my thoughts as I recollect our life in the USSR.

Back in the Soviet Union, Yan and I both worked and made enough money to support ourselves, which wasn't always the case with young families. More often than not, multiple generations—grandparents, parents, and grown-up children with kids of their own—lived together, depending on each other for financial, emotional, and physical support. The word "independence" had no meaning because it wasn't achievable.

While Yan and I stood on our own monetarily, our living

situation was very similar to most. When we got married, he moved in, and we lived with my parents and Misha, sharing a three-room, four-hundred-square-foot apartment. Yan and I occupied the smallest room; it fit a fold-out couch, a coffee table, and a crib. My parents slept in a larger room, and my brother slept on a couch in the living room, which also served as our dining room. We all shared one bathroom and a small kitchen.

To an American these accommodations may sound like tight quarters, but compared to the apartment I grew up in, our apartment on Ratmanskaya Street was luxurious. Hot water running from a faucet. A toilet behind a closed door instead of in the kitchen next to the stove. It was a dream come true. *Banya* became a thing of the past. The automated heating system proved to be heavenly during the cold Ukrainian winters. The years of fighting with my brother over whose turn it was to bring wood from the *sarai*, a storage shed, to run the *pechka* were behind us. This was a dream home! But as lovely as my parents' apartment was, Yan and I wanted to be on our own—a concept that was too painful for my mother to understand.

Children didn't leave their parents' home. That's not how it was. Everyone lived together, helped one another, and parents ran the household. But that wasn't how we wanted to live. The notion of moving out of your parents' home into your own apartment had no definition in the Soviet vocabulary. You couldn't rent a place to live or move to another city. You lived where your parents lived because your residence permit allowed you to live there and nowhere else. *Propiska* was a serious aspect of our lives. A residence permit was stamped in every citizen's passport—no moving around at your desire.

Yet we desperately wanted to be on our own. We wanted privacy. Even though the word *privacy* doesn't have an equivalent in the Russian language, we somehow understood the meaning. So as soon as Yan's mother left for America, we moved into her place, to my mother's shock. Mama told me I was crazy to leave my parents' home and move into a crumbling communal apartment where I would share the space with elderly strangers. Maybe I was insane, but I wanted to be the one to run my household and my life, and not be a child in my parents' home forever. Mama never understood that. And this step in no way prepared her for my desire to build my independence in a different country, more than six thousand miles away from home.

Yan kept his residence permit at his mother's apartment, making it possible for us to move there. Communal living or not, we found our autonomy. We now occupied two rooms in the very apartment Yan had spent his childhood, across the street from the infamous synagogue and two blocks from my parents' home. The joy of independence! The apartment with squeaky old wooden stairs, a narrow communal hallway—which housed a kitchen, a toilet, and a bathtub behind a flimsy plywood wall—was now ours. We carried groceries, a stroller, and the baby up and down four flights of stairs as they crackled under our feet—a small price to pay for a little privacy.

So by the Soviet standards, we made a decent living. Remember the crazy woman? She wasn't lying when she said Yan earned good money. He did. Our combined monthly income was around 250 rubles; we managed day-to-day necessities and did not need to borrow money to hold us over until the next payday like my parents did for as long as I can remember.

Let me give you a little context for what 250 rubles could buy. The government subsidized rent and utilities, so we paid about 20 rubles a month for both. A pair of shoes, however, cost 45 rubles, and boots 85. Owning one pair of footwear for each season and wearing them for years was the norm. As far as the rest of my wardrobe, I owned two dresses, a pair of pants, a sweater, a skirt, a blouse, a winter coat, and a spring coat. There wasn't much more than that. When I began working in America, the daily wardrobe changes by everyone around me, regardless of their financial standing, astonished me. This was not the case in the USSR. We wore the same clothes day after day with some variation by season.

Most everything, from groceries to clothing to big-ticket items—like furniture and appliances—were not only prohibitive for an average person, they required "hunting" and standing in long lines or having the right connections. If you knew somebody who knew somebody who could *dostat*—get something through a back door—you were in luck. Otherwise, you were destined to join endless lines. Shoes. Eggs. Apples. Oranges. Chicken. Toilet paper. You've probably heard the shocking stories about the Soviet lines for toilet paper. Well, they were true—in lieu of toilet paper we resorted to newspapers torn into palm-size pieces.

Lines are a widely discussed attribute of Soviet life, and for good reason. A common activity would be to get in line, not knowing what was being sold, hoping whatever it was wouldn't run out before your turn. Yan was often the one coming home with "treasures" from the lines because his job took him to different parts of the city, and he ran into lines, so to speak. He carried a briefcase to work, and sometimes the briefcase would come home with sheet music in it, and other times, whatever Yan found standing in line.

One day, he came home with a couple of kilos of onions. Let me tell you, onions don't belong in briefcases! All night, we laughed, cleaning out the smell and dirt. I had never seen clean onions until we entered the magic world of American supermarkets. Soviet onions, like the rest of the vegetables, were sold covered in the dirt they grew in.

When Zhenya was born, we faced a new set of domestic challenges. This, of course, was a time before diapers and washing machines (I didn't know anyone who owned one), which added to the daily grind. The real difficulty, however, came when it became apparent I didn't have enough milk to breastfeed. Baby formula, which saved me in America when Alik was born, would've been nice, but that was an unimaginable fantasy. Instead, every morning at six, we picked up "baby food"—allotted by a regional children's hospital only if prescribed by a pediatrician. The hospital was a thirty-minute walk from our house. It would've been a pleasant walk in the spring or summer, but Zhenya was born in October when the weather quickly changed from autumn to winter. Yan made the daily trip before going to work. The rationing of baby food—free baby food, I must add—was a reality; you got what you got, and not what the baby needed. A neighbor, who had a baby at the same time I had Zhenya, sold me her leftover breast milk for a few months. Another disaster averted.

We made our lives work without thinking about whether it was difficult. It wasn't until we had Alik in America that we appreciated how laborious and primitive mundane tasks were in the USSR. It wasn't just baby food that was limited and rationed; purchasing a crib, a stroller, a mattress, blankets, clothing, toys—you name it— required hunting and back-door connections, knowing someone who knew someone. Essentially, baby gear scarcity had been no different from the rest of life's necessities. Walking into a store and buying what we needed wasn't the reality we lived in. The experience we discovered in America of having a multitude of choices and a range of price points was mind-boggling. Even now, I don't take this abundance of choices for granted.

A Soviet childbirth requires its own mention, especially because my experience was typical. I'll start from the beginning. Even though I had regular doctor visits throughout my pregnancy, the obstetrician never explained to me what to expect and how to handle mental and physical changes that came with pregnancy, or what would happen at birth. In retrospect, I think even doctors didn't know how to handle these conversations. My mother had a difficult pregnancy with Misha and an easier one with me. I am sure she would've given me some tips, but who talked to their mothers about such topics? I had just turned twenty-two and hoped that whatever I experienced was a normal part of pregnancy. I was nauseous and sleepy most of the time, had several fainting episodes, cried when Yan ate the last spoonful of ice cream I had my eye on, and was overjoyed with the anticipation. I wanted to be a mama. That was all I ever wanted to be.

In the attempt to prepare myself for childbirth, I borrowed a book from the library and read it from cover to cover. But it wasn't any more helpful than my doctor, because when my water broke in the middle of the night, three weeks before the due date, I argued with my mother (yes, she was in the middle of it all because we lived together) that the liquid coming out of me didn't mean I was in labor. I believed it was a function of my bladder after I ate too much watermelon the night before. I doubt this part of my experience was typical; most likely it was very specific to me. Thankfully, Mama had an ally in Yan, and together they "dragged" me to the hospital in a taxi. There, at the front door, they left me and went home. Hospital rules. No one but a woman giving birth walks through the door. Period.

There I was, by myself, slimy liquid dripping down my legs, standing in front of a nurse who looked at me with disgust. "Women these days have no shame! Look at her! Wearing pants, nails painted…and she is having a baby! *Pozor!* Shame on you!"

She was right. I had on a pair of pants with cutout sides to fit my stomach. My father's suspenders held the pants in place. I wore a huge top—that I'd sewn by hand—covering my stomach, my version of a maternity blouse. The concept of maternity clothes didn't exist. Over my "provocative" outfit, I wore my mother's coat because mine no longer fit me; in fact, I'd cried over that fact the night before, while trying on Mama's coat, or maybe that was the night I cried over Yan eating the last spoon of ice cream. I can't remember. But I remember trying to swallow my tears, which blurred my vision as the nurse chastised me over my "flamboyant" outfit and painted nails, with no one around to defend me.

After an even more humiliating admission process—cutting off my nails, taking off the polish, shaving my pubic hair, and taking a cold shower as the nurse watched—I was told to go to the third floor and ask for a nurse there. So in a hospital gown (the size of which didn't consider my stomach) and hospital slippers that had seen better days, I walked up three flights of stairs. The nurse on duty took me to a room with ten beds—each separated by a nightstand. She pointed to the bed in the corner, one of the two unoccupied beds, and told me to lie down. I settled on a low, narrow, wrought-iron bed with a thin, lumpy mattress covered by a cotton sheet that had probably been white a very long time ago. Periodically, the room exploded with moans and cries of women having contractions. Once in a while, the nurse would come in and do a round of checkups to see how everyone was progressing.

The next six hours were uneventful for me; I had labor pains but wasn't dilating. I kept my eyes closed to avoid seeing anything I didn't want to see, but just listening to eight women having contractions was agonizing. In retrospect, maybe the explosive sounds of pain from others helped me ignore my own. On her routine visit the nurse determined I needed help to kick off my labor, so she walked me over to the room next door and gave me an induction shot. After twelve hours of active contractions, the nurse from the next shift told me I was ready.

"Let's go have that baby," she said, helping me get up from the bed. "The room is at the end of the corridor on your left." It was a long corridor, or so it seemed to me. I had to stop to wait out each contraction, crouching to lessen the pain. In between the contractions, I walked as fast as I could.

"I couldn't tell you were about to give birth if I didn't see you crouch like this," the nurse said matter-of-factly as we walked.

The delivery room was large and bright, with five beds placed in a circle. Yes. In a circle. Imagine a twenty-two-year-old woman—girl, really—in labor, walking into this scene.

Another nurse helped me settle onto the bed, and I closed my eyes once again, this time to avoid watching a woman across from me give birth. Yet, all was forgotten three hours later when I saw my baby boy for the first time—*saw*, not held. The delivery nurse told me the baby was fine and took him away to be checked out by the pediatrician. She said I would see him the next day for a feeding.

With no announcement or explanation, another doctor walked in—a big Armenian man with a thick accent—and said he would stitch my tears. Of course, no one had said anything about the tears before, but there he was, now sitting at my feet. As he made himself comfortable, he gave me a fair warning before he began: "It's going to hurt." With every new stitch, he repeated the warning, stretching the words as if in a song: "*Sa-a-yichas bolnooo budet.*" And again, before the next stitch. At some point, he got up and left without saying a word. I breathed a sigh of relief.

I was now by myself in the delivery room, still lying on the bed I had just given birth in, with no cover or a blanket, and no one around to tell me what was happening next. As I learned later, the hospital didn't have a bed for me in the post-delivery ward, so the nurse left me in the delivery room until one was freed up. A typical scenario.

"Better than in the corridor," a night nurse said, when she came to transfer me to the room, before the end of her shift. I contemplated whether to tell her about the encounter I had with the electrician in the middle of the night but decided not to say anything. *What would be the point?* The electrician had come into the delivery room to clean the lighting. He walked in carrying a ladder, which he propped against the bed I was on, as if the bed was empty or at least as if I were covered with a blanket, and began climbing up. I was silent for a few seconds, embarrassed and mortified, before I said: "Couldn't you come at another time?" "There is no other time in this room, my dear," he said and proceeded with his task. I was too exhausted to get upset. I drifted off to a beautiful dream where Yan and I brought our precious baby boy home.

10

Awaiting the Verdict

September 1978—Kiev

Six months after we received an invitation from Yan's "aunt" in Israel, we submitted our petition to the Kiev *OVIR* (Visa and Registration Department). We had been without jobs for four months and by then had run out of our meager savings. Yan's second job as a car mechanic had ended as soon as he told his boss about our plans. We gave our furniture to Misha, and there wasn't much else to sell. My parents received small standard pensions, and the five of us wouldn't be able to survive on their income. We didn't have enough to cover our emigration expenses, plus we wanted to make sure my parents had money for theirs when the time came. It was a lot of money we didn't have.

The "Jewish black market" became our only option, and by then it operated at full speed. While many like us didn't have enough to cover their emigration expenses, others had *extra* they had to leave behind unless they smuggled it to the US through the black market. Remember, each person was allowed to exchange ninety rubles at a Central bank a few days before departure, giving them 120 US dollars.

The black market scheme was clever. One borrowed rubles in the Soviet Union to repay with US dollars in America. The rate was four rubles for one dollar. We began looking for someone from whom to borrow the money, but my mother-in-law surprised us by organizing a money transfer for us. She paid one thousand dollars to a family in Miami Beach whose relatives in Riga, Latvia, wanted to smuggle their "leftover" money to America. She arranged for us to pick up four thousand rubles in Riga. At sixty-three, Rita took a job at a factory, earning $2.30 an hour. She lived with Sofia, contributing to the household, and by 1978 she had saved enough to help pay our way. We are forever grateful to her for that. When Rita was leaving in 1976, she also had limited resources and was struggling to manage her expenses. Yan sold his piano and expensive camping equipment to help with her emigration costs.

Four thousand rubles was an unreal amount of money, but it was the minimum we needed to cover our final expenses. Since none of the costs or steps had been documented, we expected both to change without notice. The bits and pieces of information we'd picked up from others who had gone before us gave us some idea of the upcoming costs. The price of an exit visa was 360 rubles for each visa holder (children under four didn't need their own visa, and Zhenya was three and a half). Renouncing Soviet citizenship would cost us five hundred rubles per person. The three of us would exchange 270 rubles into US dollars. Per a friend's advice, we hired a lawyer to see us through the process. Another three hundred rubles. We paid an unexpected five hundred rubles to *Upravdom*—the House Management office—for "repairs," which was, in reality, an exchange for a reference letter stating we had turned in the keys to our apartment.

That was not all. From the letters of émigrés who had recently left, and from Sofia's earlier letters, we expected to spend several months in Italy waiting for permission to enter the United States. An organization called the American Jewish Joint Distribution Committee subsidized émigrés, but their allowance only partially covered living expenses, and we would need to bring some items to sell in order to survive. Soviet champagne, vodka, linen, *matryoshkas*, photo cameras, men's cologne (which saved us in Bratislava!), coral, and other precious stones were among the important items to have.

So the four thousand rubles were barely enough to cover the immigration costs and our living expenses in Kiev for an unknown period. But borrowing any more for ourselves was out of the question, as we wanted to leave my parents two thousand rubles to pay their way out once they were ready to leave. To cover their future expenses, we borrowed an additional two thousand rubles from Yan's uncle, who was also on his way to America. His grandkids knocked on our door to pay "him" back during our first month in Los Angeles.

Over the years, we used the black exchange market in reverse— we sent money to my parents, mostly for medical expenses. "Free medical care" meant no care unless you paid, and for my parents, medical expenses would have been insurmountable without our help. The two thousand rubles we left them helped in the beginning, but over the nine years we were apart, they needed more. They never asked for help, but we remembered how life worked in that world.

It was inconceivable that the government wasn't aware of the money exchange scheme, but they allowed it to go on. It was a Communist society paradox (there were a few): the state created the strictest, most unreasonable rules, and then decided which ones they would overlook, which they would enforce, and who they would enforce them with. This was one of the allowable rule-breakers, and yet, the correspondence about the money exchange was vague and cryptic for fear of exposure. The exposure was a real threat, though it was unclear who might be the target.

One letter from Rita was unusually short, formal, and mysterious, but after staring at each other for a minute, we figured out what she was talking about. It read: "My dearest Yanick and Gala (she was the only one who called me that), I want to give you a gift—four books you need right now. My friends in Riga have the books, but you must go to them to pick them up. You must go right away, or they will give them to someone else. Call this number: 371-6-... Please call immediately. I love you. Mama Rita."

With so much of the mail being intercepted by the authorities, this one would've been an easy catch. Why wasn't it? We decided not to question our luck and called the number in Riga to schedule the pickup of the "four books," which translated into four thousand rubles, making it possible for us to proceed toward our journey. The woman on the other line told us to memorize her address and phone number, and not have them written anywhere. Both parties in these transactions took an enormous risk, and if discovered, had a good chance of ending up in prison for a long time.

Yan left the day after Zhenya's third birthday—the last birthday Zhenya celebrated with both of his grandparents. As she did on the 10th of every month for the last three years, on the 10th of October 1978, Mama bought a sponge cake decorated with yellow and green flowers—cakes with custom decorations were a thing of the distant future. After dinner, we cheered our birthday boy with tea and cake.

As much as we wanted to make a short holiday out of the trip to Riga, Yan and I decided he would go alone. For one thing, we didn't have money for two train tickets; for another, calling unnecessary attention to ourselves from the KGB, or whomever else may have been watching us, would be unwise. The Soviet organs watched everyone in the petition process (not officially but not secretly either), so we took no more chances than absolutely necessary.

"Just wait until we get to America," Yan said as we sat down for a cup of coffee in the kitchen. "You will see things you never dreamed of! We will travel the world. I promise you." He came through on his promise tenfold. But that week he traveled forty hours (to Riga and back) to bring home the four thousand rubles that our lives depended on.

The sun filtered through the puffy clouds in the October sky as we walked outside together. A beautiful, crisp, sunny day was taking shape in front of our eyes. Most likely, it would be rainy and freezing in Riga. Yan wore his black and gray checkered coat, navy wool slacks, a sweater, and a dark blue fedora hat. Under his sweater, he wore the money bag we'd sewn from an old pillowcase. He took no luggage, as he was planning to get on the return ride home the next day.

Yan knew from traveling in his youth that, for a bribe, conductors were happy to find you a seat without a ticket. Some things changed little over the years, and for ten rubles, he got a top bed in a cabin at the tail end of the car. As he would later recount to me, he climbed up without taking off his coat and tried not to move until the train reached Riga. Instead, he repeated in his head the phone number and address of the people he was going to visit. Eighteen hours later, around eight in the morning, the train came to a stop at the Riga station. He jumped off the car onto the platform, into the stinging cold air, in a rush to find a phone booth. Early morning fog loomed as far as he could see, and the city looked blurry, like an old painting. If it hadn't been for the streetlights occasionally breaking through the fog, he would have probably missed the phone booth across the street from the main entrance. He didn't want to use the one inside the train station for fear of someone overhearing him. The station was buzzing with people by then.

The woman on the other line sounded friendly and said she and her husband were ready to see Yan. She asked him to tell her the address (another precaution), and only then did she give him directions to their apartment. Yan looked around for anything suspicious before he started walking. The Riga train station was in the center of the city, and it was easy to get to any part of town from there. The couple lived a thirty-minute walk from the station.

"To be honest, I was nervous," Yan told me years later, recalling that day. "So many things could've still gone wrong." And it was true. I confessed that back at home, I worried about everything that could make this trip a complete disaster. For one thing, someone could have been following him, which meant bringing harm to the couple. Or worse, the couple might have been "fake," in place of the actual couple, who had been caught by the KGB already. And if that were the case, Yan would walk into a trap with consequences I did not want to think about.

The couple lived on the fifth floor of a nine-story apartment building. The building looked like a gigantic box with three main doors that divided it into three separate sections. Each section had thirty-six flats, four on each floor. This building looked very similar to the one where my parents lived in Kiev. These Soviet-style apartment buildings looked the same in every city: Kiev, Moscow, Leningrad, Riga, the rest of the Soviet Republics, and even in Eastern Europe where the Soviets ruled. Visiting Eastern Europe for the first time after living in America for thirty-five years, the unbearable grayness and sameness of the Soviet-era buildings struck me. They looked alike in East Berlin, Prague, Bratislava, and Budapest. A marvel of the Soviet era, which may scar the world forever.

But on that day, they looked anything but typical to Yan, who stood in front of the middle entrance, hesitating for a minute. Once inside, he ran up the stairs instead of waiting for the elevator, now wanting to get the meeting over with as soon as possible. He rang the doorbell twice, as instructed. A woman in her mid-forties or early fifties answered, glancing behind Yan, checking if he was alone. Her husband, who looked much older, was standing behind her, fidgeting. Yan gave them his name and his mother's name, told them where he was from, and repeated the amount of money he'd come to collect. To his great relief, they smiled after hearing his attestation and invited him in. A stack of money the size he had never seen in his life was sitting on the dining table. "Please check," offered the woman and gestured to a chair for Yan to sit down on. He counted the money as quickly as possible and left their apartment a few minutes later with four thousand rubles tucked in the money bag inside his underwear.

By nine that morning, Yan was back on the streets of Riga. The fog was still thick, and the air was biting cold, chilling his face and hands as he retraced his steps back to the station, thinking of a place along the way to kill the next few hours. The train wasn't scheduled to depart until three in the afternoon, and Yan didn't want to wait at the station with all that money on him. A movie theater across the street seemed like a brilliant solution. "The first show started at ten," Yan remembers. "Perfect! In a few minutes, I was in a warm, empty theater sitting in the last row, next to the exit. Suddenly, I felt exhausted and my eyes wouldn't stay open… I must've drifted off to sleep, because the next thing I saw was the bright lights over my head. The movie had ended. I frantically brushed my hands across my body, searching for the money bag. Still there. I looked at my watch. It was time to make my way home."

Over the next several months, we spent a lot of time at home playing with Zhenya and helping around the house. Yan built shelves in a closet, impressing my parents with his handyman abilities once again. When he overheard Mama commenting about the cracked wood on the living room floor, Yan refinished and re-polished the floor.

"They will kick me out and leave you here forever if you don't stop! As it is, they love you more than me," I joked.

Late evenings, after my parents went to bed, Yan listened to the Voice of America. He sat in the dark kitchen holding the radio in his hands, with his ear pressed against it. That was how Papa found him one night when he came into the kitchen for a cup of tea.

"I'll turn it off, Papa, if it bothers you," Yan said.

"Please, don't." Papa pulled his chair closer and gestured to Yan to make the sound louder. That was it. The men spent many nights listening to the Voice of America in the dark kitchen, side by side. From the reports on political events to social life and American music, they spent countless hours peeking into a life so far away, it seemed unreal. "This is the Voice of America," a pleasant but authoritative voice declared, bursting through the Iron Curtain and into our kitchen.

Monitoring the status of the emigration petition became a full-time job for everyone who applied, and we were no exception. To this day, I wonder why we made OVIR visits into a chore. Was it necessary for the outcome or did we all need to do something while out of work? Or did our collective mistrust of the government and the grim reality of our situation call for taking action, however insignificant? Whatever the reason, every family, or a member of the family, showed up in front of the OVIR office several times a week, hoping to find out the status of their petition. The OVIR office was on Shevchenko Boulevard, named after Taras Grigorovich Shevchenko, the beloved nineteenth-century Ukrainian poet, artist, and political activist. This was arguably one of the most beautiful streets in Kiev, stretching across the city from east to west for just under two kilometers. It ran from Kiev's main street, Khreshchatyk, through Kiev National University (the one I attempted to join, and failed so miserably), also named after Shevchenko, past the

the beloved *Zoloti Vorota* (Golden Gates) and Kiev Vokzal, and flowed into Victory Boulevard and Victory Square (both named to commemorate the Soviet victory in the Patriotic War).

Ancient chestnut trees lined the boulevard on both sides. With a height of almost forty meters (131 feet), these magnificent trees have a domed crown and stout branches, creating an enormous umbrella of shade in the summer months. The flowers bloom in spring and comprise clusters with twenty to fifty flowers on each. Chestnuts, with their bright polished mahogany shell, and inedible fruit inside a spiky green husk, are the very essence of autumn in Kiev. In September and October, the husks crack open and the fruit falls on the ground, providing hours of creative play for the local children.

During the peak of Jewish emigration, Shevchenko Boulevard around the OVIR office was packed with future émigrés during the OVIR's working hours. Dozens, maybe hundreds, of people were in the area at the same time. Some stood in a long line to OVIR's door dedicated to the Jewish emigration process, while others gathered in groups nearby. Everyone there had two goals: to find out where they were in the approval process and to get new information and tips "from the other side" that may have been passed to those in attendance.

To a bystander, the chatter near OVIR may have sounded as pure noise created by a bunch of Jews speaking all at once, but those who were there with a purpose welcomed every question, every comment, and every piece of advice.

"What's your number? How far have you moved since last week?"

"When was the last time you saw someone about your status?"

"How long have you been waiting? Six months for us."

"Have you ever seen this guy before? I think he bought his space in line."

"Where are you going? America? We are going to Israel."

"Did you buy cameras? Can I have your connection? We couldn't find them anywhere."

"Which city outside of Rome is cheaper to stay in, Ladispoli or Ostia?"

"Do you know if you can call home from Vienna? Someone said it's complicated and very expensive. How about Italy?"

The long OVIR line was managed rather well, most likely by one of the *refuseniks*. They were usually well respected by the others and considered experts. Like everyone else in the USSR, the Jews had expertise dealing with lines. We practically lived in lines! The OVIR line operated on the principle of a queue in an American restaurant that doesn't take reservations. You put your name on the list and receive a pager that buzzes when your table is ready. Here, instead of a pager, you got a piece of paper with a number representing the order in which your name appeared on the list. The "manager" kept track of the numbers as people came and went. Sometimes it took a couple of weeks to get to the front of the line, and once you did, it was wise to put your name on the list again for the next update.

Yan checked on our place in line almost every day. I joined him when we thought we'd be close enough to get an update. We also checked with the lawyer we had hired earlier. To date, we could only guess if she had any information or not, but it was reassuring to hear periodically, "Your petition is being reviewed." And a month later, "Your petition is being reviewed." Two months later, "You should receive the good news soon. Don't worry."

Of course we worried. Worried that it was taking too long. Worried we would be caught for fabricating the letter from my work. Worried our petition would be denied. Worried…worried… worried…

And waited.

11

Exit Visas

March 1979—Kiev

By mid-March, *podsnezhniki*—snowdrop flowers—began their bloom, marking the end of a cold winter and the coming of spring. From March to May, Kiev beams with blooming daffodils, tulips, and lilacs. These are followed by peonies and chestnut blossoms until the city seems to burst with white, yellow, blue, red, lavender, and purple colors. You could spend days walking around the city, soaking in the elegant fragrance and relishing in the most magnificent palette you've ever seen. This was our last spring in Kiev.

On a Wednesday afternoon, six months after submitting the application forms and required documents, a little over a year since the awful night at my parents' house, and almost five years since our blind date, we received a postcard from OVIR: "Report to OVIR on Tuesday, the 27th of March, at eleven o'clock in the morning."

Did we get permission? Refusal? Anything missing from our application? Did they discover the letter from my work was fraudulent?

We made a frantic call to our lawyer. "*Rebyata*, don't worry," she said. "This should be good news. I am sure of it. Don't worry, guys." If she already knew we had good news coming, why didn't she call us? Why did she wait for us to call her? With each question, we had more questions…

After spending nearly a week in agony, Yan and I showed up at the OVIR office early Tuesday morning, overtaxed with physical and mental fatigue. We found our place in line, after providing the line "manager" proof of our appointment time—the postcard. As the door opened, my heart started beating faster; a wave of apprehension came over me, replacing fatigue with fear. My body wanted to escape and make all of this go away. I looked up at Yan, squeezing his hand in the hope of making my panic disappear. When his eyes met mine, he whispered: "*Vse budet horosho, Galochka.* Everything will be all right."

We took a few steps forward, holding hands, and found ourselves inside a large waiting room. It was a square room with chairs placed along its perimeter. A closed door to our left was "the door" we would go in to receive our answer. We joined people standing behind the chairs against the wall to our right. A man next to Yan whispered, "The line is moving that way," pointing toward the closed door everyone was staring at. The lives of each person in this room, including ours, everyone outside, and thousands of Jews who risked everything for a chance at freedom were in the hands of the few behind this door.

The door flew open, and a young couple leaped out, laughing and crying, rushing out of the building. After them, a family of four disappeared behind a closed door. They came out in five minutes, the parents smiling as they ushered the kids toward the exit. As people were walking out, we moved against the wall, making our way closer to our verdict. An older couple emerged weeping, holding onto one another for support. The woman said to everyone and to no one in particular, "Our daughter…we can't go with our daughter and grandkids…they denied us permission." My heart dropped into my stomach, pushing a lump up into my throat. I looked away, unable to breathe. The couple shuffled their way out of the building, taking their anguish outside. I felt their agony in my bones, or was it my own agony imagining what might happen… to us, and to my parents?

We were next. A family in front of us had been inside for a few minutes. They re-emerged quickly. The woman wrapped her arms around her young sons' shoulders as they stood on both sides of her, tears streaming down her face. Her husband, the man who explained to Yan how the line worked when we first walked in, yelled, *"SVOBODA!!* Freedom!" as he opened the door, ushering his wife and the boys outside. The waiting room became dead silent once again.

Finally, the door opened, signaling us to come in. We walked into a small office where a uniformed inspector sat behind the desk, staring grimly at a stack of papers in front of him. There was no greeting. No acknowledgment of our presence. No chairs for us to sit on. We stood waiting for what seemed like an eternity. At last, the man looked up. His gaze fell somewhere below our shoulders.

"Passports!" he barked, stretching out his hand. He glanced at our passports and handed them back to us without saying a word. Then he shoved a piece of paper across the table: "Permission granted. Follow the instructions in the form."

I don't remember taking the paper with instructions—maybe Yan did. I don't remember looking at Yan for his reaction, or walking out of the building, which would've been under the sympathetic and distressed glances of those still awaiting their verdict. Outside, I heard Yan responding, "Yes! Yes!" to the question "Did you get permission?" as we walked through a crowd of Jews awaiting their fate on a frosty but, unusually for this time of year, sunny afternoon.

"*Molodtsy rebyata!*" Several voices echoed one another, as if it was our "great job" that resulted in this outcome. Some wiped their eyes and blew their noses; others patted Yan on the shoulder in approval. He was breathing fully for the first time in a year or maybe longer.

This is it. The feeling of finality overcame me as I walked through this human corridor. Some bureaucrat had just told me "permission granted" and, in an instant, I became a different person. *But who?* My new identity, which I didn't understand myself, was out in the open, for all to see and judge. *Who am I? I don't belong here anymore. But where do I belong? I belong nowhere...* The fabric I was wrapped in since birth, the only one I knew, was torn off me forever.

I was naked.

"We received approval!" I blurted to Mama as she opened the front door. Her face mirrored the emotions I so desperately tried to hide. She remained silent. Papa rushed out of the living room, joining us in the hallway. He too froze in silence for a few seconds.

"*Pozdravlyayu, detie.* Congratulations, kids...," Papa said somberly, his voice breaking. Mama was motionless. Her sorrow cut through me like a knife, crushing my heart.

"*Mama, ne volnuicya, vse budet horosho.* Don't worry, everything will be all right," I said, repeating Yan's words to me. "*Vse budet horosho.*"

We had forty-five days to pack up and leave, which gave us until the third week of May. We spent most of this time in a mad rush. From office to office, from desk to desk, providing this, signing that...another letter, another signature. We transferred the phone to our neighbors, the older couple we lived with in my mother-in-law's apartment. We cleared out the apartment and turned in the key to the House Management office, along with five hundred rubles for "cleaning." The city library confirmed we had no outstanding books; we notarized copies of the birth certificates. Besides our college diplomas, we had to leave our marriage certificate behind, but we were past the point of worrying about any of this. We learned later that some restrictions varied from city to city, and over time, others brought copies of their diplomas and reinstated them in America.

My father wanted us to take his medals for safekeeping until he and Mama joined us. Papa either believed we would reunite soon, or he believed the opposite and wanted his grandson to have cherished memories of him. But as it happened, the medals he'd earned by putting his life on the line in World War II were not actually his; they were "property of the state." Even when Mama came in 1986, she had to leave them behind…but she brought the supporting documents, hiding them in her luggage.

Once we paid 360 rubles per exit visa and five hundred rubles each for renouncing our Soviet citizenship, it was time for the last trip to OVIR. With all our documents and receipts neatly stacked in a large envelope, we arrived at OVIR to join the line for the last time. We held our breath as an inspector reviewed our papers, hoping he was in a good mood. Any error—real or imaginary—would delay or stop us altogether. *Could they still find out about the letter?* The night we forged the letter from my work was playing in my mind like a movie as I watched the clerk slowly and deliberately check each document. We were lucky. OVIR accepted our papers. After signing more forms, we turned over to the clerk our Soviet passports in a silent exchange for two exit visas.

From this point on, Yan, Zhenya, and I were nobody.

Stateless.

Between then and our departure in two weeks, our only identification would be our visas, which deemed us as enemies of the Soviet Union.

First Goodbye

May 3, 1979—Moscow

The mad rush wasn't over. We still needed to go to Moscow for a round of errands. The visas had to be stamped at the Dutch Consulate (Holland represented the state of Israel in the USSR, as Israel had no diplomats in the Soviet Union), the Austrian Consulate for our first stop in Vienna, the Ministry of Justice, and the Ministry of Foreign Affairs. We bribed the conductor and took an overnight train, arriving in Moscow at eleven in the morning. Without Soviet passports, we couldn't buy tickets even if we wanted to.

Aunt Maya and Zoya lived in Moscow, but Yan and I didn't want to stay with either of them and put them in danger for being associated with an "anti-Soviet element." But Papa asked his sister anyway and told us with pride that she insisted we spend the night at her apartment.

"What do I have to lose, Osik?" she said when my father expressed concern for her safety, should we stay with her. I loved how she called him by his childhood nickname, Osik.

"Since the night they took my husband in '34 and interrogated me at the NKVD headquarters for forty-eight hours while Zoya was home alone, I am not afraid of them. Zoya and I are not afraid."

Poor Aunt Maya! She must have been afraid at some point to change her married name back to her maiden name, Kugel, to protect herself and Zoya. How ironic and sad that forty-two years later, her niece carried the same "titles" her husband once did: "an enemy of the state...anti-Soviet element."

I adored my aunt and cousin. They always stayed with my parents when visiting Kiev, either together or separately. As a kid, I sat quietly nearby, listening to Aunt Maya and Zoya talk with

Mama and Papa. The sound of their voices mesmerized me. They spoke with a *Moskovskiy* accent, crisp and clear. The Russian spoken in Ukraine sounded softer and rounder, maybe less formal. Some interpreted the Moscow accent as pompous and authoritative, but this interpretation did not apply to Aunt Maya and Zoya; they were lovely.

We said our first of many goodbyes to Zoya at dinner, and to Aunt Maya the following morning before leaving to finish our errands and take our last walk around Moscow prior to catching the evening train home.

"*Kukolka rodnaya*, dolly dearest…" Only Aunt Maya called me that. The words draped over me like a warm shower of love every time: Write to us…don't forget us…kiss Zhenechka…*do svidaniya… proschayte, deti…farewell, kids.*"

That afternoon, we stood on Red Square, looking at the Kremlin wall with horror and dismay. The endless line of people crawling toward Lenin's mausoleum in grief sent chills down my spine as I watched men, women, and children waiting for hours to pay respect to a dead tyrant, fifty-five years later.

"We are done with all of them," Yan whispered in my ear, hugging me tightly. He put his arm on my shoulder as if to guide me toward our new life. "Let's get out of here!"

Between Two Worlds

May 8, 1979—Kiev

We met with Alla and Lenya Morgovsky in front of the Central bank for our last task before the departure: the money exchange.

With her parents and eleven-year-old daughter, Alla was leaving Kiev on the 17th, but Lenya would leave on the 15th with Zhenya and me. We would share a sleeping car. I was grateful not to be alone; rumor had it a woman by herself might not be safe on this leg of the journey. In Chop, Lenya would take over Yan's spot working at the border control area and wait for his family to arrive the following day.

Alla has been my friend since college. When we met, she was twenty-five, married, and had a three-year-old child. At eighteen, I was a child myself. I had my waist-length hair tied into a high ponytail and weaved into a simple braid, the same way I wore it throughout most of my school years. I wore no makeup or jewelry; I saw myself as an ugly duckling and thought the makeup would emphasize all my defects even more. As for jewelry, I simply didn't have any.

In contrast, Alla looked like a movie star! She showed off her beautiful figure in form-fitting skirts and silk blouses, classy suits, and high heels. Always the high heels! Her short hair, impeccably styled, had a different color every week. If it's true that there are over forty shades of blond hair, Alla experimented with all of them during the course of our college years. She was elegant and glamorous, and it was no surprise she ended up working at Cartier on Rodeo Drive many years later. Alla was my confidant and my university of life, in serious and mischievous ways. I smoked my first cigarette and had my first glass of wine under her watchful eye. She had the attention of every male professor when she walked by. One time, sitting next to her in class resulted in a better grade for me.

Our annual trips to Leningrad for finals at the main university campus (Kiev's campus was a satellite) were the best part of each school year. For those two weeks we lived like proper students on campus in cramped communal rooms (*obschezhitie*) on a budget of five rubles a day, most of which we saved to buy fancy lingerie made in Poland. We barely ate to save money, and we barely slept because no one sleeps in Leningrad in June. From mid-June through the end of July, the sky never reaches complete darkness. Around midnight, dusk gradually returns to daylight. Alla and I would not miss strolling at night by the city canals and along *Nevsky Prospect*—Leningrad's central, most famous, and beloved avenue—as if it were daytime. Leningrad is a city of bridges; over three hundred of them are drawbridges. They open each night to let through large vessels coming from the Volga River, heading toward the Gulf of Finland and the Baltic Sea. We would not miss watching the bridges open night after night, in perfect harmony, as if directed by an invisible conductor. We stood on the bank of the Neva River, watching magic occur every night, as if for the first time.

I have a deep connection to Leningrad and always have. It was my parents' favorite city ever since they were stationed there, and it was where Yan and I spent our honeymoon in November 1974. It was cold, it snowed, and the wind was chilling; we stayed in a one-room (this is not a typo) apartment with my parents' friends (hotels were reserved for business travel only)—which is a story in itself—and yet we fell in love with the city.

Alla's last vacation was a cruise we took together through Northern Europe in 2001. The itinerary included two days in Leningrad. We strolled the familiar streets, sharing the memories of our youth with our husbands, realizing that we didn't belong here anymore. We were tourists who spoke the language, but no longer related to the people around us and our surroundings. Romantic love for the city gave way to the sense of disconnect; it was eerie. Alla, in her infinite wisdom, kept reminding us how fortunate we were to not be living the Soviet life anymore. Even though the Soviet Union had fallen apart by then, it was still the same country. "*Rebyata*, just look at us! How lucky are we! Look around. Let's always remember to be grateful for the life we have," she said with tears in her eyes as we sat in a bar on the eighteenth deck of the cruise ship, saying goodbye to the city of White Nights.

Several years after our trip with Alla, Yan and I shared Leningrad and the White Nights experience with our younger son Alik and his wife, Laurie, on a similar voyage. The beauty and the magic of the city stunned them, while the "Russian phenomenon" shocked them. "Mama," said Alik, as we walked down Nevsky Prospect, "no one but us smiles in this city...what's up with that?" I didn't warn him to expect the stern, gloomy looks people exchanged while passing by one another. *The Russian phenomenon.*

Emigration put all of us to the test. Many families fell apart; friendships ended. Not ours. We made a relentless effort to find each other in Vienna and Italy, and stay together. Alla's parents helped us take care of Zhenya on our journey. Without their help, our time in Italy would've been a struggle. In America, we ended up in different cities (they in Cleveland and we in Los Angeles), but we continued comforting and supporting each other from a distance until we reunited when Alla and her family moved to Los Angeles. Alla died way too soon. She was fifty-eight. I still miss her every day. She is so much a part of my story.

Alla's parents hesitated to leave with her, not wanting to be a burden, but Yan convinced them to go. Alla's younger sister had recently settled in Cleveland with her family. Yan vigorously made his point that we might take the last train, and they shouldn't stay behind hoping to take the next one.... To this day, he regrets not being able to convince my parents to do the same.

On that May day in 1979 the four of us walked out of the bank onto Kreschatik Street, precious dollar bills tucked in men's jacket pockets, and turned left toward Lenin's Komsomol Square. We walked in silence—it was all real now. Years of anguish over the initial decision, the conflicts with my parents, the humiliation of the Komsomol expulsion, the letter from work, fear of not getting permission, and becoming *refuseniks* with no jobs, no money, and an empty apartment. With all this behind us, I was disconnecting from the life we were leaving behind, yet I wasn't part of the life ahead. At that moment and for many months after, I felt suspended between two worlds with no bridge to the other side or a road to follow.

Kreschatik was drowning in spring sunshine. Red tulips graced every inch of the ground that was not asphalted, and red Soviet flags hung off lampposts on both sides of the street in preparation for the annual Great Patriotic War Victory Day parade on May 9. The sea of red flags! *Long gone are the days of saluting the flag with pride for the Motherland,* I found myself thinking. *Now I fear them. Brainwashed, manipulated, and isolated from the world, most people around me were proud of their Soviet flag and their Soviet life. Or so they seemed—admitting otherwise would be suicidal.*

Yan remembers the walk just as vividly as I do. "My heart was pounding, ready to jump out of my chest," he recalls, closing his eyes as though to feel the remembered sunshine on his face. "My shoulders seemed wider, and I felt joy. The joy that comes from freedom…. I was free."

We stopped near Lenin Komsomol Square, and once again discussed our plans for finding each other as we made our way across Eastern Europe: Bratislava (Czechoslovakia), Vienna (Austria), Rome (Italy). There was no elegant way to achieve this as we didn't have phones (life before cell phones!) and didn't know where we might stay or the timing of our movement from one place to another. The best idea we had (borrowed from other émigrés) was to leave notes for each other, starting with the HIAS office in Vienna. We would likely get there first. Alla and Lenya would do the same when they arrived. Yan reminded Lenya again to take care of Zhenya and me on the train to Chop.

It was time to say goodbye. Yan and I would turn onto Vladimir Descent toward Podol; Alla and Lenya would go the opposite direction to get on a Metro.

"*Rebyata*, this is it," said Alla, as a single tear slid down her cheek from under her sunglasses. "Good luck to us…"

"*Do vstrechi, rebyata.* See you soon, guys!" I echoed, hugging my friend and kissing her on the cheek, tasting the salt of her tears. She returned the kiss, wiping my wet cheeks with her fingers. The men shook hands and embraced in a long bear hug, with their arms wrapped around each other. *Do vstrechi rebyata!* Be safe…

I Know No Other Country Where a Man Can Breathe So Freely

Farewell, My Kiev

May 15, 1979—Kiev-Chop-Uzhgorod Train

I looked behind me, climbing up the stairs of the car, hoping to glance at my family and friends once again, but the "Jewish" car was too far from the platform, and I saw nothing but train tracks.

In our sleeper car, I found Misha sitting on the lower bed, squeezing Zhenya in a tight hug, rocking side to side.

"Misha, you are smothering him! Let go! You have to go. Now! The train is leaving in five minutes! Go, Misha!" I yelled, shaking his shoulder. He attempted to release Zhenya, who threw his arms around his uncle's neck, not wanting to let go.

"Misha, don't go!" Large teardrops slid down my son's face.

Misha held him for another minute before setting him down. Zhenya grabbed onto my leg with all his limbs, throwing his head back to find his mama and uncle staring at each other without saying a word. In that moment our longstanding sibling rivalry— endless arguments and all of Misha's mischief over the years—was all forgotten.

"Go, Misha..." He kissed me on the cheek as if we were going to see each other the next day and rushed out of the car, not waiting for me to hug or kiss him back. A few seconds later, I saw him through the window, running away from the platform, never looking back.

Goodbye, Misha... I had no way of knowing that it would be nine years before we would see each other again.

"Let's open the window and wave goodbye to everyone," I said to Zhenya, as my body shook. My stomach tightened like it often did before school exams and music recitals, but a thousand times worse. I tasted the salt of my tears in my mouth combined with the slimy liquid dripping out of my nose, down my neck, and onto my chest.

"Mama, where is Misha? I want Misha... Maamaa... Maamaa!" My gentle and patient son finally succumbed to the intensity of the day. His trembling lower lip warned me of a potential meltdown if I didn't react quickly.

"Come here, my darling." I picked him up, smiling through tears, and kissed his wet, rosy cheeks until he started giggling and pulling my face closer to return my kisses. I pretended to pull away, and we both laughed. Holding Zhenya on my left hip with my left arm, I used my right arm to pull down a fold-out table underneath the window for him to stand on. The rule "We don't stand on tables" didn't apply at the moment. "Let's wave to Babulya, Dedulya, and Misha. They are waiting..." We both leaned into the open window, searching for the familiar faces, as the train moved, slowly and silently.

I saw Misha walking, then running toward the train, jumping over the train tracks, waving his arms. His jacket flew open on both sides of his body, making him look like a giant bird helplessly trying to get up in the air. My parents stood where I left them, stoic and dignified. They were waving and blowing kisses to their only grandchild.

"Goodbye! I am going to live in Moscow. I will never see you again!" yelled Zhenya, sticking his head out the window. His voice carried onto the platform and into the warm spring Kiev air as the train gained speed, blurring the faces of our loved ones until they disappeared from sight.

"Where is Lenya?" I looked around as if I could've possibly missed him in this tiny space. "What happened? Hope he is all right..." But before my thoughts took me into a complete panic mode, the door slid open, and Lenya stepped inside; his boxer-built body barely made it through the narrow door.

"Galochka...*izveni*...I am sorry...I was late...jumped onto the... train...walked into the wrong car, I am sorry...*izveni*.... Don't worry, I am here now.... I will take care of...you...and Zhenechka..." He was slurring his words. His face was flushed, and he was struggling to keep balance, even though he was holding onto the vertical bed rail with both hands. Lenya was drunk—and not just drunk, hammered. I helped him sit down on the bed as he hopelessly tried to sit up straight. When my feeble attempt to sober him up with a cup of strong, hot tea failed, I talked him into lying down to "rest." After a few minutes of trying to climb up to the upper bed, he crashed down to the lower bed instead and instantly passed out. The sound of his loud snoring and the smell of alcohol accompanied us all the way to Chop.

Years later, we had many laughs about that night as I told and retold the story of "how Lenya took care of me and Zhenya on the way to Chop," but that night there was no laughter, just sadness.

The sleeper car looked just like I remembered it from my childhood. There were two bunk beds with a window between them and space for luggage underneath the lower beds. There was only three feet between the beds (enough space for the foldout table to fit), and another three feet from the end of the beds to the door. The "beds" weren't actually beds, but rather large, wooden benches. The two lower benches provided seating space, while the two upper benches hung flat against the wall during the day, and had to be pulled out at night. For overnight travel, a thin mattress, a blanket, and a pillow were supplied for each bed. However, we didn't find any.

I must've dozed off with Zhenya sleeping in my arms when a sharp change in the train's speed startled me. The train was losing speed, and within seconds came to an abrupt stop with violent force and a screeching sound of the brakes. Clasping Zhenya in my arms, I stretched my legs and grabbed onto the edge of Lenya's bed with my feet, holding on for dear life. Zhenya lazily opened his eyes, looked at me, and smiled before closing them again as I rocked him side to side, trying to catch my breath. Lenya never moved.

The commotion outside got louder, but I couldn't make out what was going on. It seemed like hours had passed before the train moved again. *But wait... Are we going in the reverse direction? Are we turning back to Kiev? What's happening?* There was no one to ask. The night was dark, and as the train settled into its rhythm once again, I closed my eyes, trying to quiet my mind, which was bringing up stories and pictures of Jews being transported by trains to concentration camps during World War II. *The times are different, and this is hardly the same type of train,* I argued with myself, but the pictures kept creeping up in my mind.

The blackness of the night began surrendering to the light of early morning, and through the window I saw the sunlight filling the sky. My body was stiff, and my arms numb from holding Zhenechka all night. I was disoriented, having lost track of time somewhere during the night. *I should've kept my watch instead of selling it.* At least I no longer thought we might return to Kiev. We would've been there by now if that was the case. But it was also clear we weren't arriving in Chop early in the morning as scheduled. As it turned out, the train would stop in Chop for ten minutes to let us out and continue on to Uzhgorod, a city in Western Ukraine. After the fact, we learned that the "Jewish car" was the only one opened in Chop. The rest of the train was locked, so no one else attempted to escape. The train from Chop to Bratislava arrived late in the evening.

We must make it onto that train! We must make it!

Does the Kid Have Earrings?

May 16, 1979—Chop
Ten-Minute Stop

The train slowed down entering the railway station. "Chop," the sign read. I saw Yan through the cabin window while getting Zhenechka dressed. Zhenya had a runny nose, and I felt his warm forehead, the familiar signs of him getting sick. I ignored what was coming. I tied the strings of his cotton hat under his chin before he protested. The hat was my "secret" weapon and the one desperate measure I used to protect his ears from an infection. It never worked, but I continued to have him wear his hat at the slightest sign of a cold. I hoped my mother would be wrong, but she saw this coming before I was ready to. I tried not to be annoyed with her for her "prediction."

I turned my attention to Lenya, who was now awake, sober, and embarrassed. Regardless of what had happened last night, I was grateful he was here with us now. He checked our luggage, piece by piece, reminding me of Misha's "inspection" less than twenty-four hours ago. Has it only been that long? I felt we just left Kiev, but in a more profound way, I was a lifetime away from the life I knew and the people I loved.

Lenya stacked the luggage against the door; we were ready for as quick an exit as possible. He looked at his watch: "We are three hours late." I saw Yan again; he walked fast, his eyes scanning every window of the gradually approaching train. Six feet, three inches tall, he was easy to spot from a distance. He saw me too, waved, and ran toward our car as the train came to a full stop, hissing and screeching. I exhaled for the first time since we'd said goodbye two days ago. *He was here.... I could breathe again...*

"Galochka, take Zhenya and get off the train. I'll explain later. Just go," Yan said, giving me a brief hug and kissing Zhenya on the head. As we stepped off the train, he stayed behind. "This is a brief stop, people, only ten minutes. We will work together to make sure everyone gets off in time. The train will not wait! Women, children, and *stariki*, elderly, go to the nearest exit from your cabin and get off the train now! Men, stay!" Yan's voice was uncharacteristically stern. He gave no further explanation or reasoning, which only made my heart hammer faster.

I stood on the platform, holding Zhenya, watching women climb down the steps with small children in their arms, looking behind to make sure older kids followed, helping their parents and grandparents climb down at the same time. The buzz got louder as more people made their way off the train.

"Sasha, wait for *Babushka*. Don't run off..."

"Mama, where are you...?"

"Papa, give me your hand. I'll help you down..."

"I don't need any help!"

"Don't worry about your suitcases...just wait here..."

"Come here, you *idiot*!"

"*Sinok*, sonny...please...stop crying.... I know you are hungry—I don't have any food right now..."

"What do you mean, you don't know where your medications are?"

"Mama, where is Papa? I want to stay with Papa!"

"People, don't push…. I am moving as fast as I can…"

What was happening around me was surreal. In an instant, life became strikingly clear in its simplicity: I must protect my baby from the crowd and hysteria, while Yan got our luggage. Nothing else mattered.

Yan jumped off the train, followed by two other young men. As if on cue, all the windows in our car slid open, and bags, boxes, and suitcases came tumbling onto the platform unless Yan and his "team" caught them first. A large *baul* came flying through the door, landing on the edge of the platform, followed by another one and a few more. A startled gasp filled the air as another piece of luggage smashed against the cement platform floor. *What in our luggage had a chance of breaking?* Photo cameras, a thermos, delicate wooden souvenirs, a small saucepan, an eclectic burner…it didn't seem to matter.

This continued until all the luggage was out, seconds before the train moved, with no warning or announcement. The chaos amplified. People were pushing and shoving each other to grab their belongings and drag them to customs, the last step before boarding a train to Bratislava.

Yan pulled our luggage from the pile closer to where I was standing with Zhenya, away from the madness. After disappearing for a few minutes, he came back with an old, squeaky luggage cart he'd hidden while waiting for us to arrive. With our two suitcases and *baul* loaded, Yan pushed the cart toward the customs area. I followed, carrying Zhenya, who was resting his head on my shoulder, arms locked around my neck. The heat of his body transferred onto my chest. *We would be on the train soon, and I'd give him medication and some tea. The tea would cheer him up. Everything would be all right as soon as we got on that train…*

We said goodbye to Lenya and followed a uniformed guard to a large waiting room filled with people sitting on their luggage or standing around it. Everyone was waiting to enter the customs area on the other side of the exit door. Mothers comforted screaming babies by breastfeeding or rocking them back and forth. Elderly men and women leaned against the walls for support, and young men talked quietly in small groups. This was a sight I would see again and again through our journey: exhausted, hungry, thirsty, disheveled, and frightened people of different ages and social standings (if there was such a thing), stripped of their dignity, robbed down to their bones, awaiting their fate.

Soviet citizens were barred from the city of Chop, the train station, and the customs office. Only the Jews on their way to Israel—as the destination listed in their visas—were allowed in the designated areas. Sometimes, relatives and friends attempted to see their loved ones off by buying a train ticket to Uzhhorod, sneaking into the "Jewish car" toward the end of the trip, and getting off with them in Chop. When caught by the local police, which happened often, they paid a fine and remained locked up until the next train in the reverse direction came through, but some were lucky to see their loved ones off before getting arrested. Misha, too, wanted to go to Chop with us, but I talked him out of taking this risk, for himself and for our parents, fearing they wouldn't get permission to leave because of his "illegal" trip. There was also a strong possibility of him being reprimanded at work and risking future advancement, or—even worse—being fired. Neither was a pleasant prospect for someone who planned to live in the USSR.

Because the train from Kiev was late, Yan lost his space in the line for customs, so we joined people in the waiting room, hoping the afternoon shift would be the "nice" team instead of the awful morning team people were still talking about. The task of the customs office was simple, to make sure émigrés didn't hide any "prohibited" items and didn't have in their possession anything over the quantity or weight limits. The rigor with which the customs officials did their job varied from team to team, day to day, hour to hour. There was no rhyme or reason. Everything was already taken from us; what could we possibly hide in a piece of luggage?

The door to the customs swung open. "You! This way!" The official pointed his finger first at us, then at the door. Yan pushed our cart through, and we found ourselves on the open platform, surrounded by uniformed soldiers armed with Kalashnikov machine guns, holding guard dogs by their chains. The soldiers formed a large circle around the customs area, where four of their peers conducted the luggage search.

"Here. Put your suitcases on the table," came another order. I let Zhenya down to help Yan. Without looking at us, a young officer (a kid in a uniform) opened one suitcase after another, pulled random items out, and threw them onto the platform, tossing the half-empty suitcase on top.

"What is this?" he said, holding up a three-piece set of flatware.

"*Stolovy pribor.*"

"I can see that. What it's made of?"

"Silver."

"Where did you get it?"

"My parents gave it to me as a gift." This was half of the six-piece set my mother divided between Misha and me.

"What are the letters on each piece?"

"My parents' initials."

"So, it's a custom-made silver set?"

"Yes."

"You can't take it out of the country. This is artwork, and I declare it the property of the state. If someone is here with you, you can give it to them. Otherwise it will remain here."

If this was not a contradiction in the law, I don't know what was. On one hand, no one could come with their families to Chop, and yet, he asked if we had someone with us. Once again, some Soviet laws were meant to be broken.

"Is anyone here from Kiev?" I yelled, peeking through the door into the waiting room.

"Yes! What do you need?"

"Can you please return this to my parents? Podol…Ratmanskaya 25, *kvartira* 3."

"*Nyet problem, will return.*" A man with curly red hair stepped toward me, extending his hand.

"Thank you so much. My name is Galya. Please tell them not to worry…tell them everything is fine here…"

I hugged this stranger (who kept his promise) and returned inside, where all of our luggage was now on the platform in complete disarray. Yan was holding the thermos, shaking it to show me it was broken. I had hoped to get some hot water for Zhenya before getting on the train, but that was not happening anymore.

"What's in your pockets?"

I put both hands in the pockets of my cardigan, pulling out a broken string of coral from one and a few loose coral pieces from another.

"Leave this. You can't take it. It's over the limit."

I handed him the corals, not asking how he came to his conclusion without weighing the string.

"What about the kid? Does the kid have earrings?"

"The kid is a boy…" As if it wasn't clear…

"I am not asking if he is a boy. I am asking if the kid has earrings. Would you like me to check?"

I leaped to Zhenya, who was now "helping" Yan collect our belongings from the floor. I picked him up, gently but swiftly taking off his hat. I took a few steps forward, close enough to the officer for him to see the absence of earrings. I said nothing, but I screamed inside: "I hate you!... I despise your country!... *Ya vas nenavizhu!*"

The darkness of the night fell without warning. The sky was barren, with not a star shining through. The air was cool and damp. A few dim streetlights lit the platform. Together with other families, we dragged our luggage toward the upcoming train through a corridor of armed Soviet soldiers, pointing their AKs inward, slightly lowered to the ground. Inward. On to the crowd of women, children, and elderly. Members of the very same military that my father, my husband, and my brother had served in were pointing machine guns at my son.

These Are Pictures of Russia— ## It's the Homeland of Mine

Once again, chaos erupted with the arrival of the train. And once again, the men in our group took charge, separating people from their luggage, throwing and shoving belongings through the windows of the train to Bratislava, which stopped in Chop for twenty minutes.

Women, children, and the elderly stood in front of the train, with their backs to a row of armed soldiers. Once the luggage was in, the men helped older people board first, followed by the women and children. Yan pushed me and Zhenya inside the slow-moving train, jumping in behind us.

The train approached the Soviet border as we shoved our luggage into the sleeping cabin appointed by the conductor. The window was open, but the view outside made me gag, sending chills down my spine. Yan and I froze, staring in horror at the barbed wire fence—curled inward at the top—stretching for eternity. Uniformed

Soviet soldiers stood in a row inside the fence about five meters apart, facing the train, each holding an AK-47 in one hand and a dog leash in the other. This could've been a set for a movie about Nazi Germany, but it wasn't. This was real. This was us.

"Remember how we were taught that the country must be protected from the outside enemy and the West? But these barbed wires are not for the people who want to come into the country; this is for the citizens of the Union of Soviet Socialist Republics...to make sure no one escapes...," Yan whispered, hugging Zhenechka in his arms. I stood next to him in silence.

The train stopped. I leaned out the window to witness the boom barrier rise under the sharp eyes of more soldiers with machine guns and dogs. One last signal by the border patrol officer and the train began to move again, now rapidly gaining speed.

We crossed the Soviet border for the first and last time in our lives.

I remember looking into the darkness, clenching my fists inside the pockets of the cardigan that I hadn't taken off in two days. I stood crippled, rocking to keep my balance on the moving train. A strong draft blowing inside the cabin through the open window brought me back, and I rushed to close the window, maneuvering in the small space around Yan, who was settling our luggage. Zhenya curled up on the lower bed, pressing Cheburashka to his chest with both hands, shivering. What happened next pushed my own emotions to the back burner of life for many years.

"There is no window... nothing to close!" I yelled, turning to Yan.

"What do you mean?" Yan stopped what he was doing and made his way to the window. The train was moving full speed, which would most likely be at 45-55 mph, and the bitter wind was now blasting inside the sleeper car.

"There is no window..." Yan looked at me in disbelief.

"I'll be right back!" I rushed out of the cabin into a narrow hallway to find a conductor—she would help.

"Excuse me, please…our son is sick. We have a broken window in our car. There is no glass. Please, move us to another car…," I said to the woman, who looked like she was in charge.

"No. Go back to your car. You can't be in the hallway," she said, looking over my shoulder, taking a few steps toward me to show I needed to turn around.

Back in the car, Yan laid Zhenya down, covering him and *Cheburashka* from head to toe with a blanket he had pulled out of the *baul*. He stood with his back to the window, trying to block the thrashing wind, which lashed inside the cabin like a tornado.

"Mama…*chayok*…tea…*hochu chayok*… I want tea." A tiny tear slid down his red-from-fever cheek. I touched his forehead with my lips and guessed the fever to be about thirty-nine degrees Celsius—equivalent to a little over 102 Fahrenheit. His porcelain cup, a tea bag, and the medicine were in my purse. I grabbed the cup and stepped out into the corridor to get hot water, which I knew from my train travel experience would be in a large metal bin located in a small hallway next to the stairs.

"Where are you going?" A familiar voice barked over my shoulder.

"I need hot water to make tea for my son." When I turned around to face her, I noticed she was wearing a military uniform, not a railroad employee one. Or was it her attitude that reminded me of the military border personnel that I assumed the uniform was military?

"There is no hot water…go back to your car." Naively, I thought she didn't know about the hot water container since she was not a railroad worker after all.

"But there is always hot water right outside that door." I pointed at the door behind me.

"If you don't return to your cabin right away, I will stop this train." She walked past me in a narrow hallway, pushing me into the wall with her shoulder and locking the door to the hot water chamber; then she pivoted and walked to the other end of the car, I presumed, to do the same. I hurried back to the cabin, remembering we had a small electric immersion heater.... *There must be an electric outlet in the bathroom. I will heat some water there.* But I wasn't able to outsmart a Soviet Nazi conductor—that's the only name I have for her. As soon as I began heating the water in the restroom, the electricity in the entire car switched off. *Nazi. Svoloch. Witch.*

In the car, Yan still stood with his back to the window, running a hand through his hair in exhaustion and desperation. A knock on the door startled both of us. Sliding the door open against the wind, a woman poked her head inside.

"I heard the commotion outside. Is everything okay? I am a doctor. Can I be of any help?" She was a young woman with a soothing voice. I fought my sobs, telling her about Zhenya being sick, the broken window, and the Nazi conductor. "Wait, I'll be right back.... I have some warm water left in my thermos." She came back with half a cup of warm water and began examining Zhenya while I made him tea. She reassured me it was just a virus, and he would be much better once the fever broke. I hugged her, thanking her for her help. Yan continued to block the window, holding on to the two upper beds for stability, smiling, relieved. I sat down next to him on Zhenya's bed, blocking the draft that still came through. Zhenechka was asleep.

Dawn came, gradually erasing endless darkness with the rays of sunlight and replacing the horrors of the night with signs of a new day. Zhenya's fever broke, and he was a little more interested in his surroundings. Yan carried him into the corridor to look out the window.

We were passing through the Czechoslovakian countryside, with lush green fields as far as the eye could see. Small, immaculate houses dotted the fields, with bright orange rooftops reflecting sunlight. Used to the Soviet countryside with its drab, gray tones, Yan and I had never seen anything like it.

13

Bratislava

May 17, 1979

We arrived in Bratislava mid-morning. The men used the now proven strategy and unloaded people and luggage in minutes. Two trains made a stop in Bratislava on their way to Vienna, one in the early afternoon and another one in the evening—information passed from prior refugees. Our hope was to make the noon train to Vienna.

By now, we had bonded with our traveling companions, nine adults and five children. There was a young couple going to Israel (the wife was the doctor who had checked on Zhenya the night before); a husband and wife in their seventies joining their children in America; a widow with three kids between the ages of four and ten, on the way to reunite with her sister and parents; and another couple, close to our age, with a five-year-old daughter. With that many people, it took a while to make our way across the train station, schlepping our luggage and helping the single mom and the elderly couple with theirs. We missed the first train by ten minutes. Exhausted, we settled around the closest bench to the train tracks to wait for the evening train.

Zhenya was now running a low-grade fever and appeared lethargic and clammy. Yan and I took turns carrying him wrapped in a blanket, trying to distance ourselves from the others. The women and the older man sat on the bench, having a quiet conversation as the guys stood nearby, smoking cigarettes and monitoring the luggage. Suddenly, the older woman began to cry. The cry turned into a sob as her husband tried to console her.

"He is a diabetic and needs to eat," she said through tears, pointing at her husband. "They took all of our food…I have nothing to give him…" The husband lowered his head and looked away.

The woman with three kids started crying, too. "I don't have any food to give my kids. They threw it all away in front of our eyes… *svolochi*…scum…!"

Seeing her mother so upset, her four-year-old daughter climbed on her lap, hugging her tight around the neck. She was now crying, too, hiding her face on her mother's shoulder. I looked at Yan, who was holding our sick child a few meters away, and nearly lost it myself.

Then Mama's voice echoed in my head. "If you're old enough to embark on this journey, you're old enough to handle the process." *Thanks, Mama!*

I ran to the luggage pile and pulled out our *baul* from the heap, unzipping it in a hurry. My heart was beating fast, and my hands were shaking as I took out a sheet and grabbed a small bag of leftover food. In a few minutes, my sheet became a tablecloth, presenting several pieces of bread, an unfinished box of cookies, a piece of dry salami, and a large tomato. The doctor followed suit and brought out what she had: a homemade sponge cake, a couple of apples, and a can of sardines. The mother of the five-year-old girl did the same: two more apples, another can of sardines, and a loaf of bread. Someone had butter. As the sheet became filled with food, an old Russian folktale, *Skatert-Samobranka*, came to mind—a story

147

of three brothers where the thoughtful brother was rewarded with a magic tablecloth filled with the most exquisite delicacies. The food on our "magic tablecloth" was far from exquisite, but in that moment, it brought a sense of abundance and a great relief. And in that way it was just as magical.

I made fourteen portions for everyone to have a snack and saved a few leftovers for later. The older woman wept, watching me slice the bread, cut the apples, and divide it all evenly.

"This is how it was during the war," she said, with anguish and sorrow in her voice. "We had to run away from home, hide, share the food, and help one another to survive the Nazis..." My heart wept with her. I knew these stories all too well, as if I were there in person. These stories lived in my soul; they still do.

Later in the day, Zhenya got worse; his fever came back, he coughed, and he complained of an earache. A cup of hot tea and chicken soup would have been nice, but we had no money in local currency (it was krone/korona at the time), didn't speak Czech or Polish (languages spoken in Bratislava), and with a sick child on our hands and our luggage scattered on the platform, we were completely immobile.

"Galochka, take Zhenya to the cafeteria around the corner, and I will meet you there soon. The guys will look after our luggage." Yan had a plan. He remembered a bottle of men's cologne, *odekolon*, that we had brought with us to sell or exchange for food along the way, and he thought this might be a good place to do so. Why *odekolon*? I can't tell you. Many items we were told would be valuable for exchange were random. *Odekolon* was one of them. Some suggested there was enough alcohol in the cologne that it was used for purposes not intended. I wouldn't be surprised if it were true. The liquid had a strong smell of alcohol and antiseptic. But this large bottle with green substance turned out to be the most valuable item we had.

I don't remember how much time had passed before Yan returned beaming—he'd sold the bottle. Whatever he sold it for was enough to buy Zhenya a bowl of soup, and that was all that mattered. Yan later told me: "I ran outside the train station and noticed an underground walkway across the street. I guessed it might be a place to sell *odekolon*. I ran down a flight of stairs and found myself in an empty, dingy space, not a single person in sight.... Suddenly, this guy showed up out of nowhere and pointed at the bottle in my hand. I handed him the bottle. He reached into his pocket and gave me a bunch of coins and a few paper denominations."

Victory.

14

Vienna

The Pension

May 17-18, 1979

When we boarded the train to Vienna, we were veteran-émigré-travelers and a group of friends bonded by the most extraordinary circumstances. Our friendship didn't last beyond those trying days, but for the time it lasted, we trusted each other with our livelihood so we didn't think twice about leaving all of our belongings with them. While we fed Zhenya in the cafeteria, the guys loaded our luggage and saved us the seats inside the train. I had never been on a train like this! It looked new and clean, with soft seats that reclined. *No yelling and screaming. No pushing and shoving. Is this what a civilized society looked like?*

Thirty minutes after the departure, we stopped before crossing the Austrian border. The border checkpoint looked unremarkable: no barbed wires, no heavy projectors, no perfectly smoothed-out sand…just a small border booth with half a dozen armed soldiers standing outside. Still, the sight of the military was unnerving, and when the two of them climbed inside the train, I gasped. The men stopped at the door, talking before making their way across the aisle, maneuvering between random pieces of luggage stacked on top of one another between the rows. We watched them, holding our breath, anticipating that something bad was bound to happen any second. I felt a wave of collective fear encasing us all. One soldier stopped next to us and smiled at Zhenya, who smiled back, lifting Cheburashka with both hands over his head to show him off. I held my breath. Both soldiers jumped off at the back door as two dozen pairs of eyes looked on. We breathed a sigh of relief. The rest of the two-hour ride was uneventful, a brief intermission before our next emotional test.

Neither Yan nor I remember who ushered us off the train when we arrived in Vienna. Someone must have, because we schlepped our bags across the station once again. That we both remember. Our mutual memory is more vivid of the waiting area we found ourselves in, surrounded by our luggage and our travel companions. We were met with a now familiar picture of mothers feeding babies, kids running around, and people asking for food, water, and bathrooms. We must've looked like gypsies traveling through life with our miserable possessions. But unlike gypsies, who we saw on the streets of Kiev from time to time, we didn't sing or dance—we sat in an alien place, lost between two worlds, unaware of our fate.

"Anyone here going to Israel? Come with me... Bring your bags," a woman commanded in broken Russian, standing at the door. Her accent reminded me of the Israeli woman my mother and I met in the synagogue when I was little. Several families rushed to collect their belongings, including one from our group. Those who declared Israel as their ultimate destination went to the airport straight from the train station.

What about us? The woman was gone.

Zhenya fell asleep in Yan's arms. I stood next to them, listening to the rambling chatter in my head: *What day is it? We haven't*

changed our clothes or showered since we left Kiev.... Three days?...
Has it been only three days? My parents must be worried sick... I
promised to write, and I didn't.... It never occurred to me I wouldn't be
able to send them a letter right away. How long have we been here? An
hour? Two hours? Three? Now what? What if no one comes? Should
we call someone? But who? We have no phone number or address for
where we are going.... Nothing.

Vienna was where we headed from Bratislava. That's all we
knew. If all goes well, we will spend the next two weeks here before
moving on to Italy.

The wait seemed endless until they came. Two men walked into
the room: "*Poshli, poshli, poshli!* Let's go, let's go! Get your things.
Let's go! Hurry! Hurry! Hurry!" They also spoke broken Russian,
but the accent sounded different from the woman's earlier. *Maybe*
English?

Since most HIAS volunteers were Americans, it is safe to conclude that they spoke with an English accent. What they did daily
was nothing short of miraculous. There is simply no other way to
describe their effort. Without knowing who was coming on these
trains and when, they accounted for everyone and didn't lose a
single person. Not a single one. Each family had to be housed;
some people needed immediate medical care; there were pregnant
women and women with babies who needed basic supplies; they
dealt with sudden heart attacks, childbirth, and broken bones;
and everyone had gone through a deep interview process with
extensive paperwork in order to be approved to continue to our
next destination, Italy. All within a ten-day period (a typical time
spent in Vienna during our wave of emigration). A heartfelt "thank
you" doesn't come close to expressing my gratitude to each person
who made this part of our journey possible, but that's all I can do.

Thank you. Thank you. Thank you. Spasibo.

We rushed to follow the men heading outside, where two large buses waited for us. I now carried sleeping Zhenya, leaving Yan to drag our belongings to the bus. Somehow, he did, and so did the others. For the first time since we left Kiev, we parted with our suitcases, loading them in the bottom section of the bus intended for luggage. A novelty! In the passenger salon, we found soft, leisurely chairs with high backs and a head pillow. If the train to Vienna was fancy, these buses looked like vehicles from an unknown and distant future—spaceships promising a magical voyage ahead.

Disturbed by the commotion and the bright lights, Zhenya woke up and, after getting his bearings, climbed onto Papa's lap to be closer to the window, settling Cheburashka in his. To our relief, Zhenya seemed to feel much better. Our little boy was his usual curious self.

At such a young age, Zhenechka had an acute awareness of this being a complex time for our family. We hadn't prepared him for any of this. How could we? I have to admit, we took his mature behavior for granted because that's who he was in any situation—a thoughtful, loving little boy who seemed to understand life way beyond his years. He expressed himself with well-crafted, long sentences and reasoned his points of view instead of screaming his demands, which would have been more appropriate at his age. He had his one and only tantrum when he was two. A huge, loud, body on the floor, limbs shaking in the air, yelling and screaming kind of tantrum. After hesitating for a moment, I left the room—a twenty-four-year-old mom's desperate attempt to discipline a toddler. It seemed he screamed for hours, but in reality, the drama lasted only a minute before he came out with a big smile on his face. *Bravo, Mama! Your brilliant strategy worked!* I expected to use this technique again and again until he learned, but he never gave me another chance. Not once.

The three of us relaxed in our seats. Tinted glass, stretched from the ceiling to the floor, provided an expansive view. Our faces were glued to the window as we immersed ourselves in the elegance and the enchantment of the outside world, bursting in the extraordinary refinement of the evening lights.

It was past midnight when the buses brought us to the HIAS office, where we unloaded our luggage—for the fifth time in twenty-four hours. This time, the waiting area was a long, narrow hallway. It is possible that I missed instructions or information provided to us. Be that as it may, we sat and waited for something else to happen next.

"Yan, there is a man downstairs asking if anyone wants to sell their vodka bottles to him...are you interested?" one of our travel buddies shouted from the other end of the corridor. Yan and I answered in unison: "Yes!" Only a few people did the same. Some suggested selling vodka at another location for a better price. We were happy to lighten our load a bit and have some cash in exchange.

One by one, families registered with HIAS and three vans began taking people in small groups to their respective accommodations. A HIAS worker directed each family to their van, depending on the housing assignment. A young man guided us into a van with another family of three. They too were from Kiev, Podol district. The husband's name was Sasha. His wife (I don't remember her name) looked tired, scared, and lost, holding their five-year-old daughter on her knees. I imagine I looked like Sasha's wife as well.

The van stopped in front of a large five-story building, and the driver told us, with gesticulations, to go up to the third floor. Before driving away, he handed Yan a piece of paper, the address of HIAS written in German, and said to arrive at eight o'clock in the morning, which was just a few hours away.

The building didn't have an elevator, so we dragged our possessions and two sleeping children up three long flights of stairs, maybe the longest I had ever climbed. An older woman met us by the door on the third-floor landing. She gave each family a pair of keys and said in German, "All neighbors share the toilet and the shower. They are on the second floor. There is no kitchen."

Yan remembered some German from his school years and translated what she said. Too exhausted to react, we unlocked the door and walked into a narrow hallway that opened into a large room with a dark, wooden dining table and four chairs.

"Is this it? Where do we sleep?" said Sasha's wife, her chin trembling. I looked around; two doors led from the dining room into two small rooms with a bed in each. We had a place to sleep, after all.

A Version of Truth

21 May 1979—Vienna

Dorogie Mama, Papa, i Misha,

This is my first letter since we left Kiev. I am sorry I didn't write sooner, but I couldn't mail a letter until now. We bought stamps today at the post office—it was closed over the weekend, and before that we had nowhere to purchase stamps.

U nas vse horosho—all is well with us. The voyage from Kiev to Vienna was pleasant, without incident, bez problem. The train arrived in Chop on schedule and we left for Bratislava the same day. From there, it was a short train ride to Vienna. Zhenechka did great throughout the trip. He loved the trains just like I did when I was little. He misses you and every day asks when you are coming to us. I hope very soon.

By late evening on the 18th, we arrived in Vienna. A

small bus brought us to a hotel. We are sharing a large space with a couple who has a five-year-old girl, so Zhenechka has a friend to play with. You may know the girl's father, Sasha, or his parents. They lived on Spasskaya 24, across the street from us. If you run into his parents, tell them not to worry.

We will try to call in the next couple of days—someone said we may be able to do that at the post office. Hope to hear your voices before you get this letter.

Please don't worry about us. Everyone is doing well and we have plenty of food. I cook for the two families on the little burner we brought. Sasha's wife can't cook, but she helps as much as she can. She is very nice. Yesterday, we bought some fruit at the farmers' market, like our bazaar. Yan bought Zhenya a banana and strawberries. Remember, he tried a banana once and asked for more, but we didn't find them anywhere? Looks like there are plenty here.

Uncle Vova left for Rome two weeks ago. We will find him there. Alla and her family should arrive in Vienna today.

Turns out Yan remembers some German from studying it at school. He is now our putevoditel, a guide! It's been great! Mama, you will remember German too, once you are here. Papa always said you spoke it well when you two lived in Dresden after the war.

We have seen little of Vienna, just what we could glance at from the trolley to HIAS and on our walk back to the hotel—it's a long walk. We walked until Zhenya got tired. Every street is clean as if scrubbed by hand; every building seems recently painted, every tree is groomed, and people look just as neat as the city itself. Oh, and the smell… Vienna smells like someone bathed it in the most expensive perfume. Don't laugh, I am serious! We will try to explore

*while we are here. But most of all, we want to be cleared for
Italy soon...*

*How are you? Any news? How is everyone? Bella, Basya,
Aunt Katya? We miss everyone.*

*Don't write back to this address. We would most likely
be in Italy by the time your letter arrives. It would just be
lost. I'll write again the day after tomorrow. Please don't
worry about us.*

Privet vsem. Say hello to everyone.

Obnimayem, celuem. Sending hugs and kisses.

Yours always, Galya, Yan, i Zhenechka

*P.S. Zhenechka drew you a picture while I was writing,
and I traced his right hand—like Papa used to do—on the
other side of the page.*

With this letter, I began my written account of a version of our
journey that looked slightly different from the reality. Nothing
about the Soviet border crossing. The armed Soviet guards. The
dogs. The treatment we received on the train to Bratislava. Zhenya
being sick, especially not that. If I had shared those details while
they were still fresh, I would've given myself an excuse to dwell
on them and feel sorry for our misfortunes. I would've given Papa
more reasons to chain smoke, pace around the house, or sit on a
chair in the hallway by the front door. My real tale of our exodus
would give Mama more reasons to pound on her pots and pans in
the kitchen—*click, click, bang, bang*—and take her heart medications while lying on the couch in the living room with her hand over
her face. I could hear her say to Aunt Katya: "Why is she putting
her family through this hardship? For what?"

I locked up these memories far, far away, wherever one's struggles live. So far, in fact, that it has taken me forty years to bring them

back, one by one by one. I transcribed the letters in this book from memory and translated them from Russian. Mama saved each one of them and brought many with her when she came to America. I reread them again, but when I cleared Mama's apartment after she died, I didn't find them. Nevertheless, I include their content here; I wrote to my parents four letters a week for eight years, and many of those letters are etched in my memory.

In the first one, I said we lived in a hotel in Vienna. In reality, the place was more like a boarding house, a pension. People came and went at all hours of the day. We joked about this establishment being of a "suspicious" nature. Except for Sasha's wife, we all managed the inconvenience of living without a kitchen and a bathroom nearby—not being spoiled by a life of luxury came in handy. My electric burner served as a stove, and I made food for six of us every day. The adults ate canned meat (resembling SPAM, which we later ate in America to stretch our budget) mixed with a few potatoes if we had them…a stew of sorts. For the kids, I often made cream of wheat hot cereal, and we bought them fruit. We must've bought a few other types of produce, but neither Yan nor I remember what they were. We used the few kitchen utensils we'd brought, but there wasn't enough for everyone to eat together, so we took turns. Sasha's wife cried a lot, and Yan and I often took care of both kids while Sasha consoled her. She missed her parents and had a tough time adjusting to our less-than-comfortable surroundings.

But we also had some beautiful moments in Vienna. We lived just a few trolley stops from the Schönbrunn Palace, where entry was free once a week. The eighteenth-century summer palace with its late Baroque architecture reminded me of the Winter and Summer Palace in Leningrad. It had similarly grandiose and elaborate architecture, charming gardens with hidden passages, and spectacular fountains throughout the grounds. Another memorable place was Stadtpark (we called it Strauss Park), a city park where a gold-plated statue of Johann Strauss playing violin graced the central allée.

Thirty-nine years later, Yan and I returned to Vienna for a brief visit. Our first stop was Strauss Park. We found "our bench," the closest one to the Johann Strauss statue—on the left side of an allée lined with trees and benches if you are facing the statue. On this spot, thirty-nine years ago, we had our first encounter with the "real West." Our entire lives, we had been taught that people were mean and horrible to each other outside the Soviet border. "You will die on the street, and no one will offer help." Soviet leaders and schoolteachers drilled this message into our heads from childhood through education, books, movies, radio, and newspapers.

Relaxing on this very park bench one May afternoon in 1979— as Zhenya played nearby—we learned it wasn't true: an older gentleman walked toward us, leaning on his cane, more and more with every laborious step he took. We both rushed toward him to help, but he fell to the ground before we reached him, and there were half a dozen people around him already trying to assist. To everyone's relief, he recuperated once a man helped him get up, and a woman gave him water.

Thinking back on that experience as I was writing this book, I asked Yan if he remembered how shocked we both were, watching the bystanders' reactions. "So much for 'no one will give you a hand if you fall,'" I said with a wry smile.

Yan nodded. "If we had listened to everything we were told by the Soviets, we would still be there, and what a calamity that would've been! Can you imagine?"

I certainly could imagine. The financial help we had given to my parents and Misha from America sustained them during the years we were apart. No saying how they would've survived. We would've been in Kiev for the Chernobyl disaster, living only sixty miles away from the explosion that killed my father. I have no medical proof of this statement but I don't need one. He died a few days after it happened, and that was no coincidence. He wasn't well, but he would have made it to America were it not for that disaster and the misinformation that accompanied the dreadful event. The radiation—coming through the open doors and windows into their apartment—killed him. Of course, he and Mama were in the dark about what was happening. What did she say when I called to warn them? "You're spreading propaganda." Some propaganda!

To this day, these memories outrage Yan whenever I mention them. We both talk about this period with anger and sadness.

"You know what else I am horrified about?" I said. "If we never applied to leave, or worse, became *refuseniks*, the boys would've served in the Soviet Army, and I can't imagine that. What is scarier than that? Would we even be brave enough to have Alik in the USSR?"

"Are you serious? If we—you—were brave enough to have him two years after the arrival in the US when we still had nothing, you would have him anywhere on the planet." Yan wrapped his arm around my shoulder and we both laughed. He was right.

We reminisced about the smell of Vienna. Yan said the cleaning people added perfume to the water they hosed the streets with, and that's why the city smelled of an exquisite perfume. I think he was almost serious. I remembered standing in a small delicatessen, lightheaded from the abundance and the variety of meats, cheeses, and breads. We walked out of the store empty-handed and Yan said, "Imagine, what will life be like in America if it's like this here?"

Naive? Maybe a little, but largely, he was right.

The incident at the market, all those years ago, reminds me of an animated movie we watched with the kids, *An American Tail*. Zhenya was eleven, and Alik was four when the movie first came out. We wanted them to appreciate our family story, and this film

160

fable was a wonderful way to do so. We explained to the boys that, like the mice family, we also came to America in hope of a better life. Just like the mice family, the four of us sang together: "There are no cats in America, and the streets are paved with cheese…"

Why Would Anyone Lie?

We arrived on time for our interview at HIAS, writing down the names of every street and trolley stop along the way, to trace our steps back. With Yan's newly discovered knowledge of German, however limited, we enjoyed being on our own.

The visit to HIAS lasted several hours. They required all three of us to be present. First, we underwent a medical examination, which included a physical exam and answering questions about our medical history. During the long hours spent at HIAS that day, Zhenya didn't take part in the wild play of other kids, whose patience ran out the minute they walked in, possibly causing their parents to develop an ulcer or—at a minimum—to lose their voice from constant yelling: "Stop! This is not a park. Stop running!" I felt bad for these parents and the kids. What a twist of fate we all experienced in a few days. I hugged Zhenya tighter as he sat on my lap listening to my stories about *Babulya* and *Dedulya*. When I'd exhausted all the stories, he told me his—about how they would soon come and live with us, asking a million questions along the way. *Was our child really three and a half?*

After the medical exam, we waited for the second step, an interview. A HIAS caseworker, whose Russian was good enough for us to understand each other, conducted the interview. This was a relief because neither Yan nor I could have handled this conversation in English. Let's be real, we couldn't handle *any* conversation in English.

The caseworker had a friendly smile but seemed a no-nonsense kind of person. Very direct. His first comment to us was a request to be truthful in our responses. He began with several generic questions about our place of residence and work, our education; he asked if we had any family left behind in the USSR and if any close family members lived in the US. Yan and I took turns answering these questions with some level of confidence that we were on the right track. Honest. Truthful. Nothing to hide. Then came more provocative questions.

When the caseworker asked us to be truthful, it wasn't without a reason. Why would anyone lie? Two reasons.

First, we were applying for a refugee asylum in the US based on religious persecution. Were we persecuted? That was a tough fact to prove. The persecution was not visible to the naked eye; we lived with it, not noticing or rebelling. There was nothing to see… no proof; just some anecdotal stories from our daily lives. The Soviet Jews were a special breed, and many of us still are. We didn't know what we didn't have, and subconsciously, we wanted it this way because we needed to survive. Be like everyone else. Sound like everyone else. Look like everyone else. Celebrate the same holidays as everyone else. I didn't know about a Jewish wedding, the one with a rabbi and a chuppah. It didn't occur to me to circumcise our son, or to invite a friend to a Passover dinner. Or to even have a Passover dinner. Soviet Jews! We had no connection to our heritage, language, tradition, or roots. We were strangers in our own land and had no ties to Jewish communities anywhere in the world.

We didn't understand Jewish life when we came to America, and to this day, I am not entirely comfortable among the American Jews lucky to be born here or in Israel. For me, the proof of persecution was the absence of visible persecution because there was nothing to persecute…we didn't know what we didn't have. The only Jewish identity the Soviet Jews had was their nationality stated as Jewish in the Soviet passport. Did every Jew in the USSR have the same experience? Maybe not, but I didn't know anyone who hadn't.

The second reason to lie in the interview was to hide former association with the Communist Party. Keep in mind, the Cold War between the USSR and the US (with their respective allies) was still alive and well in 1979. Allowing former Communists into the United States wasn't on the priority list of the US government. I can imagine that the Communist Party association questioning also helped weed out potential spies. It would be naïve to think the Soviets didn't attempt to plant spies amid two million people coming to America. Wasn't it Winston Churchill who famously said, "Never let a good crisis go to waste"?

We were aware by then that the HIAS personnel were knowledgeable about the Soviet system and the Communist establishments. They understood that every Soviet kid was at least in the Young Octobrist and the Pioneer organizations. It would be foolish to lie about that. Most young people were Komsomol members. Also not wise to hide. It got complicated with the Communist Party membership. Many professional positions required membership in the Party (not officially, but widely known) – heads of large companies, university deans, history and political science teachers, military personnel above a certain rank, among others. So for me to deny that my father, a retired major of the Soviet Army, and my mother, a military wife, were Communists would be suicidal. Admitting these facts could deny us entry to the US.

"Can you prove you are Jews?" asked the caseworker. *Did I hear that right? He asked us to prove that we're Jews?* For the first time in our lives, being Jewish had an enormous privilege—the right to leave the Soviet Union and be considered for a life in the United States. Our Soviet passports with the fifth paragraph would be proof, but we didn't have them, and our visas didn't state our nationality. But Yan had proof—the proof of a Jewish man. He was circumcised. And the rest of our answers provided the remaining evidence.

"Why did you decide to leave the USSR?" The caseworker continued his inquiry. Yan spoke first. He talked about his family's plan to send him to America when he was thirteen, and how the plan never came to fruition. He explained his desire to immigrate to America rather than Israel with the truth. He believed that in America, we would have a broader perspective of the world, learn a Jewish life, and also be part of the American tradition. I had a simple reason: meeting Yan had opened my eyes to the limitations Jews experienced in the Soviet Union.

"As Jews, how were you persecuted?" was his next question. I took this one. I talked about my mother's family. They were from Chernobyl, a *shtetl* outside of Kiev (made famous by the 1986 nuclear disaster). My grandfather was a tailor whose great reputation with the gentiles must have saved his family from the 1919 pogroms. The town was under the occupation of Ilya Struk, a Chernobyl native who headed a gang of armed Cossacks who collectively murdered 150 Chernobyl Jews, raped Jewish women, and looted or destroyed Jewish homes and shops. My family attributed their survival to my grandfather. My grandmother kept a Jewish home and was famous for her generosity; she shared Shabbat dinners with strangers passing through the *shtetl*, and neighbors who were poor or lived alone. Everyone in the family spoke Yiddish and lived a simple life until they moved to Kiev in 1926. Here, their Jewish life gave way to Soviet doctrine, and by the time I was born, there was no trace of it. Not the language. Not the holidays. Not the Shabbat. Gone were the traditions. Gone was the Jewish life. That's how we were persecuted.

"What are your and your parents' affiliations with the Communist Party?" This one was easy for Yan. His parents were never Party members; they were more of Party haters, and he escaped Komsomol altogether. But I had a story to tell. Yes, I was a member of the Soviet youth Communist organizations and had been expelled from Komsomol when we decided to emigrate. My parents were both Communist Party members. (Somehow it sounded better to say "my parents were Communist Party members" and not "my parents were both Communists.") My father was the youngest of thirteen siblings and grew up without a father. He lost much of his family to Stalin's persecutions and found a new family in the Soviet Army. As he moved up in rank, it was a given he would have to join the Party. My mother joined when he became a major; at that point, she had no choice if he were to progress any further, so she followed another unspoken rule.

I paused.

"Did your father get another promotion?"

"No. They pushed him into retirement, and he had a hard time finding a civilian job. Now, because we left, my parents will be expelled from the Party, as a punishment for them, and a lesson for others. They were prepared for that; they are both retired; they are ready to leave too and reunite with us in America."

"No more questions. Thank you. You may go. Someone outside will give you your allowance to use for transportation and food. We paid your living accommodations and will be in touch regarding your status in about a week."

"Hope we convinced him we are Jewish," I said to Yan.

We lived our lives hiding that fact as much as possible, avoiding saying the word *Yevryei*, and now we had to say it a number of times out loud and pretend were completely comfortable doing that.

Another box checked. One step closer to America.

GALINA CHERNY

The Meltdown

Armed with 392 shillings of HIAS allowance (three dollars a day—according to the exchange rate of the time—for the remaining nine days we spent in Vienna), plus another 15 shillings from selling two bottles of Soviet champagne, thanks to Sasha, and with zero knowledge of the currency value and the cost of anything, we stopped at the farmers' market, a few blocks away.

In Kiev, we lived close to the bazaar and made frequent trips there to buy fruit and vegetables in season, sometimes fresh chicken parts. Since I was a kid, Mama brought me along, so I learned the system very well. For instance, if strawberries were in season, we checked the price with each seller and purchased from the cheapest one. Bargaining was a necessary part of the shopping, but it was Mama's job; I was too shy.

Podolskiy Bazaar, named after its location, the old Podol neighborhood, was an open-air market. This meant that when it rained, it rained, and when it snowed, it snowed. Those were the best times to shop, since bad weather gave better opportunities for price negotiation. But you had to come early or your chances of getting something of a decent quality were slim. The packaging would horrify any American; the merchants, Ukrainian women looking as disheveled as the produce they sold, used newspaper scraps to wrap the delicate items, like berries. The rest, they handed to you, unwrapped and soiled. There was an indoor *bazaar* on Kreschatik Street called *Pechersky Bazaar* where things were a little more civilized and the quality of produce was better, but everything was much more expensive, way out of our budget.

That sunny May afternoon in Vienna—relieved to be done with the interview and hoping we did a good enough job proving our Jewishness—we walked toward the market holding hands, Zhenya in the middle, hopping and skipping. "I want to jump! Mama, Papa, say, '*raz, dva, tri*,'" he demanded, giggling and squeezing our hands to make his request non-negotiable.

"One, two, three." We pulled him up in the air, to his complete and utter delight. We laughed and did it again and again until we reached a two-story building that looked like the description we had.

I don't remember the address of the market or of the HIAS office to give a better orientation of these places in Vienna. I wish I had it all scribbled, but documenting our whereabouts was the furthest thing from my mind.

Yan held the door, and I followed Zhenechka inside. *What is this?* My breath trapped in my throat, making me gasp. All around us, rows and rows of long tables drowned in a rainbow of colors: purple huckleberries, ruby-red raspberries and strawberries, dark red and flushed yellow cherries, and other small fruit I didn't recognize. Light green and wine-colored apples shone as if someone had polished them by hand. Heaps of beaming golden bananas towered over each table. Colors, shapes, and smells blended into one another, making me dizzy. Vendors, women, dressed in crisp white aprons over colorful dresses. *Are they smiling? Who are these people? What are these things? This must all be plastic! Even the people!*

Before I recovered from my shock, I heard: "Ma-amaa!... Ma-amaa! Bana-nas! Straw-berries! Straw-berries! Ba-nanas!" Zhenya stood in a wide space between the front door and the first long table packed with exquisite goodness, screaming in agony, repeating again and again: "M-maa!... M-maa! Ba-nanas! Straw-berries! Ba-nanas!" My heart sank. For the first time, I didn't know how to console my son.

"*Sinulya*, stop please; sonny, don't cry." I leaned to him, cupping both hands underneath his face, causing him to look up at me. "Papa will find out how much strawberries and bananas cost, and we'll see if we can buy them. Please, darling, be patient for one minute." This reasoning would've worked with Zhenya on any other day, but not that day. He wiggled his head from my hold. "Bana-naas! Straw-berries!" He interrupted his screaming every few seconds to catch his breath after each word before it continued with a vengeance. His little body convulsed. I dropped to my knees in front of him, hugging him tightly, sobbing, swaying with him from side to side as short, sudden expulsions of breath pushed their way out of my chest, again and again. *How long were we like this? Hours? Minutes? How many people walked by or stood around?*

"Here, here, *sinok*." Yan was squatting next to us, holding a small basket of ripe strawberries and a shiny banana in his hand.

Goodbye, Vienna!

26 May 1979—Vienna
Dorogie Mama and Papa, this is my third letter.
We are so happy we talked this morning! It was won-derful to hear your voices even though it was only for three minutes. Zhenechka loved talking to both of you. On the way home, Zhenya kept asking: "How did dedulya get inside the phone?" We tried to explain, but he insisted Deda was inside the phone. Papa, did you tell him that? What story did you tell your grandson in the one minute the two of you spent on the phone? I think you were singing, too. He is a very lucky boy to have you two as his grandparents.
I have some good news—we found Alla and her family! So yesterday, we showed up at their hotel and surprised her with a single red rose for her birthday. We spent an afternoon together, walking around their neighborhood. Zhenya en-joyed all the attention he got from Lenya and Alla's parents.

We've been exploring Vienna on foot as much as we can. The city is beautiful, with lots of parks and elegant architecture. No two buildings look alike. We visited Strauss Park twice now, and one evening, an orchestra was playing Goluboi Dunai. You would've loved to experience "The Blue Danube" in Vienna. People got up and danced. Just like that. We just sat and watched...

Another surprise: there are no signs that say "Do not walk on grass" anywhere! Kids play on the grass. Families have picnics in the city parks. Imagine that! Zhenya jumped with excitement when we told him to play on the grass like other kids.

We should hear from HIAS in the next couple of days. We'll call you when it happens. I am sure they will approve us for Rome, so don't worry. In the meantime, we eat well and have enough money to last us through our stay.

You didn't say anything on the phone about your recent ordeal with the Party.... I am relieved this is behind you.

Please give our love to the family. Tell them we are thinking of them and love them very much. I will write another letter before we leave Vienna.

Vsem privet. Say hello to everyone. Mi vas lubim. We love you.

Vashi,

Galya, Yan, i Zhenechka

The approval to proceed to Rome came on the 28th, and we were scheduled to depart the following day. When I told my parents "not to worry... they would approve us for Rome," that was my wishful thinking, a desire, a dream. We knew some people were detained in Vienna, but the thought of not moving through the process "as planned" was terrifying. Yan and I analyzed our interview, going back and forth, recalling our answers and trying to interpret what the result might be, but we didn't know. "We have enough money" was a bit of a stretch as well, although our expectation of what was "enough" was so low, we were fine with only being able to buy very limited necessities. We ate canned food and bought some fruit for Zhenya a few times. To save money, we walked everywhere instead of using public transportation.

Late in the afternoon on May 29, we stood on the platform of the Wien Hauptbahnhof in front of the Vienna-Rome train. We stored our luggage on a cart and had plenty of time before the departure to settle for the twelve-hour ride to Rome. There were no guards, customs, or border patrol. We breathed.

Thank you, exquisite Vienna, for your hospitality. Thank you for calming our souls by letting us stroll your elegant streets. Thank you for welcoming us into your enchanting parks where the sounds of Johann Strauss's "The Blue Danube" waltz made us forget the struggles behind and the uncertainty ahead, even if just for a little while.

Goodbye, Vienna! *Auf Wiedersehen*! Until we meet again.

15

Hardly a Roman Holiday

Somewhere in the Heart of Rome

"*Kusit! Kusit!*" Mima's call to meals caused an uproar of laughter among the guests of a rundown flophouse a few blocks from the Roma Termini train station. The residents were our former compatriots, Soviet Jews immigrating to America, Canada, or Australia, on the last leg of their journey. "*Kusit*" was Mima's butchered pronunciation of a Russian word, "*kushat*," which means "Eat, let's eat, come to eat." Zhenya picked up the "new" word from Mima, and it became part of our family's lexicon. Even today, "*kusit*" is how we often call people to our family dinners.

Mima was Portuguese (or so we were told), a short, grumpy-looking young man whose gloomy disposition intimidated many. He was managing the kitchen, and as such, was the most important person at the hotel. Mima became my best friend, and I adored him. (Thank you, Mima, for breaking the rules and letting me make Zhenya tea in your kitchen every night.) However, I won't praise Mima for the meals he served: bread with strawberry jam and coffee for breakfast, plain pasta for lunch, and pasta with tomato sauce for dinner. This wasn't a big step up from the canned food we had eaten in Vienna, but we were grateful to the Joint—the American Joint Distribution Committee—which provided shelter in Rome for ten days, giving us time to find more permanent housing for the rest of our stay in Italy. Of course, at the time, gratitude toward the Joint was not at the forefront of my mind, since I could only process the things right in front of me. I remember calculating the maximum rent we could pay for an apartment and realizing we wouldn't have enough money. I couldn't process anything outside of these immediate measures. The Joint paid us an allowance to help cover living expenses once we moved out of the hotel. We didn't know how strict the "ten-day" hotel stay limit was, and we had not heard of anyone being kicked out on the street if they didn't find a place to live in time, but we didn't want to be the first to find out. We intended to rent an apartment before the ten days were up.

Very few people remained in Rome for the duration of the entire stay. It was too expensive. The time spent in Italy was unpredictable—it took anywhere from several weeks to months for the embassy to approve individual requests for immigration to the United States. Our choices for housing were one of the two seaside cities outside of Rome, which became major transit points for Jewish émigrés—Lido Di Ostia (called "Ostia" by the Soviet refugees) and Ladispoli. Ostia, the original settlement site, was located ten kilometers closer to Rome than Ladispoli, but it was much more expensive.

Decision made. Ladispoli it was.

Finding a place in Ladispoli, however, turned out to be more difficult than we'd expected. Every morning, armed with a train ticket and a few phrases commonly used to rent an apartment— *appartamento in affitto,* and *quanto costa l'affitto*—Yan took a forty-minute train ride from Rome to Ladispoli while Zhenya and I waited for him at the hotel. You'd think I might have passed the time by taking my son for a walk to explore the majesty of the eternal city. The city, which according to Mark Twain was "beautiful to the eye, more illustrious in history than any other in Europe." Why not do some sightseeing? But I opted to stay inside and not risk having to ask simple directions in fear of "getting it wrong" or "being laughed at." While others bragged about the ease with which they learned Italian, I couldn't say "*ciao*" or "*grazie*" out loud, or any other words that came effortlessly to everyone else. Who was I afraid to disappoint? My father? Myself? Perhaps both.

Day after day, Yan came back from Ladispoli empty-handed. "*Nessun appartamento in affitto.*" *No apartment for rent? Did the entire world come to Italy for the summer?* With our limited resources, $300 worth of mili lira a month, finding an apartment and having some money left for groceries and train tickets to Rome for INS interviews was challenging. But we needed to get out of the hotel, especially because I feared Zhenya wasn't getting enough to eat at the flophouse. He wasn't used to this type of food and barely touched his lunch and dinner, so I began saving my breakfast roll to give him in the evening. He liked it soaked in tea. At home, he loved a mixture of warm milk with soaked white bread, so my version of this "dish" invented by *babulya* must have tasted more familiar to him than pasta. The sooner we could find a place, the sooner we'd receive our three hundred dollars allowance, which would give us a little more flexibility. *My baby needs some soup!*

All Roads Lead to Ladispoli

4 June 1979
Our dearest Mama and Papa! This is my first letter from Ladispoli.

173

The letter before this, I sent from Rome and asked you not to write back because we were only going to be there for ten days. Now you can write to us! Use the address on the envelope (copy exactly). Guess whose address this is? Uncle Vova's! You wouldn't believe what happened!

Last night after dinner at the hotel, there was a knock on the door. I opened it, and there was Uncle Vova in the flesh! Imagine our surprise! After lots of hugs and kisses, he told us he came to Rome several times to look for us, checking every hotel and pension where he was told our people might be staying. It was getting to be dusk, but he decided to check one more place before heading back to the train station. He ran into Mima (I told you about Mima and his tea) at the entrance, and he pointed Vova to our room. How they communicated is a mystery. Maybe "kusit" wasn't the only Russian word Mima knew, and maybe Uncle Vova learned some Italian by now, seeing as they've been in Italy since the middle of March.

Uncle Vova insisted we come with him right away. We didn't hesitate for a moment! We packed our bags and took the last train to Ladispoli. Imagine Aunt Lillia's and Sonia's surprise when we all showed up at the door! They are renting one room in a three-room apartment, sharing a kitchen and bathroom with two other families. I worried it might upset the neighbors to have additional people in the space, but Sonia said nobody complained. We will try to find our own place soon—it should be easier now without having to schlep on the train back and forth. In the meantime, last night, Aunt Lillia made us a bed on the floor using all our blankets and a few of theirs, and we had a wonderful night. These marble floors get cold during the winter months, but now they are refreshing, just very hard...good thing we had the blankets.

We offered Vova to pay a portion of the rent while we stayed with them, but he wouldn't hear of it, and when we went to the market this morning, he wouldn't take our money, either. He said, "I won't let my niece pay for a bowl of soup I share with her and her family." I know how much you love your cousin, and his generosity toward me is no surprise to you.... I can hear you say, "He adores you, Galochka!" And I know that, too. I've always felt loved in his presence.

I hope we can find a place of our own in the next couple of days, but first, we need to find Alla and Lenya. We want to share an apartment with them.

Please write and tell us how you are doing. We miss you and can't wait to see you soon. How is Misha? Aunt Katia? Bella? Everyone else? We will try to call in a couple of days. Yan sends his love.

Don't worry about us. We are doing well. Everyone is healthy and eating. Zhenechka is great. He drew another picture for you and asked me to "not to forget to put it in the envelope and seal it really, really hard so the picture doesn't fall out when the letter travels on the train to babulya and dedulya."

We love you.

Do skorogo svidaniya. Until we meet soon,
Galya, Yan, i Zhenya

16

Summer in Ladispoli

June 28, 1979

"*V tesnote da ne v obide*—cramped, but not put out," said Alla, helping me set the kitchen table for Yan's birthday dinner. Our families shared a two-room apartment with one bathroom, a kitchen, and a lovely balcony. Yan, Zhenya, and I occupied a small room with a single bed, and Alla's family of five lived in the larger room, sharing two double beds and a small folding bed. The apartment was on the second floor of a two-story building; the owners of the building managed a restaurant on the first floor. The restaurant must have been theirs, but the concept of owning a business wasn't in our vocabulary or our grasp, so it never occurred to any of us to inquire.

As we continued to shuffle plates, glasses, and flatware on the small kitchen table, the tender sound of an acoustic guitar and a beautiful male voice drifted into the apartment through the open window:

Sul mare luccica, l'astro d'argento
Placida è l'onda, prospero il vento;

. . .

Venite all'agile barchetta mia;
Santa Lucia, Santa Lucia!

The old Neapolitan song filled the summer air, inviting us to enjoy the fresh breeze of the Mediterranean Sea.

The silver star shimmers on the sea,
The waves are peaceful; the wind is favorable.

. . .

Come to my sprightly little boat,
Santa Lucia, Santa Lucia!

We listened to the timeless tune until the last words gracefully faded into the night, as we toasted Yan on his thirty-third birthday.

Our dinner menu that night resembled most of the meals we had those days—a hearty turkey wing stew with potatoes. Alla, her mother Maria, and I became very creative at preparing several dishes from the cheapest meat—turkey wings or *krylya sovetov*, as the entire generation of Jewish refugees from the USSR called them. Why the name "wings of Soviets" and who came up with it? I couldn't tell you. Maybe because it was reminiscent of the names for a hockey and a soccer club, Soviet aviation, or maybe because Soviet Wings was a slogan often used in speeches and patriotic songs. Either way, saying the words made us chuckle every time. We made "wings of Soviets" or "Soviet wings" into soups, stews, cutlets, and meatballs, among other dishes. Once a week, Yan or Lenya took a train to Rome with a shopping list for the two families. That saved us a little money. When possible, the men timed their trip toward the end of the day when the merchants were more likely to reduce their prices. The outdoor market was on the Piazza Vittorio Emanual, a ten-minute walk from the Termini, down Via Giovanni Giolitti. The market must have had a *real* name, but the Russian Jews called it *Kruglyy Bazaar,* Round Market, for the circular arrangement of its produce stalls.

Zhenya and I joined Yan on the market run on the days we had HIAS appointments for additional paperwork and interviews. The variety of fresh meat, poultry, fruit, vegetables, and bounty of merchandise, from clothing to sunglasses to shoes to jewelry, was still overwhelming. However, the sense of shock and panic we felt in Vienna settled down with time. In awe, we watched people buying meat with no bones and asking a butcher to trim off the fat from a piece of meat they wanted. That was unheard of in our world—you paid for the fat and the bones whether or not you wanted them, or you got nothing. And how strange it was to be thanked for our purchase! We struggled to comprehend the unfamiliar logic: The butcher did *us* a favor selling us turkey wings, and yet, he said "*grazie*" as he handed us a neatly wrapped purchase. Both were foreign: a "thank you" and a neatly wrapped purchase.

The atmosphere at the market was festive and loud. Locals negotiated with the merchants, gesticulating with broad hand movements, screaming and yelling as if they were going to engage in a fistfight at any moment. But once they settled the price, both sides laughed, shook hands, and said to each other: "*Ci vediamo domani...ci vediamo domani,* see you tomorrow..." before moving on. Women with children received special attention at the round market: "*Signora, prega, regalo per bambino! Due pezzo—una mila lira! Tre pezzo—una milla lira!* Lady, please, a present for the child! Two pieces—for one mila lira! Three pieces—for one mila."

"Mama, mama," Zhenya would ask every time we walked by a merchant selling toys. "Do we have enough money today to buy *regalo per bambino?*"

I always gave the same answer: "Not today, sweetheart."

Over the years, Yan and I visited Rome several times and never re-traced our emigration steps. We understood that *Kruglyy bazaar* moved a few blocks from its original location and became *Nuovo Mercato Esquilino*, but we didn't look for it. Perhaps we didn't want to remind ourselves of the time when we didn't belong anywhere and had nothing. Absolutely nothing. We did, however, make good on our pledge with Alla—that one day we would drink the coffee on Piazza Navona, not just smell it. We also promised ourselves that we would eat the entire portion of gelato instead of dividing it into three, between those of us with a sweet tooth: Alla, Zhenya, and Yan. And finally, we pledged to eat that famous Italian pizza, sipping a glass of Chianti in an outdoor cafe. We wouldn't fulfill these promises until years later. For now, during that long summer of 1979, we were the turkey wings family for whom even the cheapest *regalo per bambino* was an unthinkable luxury.

We ran into Alla and Lenya a few days after we moved in with Uncle Vova and Aunt Lillia. After another unsuccessful morning of looking for an apartment, they stopped at The Fountain near the Ladispoli Cerveteri train station at almost the same time as we came by to look for them. Of course, the plaza with a fountain had an Italian name, but it was renamed "The Fountain" by the Russian Jews. The Fountain was the central meeting spot for émigrés and a place to find things out: the best places to sell the Russian *tchotchkes* that occupied everyone's luggage; questions asked in the HIAS interviews, and what answers to give; the best time to shop at the round market in Rome; which landlords were crooks and how to avoid them; and how to bargain rent prices.

The scene around The Fountain reminded me of the scene by the OVIR office in Kiev, minus the lines and the chestnut trees. We avoided the area as much as possible, and finding an apartment on the other side of town was perfect. A thirty-minute walk from the train station was well worth a slightly cheaper rent and a little more privacy. After spending days and weeks schlepping our luggage from one train station to another, crammed in with large groups of people, sharing housing with strangers, we developed a herd fatigue (yes, it's a thing), which I carried with me in America for years. So when we settled away from the Russian immigrant population, we created a sense of some normality for ourselves. In the summer of 1979, this seaside resort town of 17,000 people hosted over four thousand Jewish émigrés from the USSR a month. We weren't the only ones overwhelmed by the migrant crowds—Italians were, too. Many of the locals worked in Rome, and their travel to and from work became hectic. With so many more people vehemently competing for seats on trains and buses, the quiet lives of the residents became chaotic, with Russian Jews flooding local stores, the post office, and the beaches, and taking up apartments that otherwise would've been rented by tourists. Sometimes, it seemed more people spoke Russian in Ladispoli than Italian. Here, we didn't want to be "*v tesnote*," "*cramped.*"

30 June 1979—Ladispoli
Our dear Mama and Papa! We received your letter and a birthday card for Yan. He was happy for a greeting signed by both of you. And it came right on his birthday! What were the chances? Thank you very much. Tell everyone in the family we thank them for their wishes, as well. Yan knows how much everyone loves him. How are you both doing? What's new with everyone? How is Misha?
A little about us. We are doing well. Everyone is healthy. The weather is beautiful, and we take Zhenya to the beach as much as possible. The Mediterranean air and salt seawater are good for him. He loves building sandcastles—the sand is dark, almost black—and skipping across the waves.

And don't worry—he is never alone in the water—we are watching him closely. I know you worry about these things.

I already wrote about us reuniting with Alla and her family, and that we live together now. Alla's mother, Maria Vladimirovna, has been such a great help to us with Zhenya. When we have HIAS appointments and he doesn't need to be present, he stays in Ladispoli with Babushka Musya. We are so grateful for her help. Yan and Maria Vladimirovna spend evenings studying English together. Alla and I join them sometimes, but I have a hard time learning from the book. None of us knows the language to teach the others; it's like "the blind leading the blind." Hope the few phrases I remember from school will help me when we get to America.

I must tell you what your grandson did yesterday. His singing, which came from Alla's room across the hallway, awakened us at six o'clock in the morning. I ran over and found Zhenya standing on a chair in the middle of the room singing "Arlekino" while everyone was still in their beds. When I tried to take him back to our room, Alla's father asked me to let him stay. For almost an hour, he sang and cited his entire repertoire. I am afraid this will now become a habit. Papa, he remembered every single song you taught him.

The Givertses left on the 26th. They flew to New York but did not know how they would get to New Jersey from there. They are going to the city called Cherry Hill, Vishnevyy Kholm in Russian. I wish they were coming with us to Los Angeles, but it was too late to change their destination when we realized how far the two cities were from one another. Six hours on the plane! Uncle Vova said not to worry and promised to come visit us soon. I am sure he'll want to see you both when you arrive.

Almost forgot! Yan sold all the things we brought with us. We learned the quickest way to get rid of everything at once was to sell it at the market in Naples. We may have gotten better prices on the Americano in Rome (the market's real name is Porta Portese; the immigrants gave it a new name), but Yan and I didn't want to spend days selling our trinkets. We are not good at this kind of thing. You must be nodding your heads reading this. With everything sold, we have the money to add to our allowance and pay for rent and food.

Mama, you said you began packing already, so please, please listen to my suggestions. Don't bring anything to sell. All you need is your medications, clothing, a blanket, and two pillows—traveling light would help you and Papa get through the border check easier. Nothing but the essentials. Horosho? Okay? You would need to bring some food: bread, salami, and several cans of meat and sardines to hold you over from Kiev to Vienna. Everything will be fine. Don't worry, just be prepared.

And when you get to Italy, we'll transfer American dollars to you to cover anything you may need. Who knows, we may even still be here when you come, in which case you will live with us. In each subsequent letter, I will write a few more details about what you might need along the way. Don't want to have it all in one letter—for an obvious reason. And please, don't sell the furniture until you have permission in your hands. And if you won't have the time to sell everything then, just leave it all to Misha.

That's all for today. I'll write again in a couple of days. Please write and tell us how everyone is doing. We love you and miss you very much. I am including a drawing from Zhenya, and a note from Yan. Sending you hugs and kisses.

Yours always, Yan, Zhenechka, i Galya

17

Refuseniks

July 15, 1979—Ladispoli

"Yan, look! This letter is from Papa!" I said, examining Papa's handwriting. My parents' handwriting was as different as their personalities. Mama wrote in clear and elegant calligraphy; Papa's letters fell on the page like tall soldiers in a confident fury. *He hasn't written to us before. Mama did all the writing. Why is he writing?* As my heartbeat quickened, Yan took the envelope from my clammy hands, looked it over, and gave it back to me.

"Open," he said and sat down on the edge of the bed, our only sitting spot. I sat next to him, tackling the envelope to tear off the side. My heart now pulsed aloud. Pulling out a folded page, I stared at the familiar handwriting. My father's letter was brief, not like Mama's, with pages and pages of beautiful writing describing everything and everyone and asking a million questions: about Zhenya, about our health, and what we eat—it's a Jewish mother's thing. I listened to Zhenya's laughter coming from Alla's room for another moment before my eyes began to see the words on the page.

GALINA CHERNY

20 June 1979 - Kiev

Dearest kids, Galochka, Yan, and Zhenechka.

I write to share with you that num dali otkaz. We received a denial. It will be no surprise to you that no one gave us the reason. There was no explanation, no matter how many times we asked, or how much Mama cried. She took the news hard, crying a lot. Mama began packing as soon as you left, and now we are sitting on our luggage like two old fools with nowhere to go.

That's the story. Mi otkazniki. We are refuseniks. I thought refuseniks were people with high-level security clearances. Their permission might be denied to prevent the country's military or engineering secrets from ending up abroad. But us? Why? What do they need us for? I understand my questions will remain unanswered, but Mama and I will not rest until we achieve our goal. We will appeal as soon as possible, and do it as many times as it takes until we're allowed to leave. We're retired; what else do we have to do? Our documents are intact, and we have the means, thanks to the money you left us.

We no longer have our party identifications, so we are ready to get on the train at a moment's notice. Our mission in life is to reunite with you and watch our grandson grow up. Nothing will stop us. Remember, we lived through tough times before. Your parents don't give up.

You mustn't worry about us. Your job is to get to America and build your best life there. We love you. We'll be together soon.

Kiss Zhenechka for us. We miss him very much. Don't let him forget us. Please.

Obnimayem, your mother and father.

So like Papa, to sign "your mother and father," and not "Mama and Papa"—that was Mama's way of signing. "Your mother and father" rang in my head as I reread the letter, hoping for a different story. But no matter how many times I read it, the words "*mi otkazniki*" remained engraved on the page. The couple in OVIR—who received denial the day we were there—came to mind. I remembered their faces filled with fear, sorrow, and despair. *Did my parents look like that?* I pictured how they must've looked, getting the news, and I felt in my bones the distress they must've felt.

"They are going to miss Zhenya's fourth birthday," I said, leaning on Yan's shoulder, his arm wrapped around my waist. "They are going to miss everything," I thought or said, my gaze firmly planted on the wall in front of me.

That awful night in Kiev, I told the truth when I threatened my parents to leave regardless of what they thought of our decision, and I told the truth when I said to Yan I was ready to save my family, even if it meant never seeing my parents again. But now—with the prospect of never seeing them again a vivid reality—I was broken, empty. The same thoughts cycled through my brain on repeat: *I am a homeless, stateless orphan, whose parents are alive in the world I can no longer enter.*

I knew nothing about where we were going. We left our lives behind based on Yan's hunch and a few letters that told someone else's version of the truth. And yet, we fought feverishly to escape before the Iron Curtain fell down again.

You were right, Yan—we took the last train.

Here began an eight-year quest to get my parents out of the Soviet Union. They re-applied in September 1979 and received another "permission denied" in December. This happened to be around the time when the Soviets invaded Afghanistan, provoking new tensions and increased levels of hostility between the USSR

185

and the West, starting a new period of Cold War and halting the Jewish emigration. Mama, Papa, and thousands of Soviet Jews who wanted to emigrate were caught in the middle—their lives frozen for almost a decade.

I don't intend to analyze world events during the Cold War period between 1979 and 1985. I'll only mention a few widely accepted ones as a reference for what the world looked like. For instance, the American-led boycott of the 1980 Summer Olympics in Moscow was answered by the USSR's boycott of the Los Angeles Summer Olympics in 1984. President Reagan's proposal of the Strategic Defense Initiative (Star Wars) in 1983 came to be because of the increased threat of nuclear war. The tensions exacerbated even more when later that year, Reagan called the Soviet Union an "Evil Empire." The reaction to the president's statement by the US media and politicians was mixed, with many criticizing him, but I was elated. The words rang in my ears for days. Finally, someone understood.

I have to digress and share my observations of the Americans' lack of comprehension of the Soviet regime. Americans didn't understand the socialist system and the misery it created for its citizens, who, while miserable, had no choice but to sing praises to the Communist leaders and Mother Russia. They didn't understand the power of the government's brainwashing of its citizens from birth; the power of refusing them access to news, information, books, music, travel outside of the country, and free movement inside the USSR; the power of keeping people dependent on the government by providing "free" education, health care, long vacation time, maternity leave, and unlimited sick days, but denying individual opportunities. And when you add to the above vile and open anti-Semitism, the exodus of the Soviet Jews at the first opportunity might seem more logical. It wasn't only logical—it was the only way to survive.

To this day, many Americans think the rest of the world works like America. They compare America's flaws to a utopian ideal that doesn't exist, and not to the reality of the world. America's immigrants know better, at least in the beginning. When they first come, they remember why, but sadly and maybe even tragically, even they—with time—often forget themselves or forget to teach the next generation about the uniqueness and greatness of this country; they become too comfortable, and take America for granted. This pains me.

So, in our early days living in the US, when we met new people, their fascination with our country of origin was often based on bad American movies of the time about the Russians. At least that's what it seemed like based on some questions they asked:

"Is it true that Russians drink vodka every day?" (This was a popular one.)

"Did you have a refrigerator?" (Another good one.)

"How did you live in such cold weather?" (This was only the world's largest country spanning most of Europe and Asia—so when it was cold in one part of it, inevitably, it was warmer somewhere else.)

"I met this woman. She is also from Russia. Her name is so-and-so. Do you know her?" (My coworkers asked this question repeatedly.)

"So-and-so is also from Kiev. Do you know him?" (Over two million people lived in Kiev, the third largest city in the USSR, after Moscow and Leningrad.)

Americans didn't understand the USSR until Reagan. He understood the Soviets. I know he did. Among the more obvious evidence of that fact, like his economic policies and public introduction of the USSR as the evil empire, were the Russian jokes he collected. The Soviet citizens themselves created these jokes about their life, and he told them masterfully in various settings and interactions with the American public. Here is one of my favorites:

"A man goes to the official agency, puts down his money, and is told that he can take delivery of his automobile in exactly ten years."

"Morning or afternoon?" the purchaser asks.

"Ten years from now, what difference does it make?" replies the clerk.

"Well," says the car buyer, "the plumber's coming in the morning."

Reagan's profound understanding of the Soviet system and its threat to the world was shockingly accurate. His boldness in labeling the evil regime as such gave me hope. When we fled the USSR, we were certain the country, the system, and the Iron Curtain would remain for millennia. And yet, its fall and the death of the Union was happening in front of our very eyes.

Years of writing letters to my parents piled one on top of another. I was diligent in my promise to write four letters a week, and I continued to filter what I shared. And when I didn't, I regretted it. In one of his rare letters, Papa asked how we managed money, rent, gas, etc. I loved his questions and in my next letter explained in great detail our financials: how much we made (which was minimum wage) and what we spent our money on, sharing how we were diligently tracking our expenses to live within our means. My delight with Papa taking such interest faded when Mama wrote us back. She said something like this: "We understand you are poor and barely make ends meet, so we will never ask you for anything. The few things I asked for in the past were for Papa's nurse and his medications. In the future, I won't ask for that either."

I nearly dropped the paper when I read that. *What?* I thought, stunned. *Does she not know me? What is she talking about?*

First, her recount wasn't exactly accurate. She'd also asked for wedding attire for my third cousin and an archery set for her friend's daughter, jeans of all types for people I'd never heard of, and cosmetics for whomever—all while Yan was the only one working. We fulfilled each request. But that wasn't relevant. What became clear was the fact that we no longer lived in the same universe. Our life in America and the lives of my family in Russia were no longer deeply connected and mutually understood from daily interactions, shared meals, smiles, hugs, and face-to-face arguments.

Remember, this was the time before FaceTime, Zoom, WhatsApp, mobile phones, and all the technology available today to help people stay better connected. All we had to communicate with each other were our letters, rare phone calls, and photographs. We relied on photographs a lot. Even though they were costly to develop, we thought they gave our loved ones a view into our lives. Color photos of happy, smiling faces during our year-round trips to local parks and beaches; pictures of our living room furnished with a large (comparatively) TV; our first car, then a second one for me. This lifestyle was unfathomable to anyone in the Soviet Union. It was foreign, even disturbing—an alternate reality of sorts.

"Moya tvoya ne ponimaet." "Mine doesn't understand yours." This famous Russian phrase, uttered when people completely missed each other's point of view, cynically but accurately described a growing gap in my connection with my family. And yet, we loved each other deeply.

By 1985, my father's health had deteriorated, and I worried he wouldn't be able to travel even if allowed to leave. "Don't worry about me, *dochenka*, it will be a one-way trip. I will make it," he said every time I expressed my concern.

It was then that President Reagan pressured the Soviet leader, Mikhail Gorbachev, to allow Jewish *refuseniks* to emigrate. Reagan's "list of *refuseniks*," which he handed to Gorbachev before their meetings, with a request to let these people go, had become public knowledge. On a friend's advice, I wrote a letter to the White House, asking (begging) the president to add my parents to his list. But first, I did the usual: I stressed, fretted, and doubted myself. "Who am I to write a letter to the president?" I said to my friend.

"Here is the thing, Galina," my friend Alexandra told me. "In America, the president works for you. You pay his salary, and you have every right to send him a letter or criticize his policies if you disagree with them." This explanation sent tingles down my arms, and to this day, it is the best explanation I've ever heard of how America works. Thank you for that, Alexandra!

I wrote a letter telling President Reagan our story. Alexandra edited, and her mother, who was politically active, insisted I send it immediately. The response came within a month. A letter from the White House! I regret not saving the letter but the moment it arrived is as vivid in my mind as if it were yesterday. What a moment!

For a minute, I held the white envelope in the palm of one hand, sliding the index finger of another over the one-line address that said "The White House." With my hands shaking, I opened the envelope and pulled out the letter. "Dear Mrs. Cherny…," I read out loud, but the lump in my throat blocked my voice and I could no longer speak. In a surreal way, this was a personal letter. Of course I realized President Reagan didn't write it himself. That didn't matter. The president expressed deep sympathy for my parents' situation and his heartfelt regret for all the years we'd been apart. He promised to add them to "the list." The letter ended with a handwritten: "Sincerely, Ronald Reagan."

By 1986 we had brought our second son into the world and become homeowners, living in a lovely townhouse on the eastside of Los Angeles in a neighborhood called San Gabriel. Yan and I both worked in the Technology sphere—which turned out to be a common path for the Soviet Jews of our emigration era—making a living we had never dreamed of: twenty-four thousand dollars a year each. The boys were thriving. Zhenya Americanized his name and was now Eugene, and Alex (Alexander), seven years younger than his brother, was called Alik or Alusha by the family—more on that later. Besides writing to my parents, we now phoned them several times a month.

My father sounded frail but remained undeterred, and my mother still believed—or wanted us to think she did—that things would work out and they would receive permission to leave. In the meantime she asked if we ate well and if the children were healthy. Zhenya loved talking to his grandparents, although he had trouble expressing himself in Russian by then, and his Russian vocabulary—once extravagant—became limited. A four-year-old Alik had to be coaxed to get on the phone; he held the receiver in his hand, alternating between looking at it and listening. He often smiled and nodded instead of responding. After spending the first two years of his life hearing mostly Russian language, Alik understood it well enough, but he didn't know the people on the other side of the line. Being "forced" to talk to them was awkward and confusing for him, but none of that mattered to my parents. They were happy with any interaction with the boys. They ended each call with *"do skoroy vstrechi"* and never said "Goodbye."

On Thursday, May 1, 1986, the US press reported that the USSR denied "wild rumors" about the devastation caused by the Chernobyl nuclear plant explosion that had occurred five days earlier. May Day parades and celebrations went ahead across the country as the reactor continued to burn, spreading radioactive dust by wind not only through Ukraine but over Belarus, and Russia, even reaching as far west as France and Italy. Later reports declared that the amount of radioactive forms of chemical elements that entered the atmosphere had several times more radioactivity than that created by the atomic bombs dropped on Hiroshima and Nagasaki in 1945.

Here in America, we followed the news in horror. The information came in bits and pieces from European countries, detecting high levels of radiation coming from the direction of the Soviet Union. After first denying the accident, the Soviets finally made a brief announcement on Monday, April 28, without providing details and refusing to accept any help from the US and other countries. My parents lived sixty miles from Chernobyl with no information or protection. Thoughts of their safety tormented me daily. *They are probably breathing radiation through open windows, thinking they are breathing fresh spring air,* I fretted. *I must call them.*

Over the years, it had become easier to call Kiev without going through an operator, but this time my calls did not go through. I was on the phone from Sunday night to Monday morning, listening to a busy signal followed by dead silence—again, and again, and again. *Soviet snakes!*

On that Monday, Yan took the boys to school and I drove to work, fighting the fatigue and ignoring my throbbing headache. *This is all my fault! I should've insisted they come with us in the first place—now they are* refuseniks, *Papa is sick, and they may die of radiation!* Several of my colleagues gathered around my cubicle, waiting for me with questions:

"Did you hear what happened in the USSR?"

"Isn't your family still there?"

"How far are they from Chernobyl?"

My boss, Gary, brought a newspaper with a European weather map, and we hovered over it, trying to understand if the wind was blowing toward Kiev or away from it.

"I haven't been able to reach my parents," I told them, almost numb. "The Soviets won't let international calls through right now."

"Have you tried calling the Red Cross?" Gary asked.

"No. It never occurred to me."

I was on my way home in less than twenty minutes with instructions, a phone number, and a mandate from Gary: "Don't come back to the office until you talk to your parents. Good luck!"

Wednesday morning Kiev time (Tuesday night in Los Angeles), we finally connected through the Red Cross. It had now been five days since the explosion. Mama told me Papa suddenly seemed worse; he had difficulty breathing.

"Mama, listen to me, please. Something happened in Chernobyl. You know what I mean... Please close all windows and doors, and stay inside. Wash the sheets, blankets, and pillowcases, and all your and Papa's clothes. Tell Misha. And everyone." I spoke fast without taking a breath, anticipating the line to "die" any minute.

"*Dochenka*, what are you talking about? This is all American propaganda! We are fine and nothing serious has happened here."

"Mama, please believe me. This is really bad. You must protect yourselves. They are not telling you the truth. Please..." Click. A busy signal quickly turned into silence on the other line.

I looked at Yan: "I just realized something: she can't do any of the things I told her to do, except close the windows. They don't have a washer and dryer to wash their clothing and linens! She can't possibly do the cleanup by hand in any reasonable amount of time. And it's not like she can hire someone to help. I forgot they don't live like we do. Can't believe I forgot."

We followed the news religiously, trying to make sense of what we read and watched on TV. Horrified, with disbelief and disgust, we watched footage of the May Day Parade in Kiev.

My childhood friend, Vera, lived a few blocks from my parents with her husband, Sasha, three-year-old daughter, Alina, and ten-year-old son, Aloysha. Her recount of the days and months following the explosion placed me back in time, right in the midst of the events of 1986, with the family I knew so well most of my life.

Late afternoon, Saturday, April 26, the extended family gathered to celebrate Alina's third birthday. The windows and the balcony door were open since early morning, and the warm spring breeze infiltrated the apartment. You could see the Dnieper and the Naberezhno-Khreschatetskaya Street running along the riverbank from the living room balcony.

The after-dinner tea brought guests back to the dining table, where a sound of something heavy rolling down the street got everyone's attention. From the balcony they saw a long chain of heavy machinery moving in a northern direction, toward the Obolon district of Kiev. "They must be going for a May Day parade rehearsal," Vera guessed, even though they'd never seen a sight like this before. These were first responders on their way to Pripyat (nine miles from Chernobyl), where the reactor caught fire.

The next day was uneventful. Like thousands of Kiev families, they spent Sunday enjoying a warm and sunny spring day outdoors with the kids.

On Monday morning, Vera learned from a coworker (whose parents lived in Pripyat, a city of 14,000) that the atomic reactor had caught fire a few days prior and was still burning. She couldn't believe what she'd heard. "If this was the case, given the proximity of Pripyat/Chernobyl from Kiev, we should've seen the debris or smelled the burn, or something…," she remembered thinking. As they learned weeks later while in Kiev, and we did in America, Kiev was spared by the favorable direction of the wind, which blew to the northern states of Russia and to Northern Europe. But in those first days following the disaster, there was nothing in the Soviet papers. No announcements on the radio. Nothing at all. Unaware, the people of Pripyat, young and old, gathered outside, close to the burning reactor to watch the "magnificent spectacle."

On May 1, thousands walked in columns along Khreshchatyk Street with patriotic signs, flowers, and portraits of the Soviet Leaders, singing "Wide is my Motherland… I know no other country where a man can breathe in such freedom," inhaling the sweet fragrance of lilac with the invisible poison—both carried across the city by the warm breeze.

All the while, tour buses, packed with the children of the government officials, headed to the Borispol airport, as if in wartime.

On May 3, the announcement finally came. People were ordered to stay home with closed doors and windows. With no breeze coming from the outside, the heat was almost unbearable. Everything inside had to be washed. "We washed and washed and washed again. Seemed like that's all we did." Vera shivered as she remembered.

Kiev became a ghost town. Rumors of the wind beginning to blow in its direction persisted, but the Victory Day parade on May 9, along with the annual cycling Peace Race (*Velogonka Mira*), took place as planned. And to reduce the growing panic, the government officials' kids were brought back to Kiev.

Finally, school children began bringing home messages, urging parents to take elementary and middle school-aged students out of the city as soon as possible. High schoolers and their teachers remained in Kiev because of their upcoming finals.

Now the panic was rising, and everyone tried to leave Kiev any way possible. Vera was lucky to get train tickets to Luga, a town in the Leningrad Region, about fourteen hours from Kiev. She left with her children and her nine-year-old nephew, renting a room in a ramshackle country house. The beauty of Luga didn't register with Vera, as the forty days she spent there, she was hunting for food, cooking nonstop, and trying to keep the kids clean. The latter turned out to be an unachievable task: Lina contracted lice first, and one by one the boys did, too. Vera cried, cutting off her daughter's beautiful chestnut curls, but she had no choice.

Upon returning to Kiev, Vera lost her job—a rarity in the Soviet Union. The same man whom she once overheard saying "Give me a gun and I will kill all the Jews" told her she was no longer needed. That moment may have determined her family's resolve to leave the USSR.

The fallout from the Chernobyl catastrophe didn't end there. Over the next many months and years, people continued to measure radiation in their homes and in their bodies, if they were lucky to obtain a measuring device for that. If the device buzzed, everything had to be washed immediately. This happened often. Shopping for produce was so much more difficult than ever before—avoiding local products proved to be nearly impossible, but everything local was contaminated, a vicious cycle of sorts. Everyone knew someone who was diagnosed with cancer shortly after the catastrophe, and later there were others diagnosed who had worked on the cleanup effort at the station.

I heard none of this from my mother. *Was she protecting Rodina or me?*

It was May 3, six days after the explosion, when I got through to my parents again and spoke with my father for the last time. His breathing was laborious. He spoke slowly, stretching each word. He asked about the boys and Yan.

"How is the weather today, Papa?" I asked.

"What a silly question, *dochenka*…. Look out the window…you are across the street and have the same weather I do," he said.

"Yes, Papa, we do."

"Are you coming over soon?" he said.

"Yes, Papa, we are. *Ya tebya lublu.* I love you. Goodbye."

Papa died the next day, two months before receiving permission to leave the Soviet Union.

A telegram from my mother read:

USSR Ukraine Kiev 12:00 4 May 1986
Papa died this morning. Stop. Funeral tomorrow. Stop.

18

What Is a Strike?

"LOS ANGELES, August 27, 1979—Public transportation in Los Angeles was crippled today by a strike of 5,000 bus drivers of the Southern California Rapid Transit District, the area's principal carrier and one of the nation's largest bus systems," reported the *New York Times*, announcing what would be a thirty-six-day strike.

We had been in the US for five weeks, confused, startled, and unhinged, while trying to not be obvious about it. Another completely "foreign" element of our new life was sprung on us without a warning. Someone said: "This will be unpleasant, especially in this heat." *How bad could it be?*

During the three summer months of June, July, and August, temperatures in Kiev vary between twenty-three and twenty-six degrees Celsius (seventy-three and seventy-nine Fahrenheit), with fluffy white and gray clouds rolling across the blue sky, taking turns blocking the sunshine and bringing warm summer rain every couple of days.

While in Kiev, we heard of Los Angeles's hot summers, but nothing prepared us for the temperatures rising to one hundred degrees Fahrenheit (almost thirty-eight degrees Celsius) during that first summer. "It gets hot in Los Angeles, but the heat is dry, so it's really not bad," we had read in the letters from our former compatriots, not having a clue what they meant. *How does "dry heat" of one hundred degrees feel?* Once outside, there is no place to hide; the blazing heat pours out of the bright blue, cloudless sky, piercing through every inch of your body, burning through your bones. That's how it felt.

I remember thinking what a terrible time it was for the buses to go on strike—after all, we didn't have a car! *What is a strike, anyway?* I wondered. It was simply not what people did in the USSR. Soviet labor unions—created in 1918—were controlled by the state, which was synonymous with the Communist Party. The unions reported to the All-Union Central Council of Trade Unions, an instrument of the Soviet government. Unlike in the capitalistic society—where union disputes are resolved between an individual and the union—in a Communist regime like the Soviet Union, a union and the state are the same. If there were brave souls who stood up for their cause with a strike, their stories were not in the news, and they most likely didn't live to tell the tale.

My sandals melted into the asphalt and the skin on my arms and legs burned as Sofia and I walked from where we lived on Stanley Avenue in West Hollywood to Western Avenue, known for the cheapest furniture stores. We covered a distance of over three miles down deserted Santa Monica Boulevard. We tried to hide from the sun in every tiny inch of shade we could find, laughing hysterically, describing to each other all the horrible ways we might, and most likely would, die before reaching our destination.

From our apartment on Stanley, Yan, Zhenya, and I made several trips to the Jewish Family Center on Wilshire Boulevard—probably a three-mile stretch each way. One such trip was memorable—outside of the walk in the heat—as it was a meeting with a social worker about "how to look for a job," a process that shocked me by its simplicity and audacity all at once. Write your resume, look for job openings in a Sunday issue of the *Los Angeles Times*, and send your resume to all the companies whose ads somewhat fit your resume. In an interview, talk about your best qualities and biggest accomplishments. *Where do I write I am Jewish?* I wondered. *How do I talk about my accomplishments when my entire life I was taught to be modest and never brag about myself? And what is a resume?* The most surprising part of the conversation with the social worker was that she didn't seem concerned with our inadequate language skills. "Everybody starts this way," she said.

It was during the transportation strike and unbearable summer heat (which became a norm over the years) when Yan did something that determined the trajectory of our lives in the US. A musician by trade and a car mechanic by necessity, he suspected that neither one of these fields would help him create the future he always wanted for his family. He had a hunch that he must get into the computer industry. His rationale was not clear to either of us, and frankly, we didn't over-analyze his intuition; instead, we took it for granted. We dismissed all the obstacles a pursuit like this would undoubtedly present for a thirty-three-year-old foreigner with no English and no background in technology, so when Yan found a twelve-month computer programming school downtown, he made an appointment for an interview.

I must explain that scheduling an appointment by phone when you don't speak the language is an endeavor not to be underestimated. We used a dictionary (one of the few treasures we brought with us) to write what Yan would say; we both had our ear to the phone (no speaker phones yet) to increase our chances of understanding what was being said. Yan asked the person on the other line to speak slowly, repeat the address, the time of the appointment, and the name of the person he would meet with. *Phew!*

On the day of his appointment, under the boiling heat of the summer sun, Yan walked seven miles to Wilshire Boulevard in downtown Los Angeles, wearing dress shoes, slacks, and a button-down shirt, while he carried his suit jacket and a tie, which accounted for his entire business wardrobe.

"I have another appointment next week. I think they said something about the finance department and a 'student loan.' I don't quite understand what that means, but don't worry, we'll figure it out," he said when he came home.

5 October 1979
Our dearest Mama and Papa,
Thank you for all the presents and birthday cards you sent to Zhenechka for his birthday. It took over a month for the parcel to arrive, but everything came in good shape, and we agreed to let him open his gifts ahead of his birthday. Zhenechka loved the candy (of course!), but the colored pencils were his favorite—I know you are not surprised. He's been drawing with them nonstop. We've been reading the Agnia Barto poems to him every night. Thank you for the book—all his favorites are in it.

A little about us. We are doing well. Everyone is healthy. It's the beginning of October, but the weather is still very warm, and it's always sunny. I haven't seen a single cloud in the sky since we arrived in July.

We've been taking Zhenya to the park and the beach, (Yes, the beach in October! Can you believe it?) on weekends, and during the week he stays with Babushka Rita. She's been watching him during the day while Yan is at work and I am at school.

Wait! I wrote about all these changes already, but from your responses it seems you may be missing some letters, so let me back up a little, and if I repeat myself, please forgive me.

Yan was accepted to a computer school and will start classes in January. The cost of the school is two thousand dollars. We don't have this money, but the school gave us a "student loan," which we will begin repaying monthly six months after he finishes. This might confuse you as it did us. You have to pay for education beyond high school, but we were lucky to get a loan, so Yan can do this. He will study at night and work during the day.

More on that in a minute—first let me tell you about our new car. We bought a car! It's called Chevrolet Impala, and it's ten years old. We paid six hundred dollars for it, which we borrowed from Sofia, but Yan works now, so we'll repay her quickly. We've never seen a car like this! Papa, you would love it. It's big and comfortable, and it rides like a Chaika. It has an air conditioner that cools the air inside the car when it's hot, and a heater that does the opposite (don't think we would ever need to use a heater here, though).

We discovered that buying a car is only the beginning; we also need to purchase car insurance to protect us in case of an accident. An insurance company would pay to repair the damage made to the cars involved in an accident (not that we will ever get into one—don't worry). Otherwise, it's very, very expensive. People here buy different insurances: car insurance, health insurance, life insurance, and many other kinds. There seems to be an "insurance" for everything. So, the car insurance will cost us two hundred dollars every six months, and it will only cover the car we might hit (not that we ever will); we can't afford to buy the kind that covers our car as well (not now, anyway). Another part of the car ownership cost is gasoline. We spend about twenty dollars to fill up the car with gas every week and probably double that when Yan starts college in January. As far as car repairs go, Yan thinks he can do all the basic ones himself.

I am including a picture of the car with Zhenya sitting on the top and hope you get to see it in person soon. By the way, Yan passed the driver's test, which included a written and driving part. The written test was "a multiple-choice test," which means they include three or four answers for each question, but only one of them is correct. So, instead of writing the correct answer, like we are used to doing, you select the correct one from the list. This is a popular form of testing in America, and most schools use it. Very unusual for us...

We bought a thick map-book called Thomas Guide, which has very detailed maps of each area of the city. Every street is included. It's like an encyclopedia for drivers. Yan's been studying it now, and I am afraid to get near it.

Now, about Yan's job. He is working at a machine tool plant as a fitter. They will pay him $3.19 an hour and his boss told him he can work an extra hour or two—beyond the regular eight hours—for which they would pay him "time-and-a-half." Last week, he worked ten extra hours, and for each extra hour, he earned $4.79. With that, he earned $176 last week. Of course, everyone pays income tax, and that money is deducted from your check. A check looks like a piece of paper. It's "bank money"—that's how employers pay you, not with cash like we are used to. We opened a bank account, and that's where we'll be able to exchange the checks for currency (cash). There is more to the banking system, which I will explain over time as we learn. I am definitely getting carried away with all this detail, but Papa always asks about every aspect of our lives, so I thought I'd share.

Papa, you asked why I need to take an English class since I had "5" at school. Well, the English I learned at school gave me some basic phrases I memorized, but not much more than that. Remember, my teacher had never talked to an English-speaking person herself (none of the foreign-language teachers did). She taught from a textbook, which isn't enough to communicate with people and understand what they are saying. That's the biggest hurdle: understanding when people have a conversation, understanding the radio, or TV. During my three-hour-a-day class, I speak English with other students (who are from different countries) and the teacher, so hopefully I will pick things up. Actually, I should've said, "I speak English with other students, excluding my comrades." There are five other "Russians" in the group, but I stay away from them because instead of practicing English, they sit in the back of the class and talk about what tchotchkes they smuggled across the border and what they sold in Italy. Listening to them once was enough for me. It takes me well over an hour of travel on two buses to get to class every day, and I leave Zhenya with Yan's mom five days a week, so I want to make the best of my effort. And at the end of the three-month course, the school will help me look for a job. It's a free program offered to new immigrants. Don't worry, I'll learn.

How is everyone? What's going on with Misha? We haven't heard anything from him. How is Aunt Katya? Mama, you said she was in the hospital. Does she need anything from here? Maybe something for the nurses, so they take good care of her? Say hello to the rest of the family. We love you and miss you very much, especially Zhenechka. He talks about you all the time.

I will write soon. Sending you hugs and kisses.

Vsem Privet. Yours, Galya, Yan, i Zhenechka.

Misha and I didn't write to one another often. When I wrote, he usually responded with a photograph or a greeting card, signed:

"*Lublyu*. Love you. *Skuchayu*. Miss you. Misha."

These few words gently touched my heart every time—they were so unlike the "rough around the edges" Misha I knew.

> *15 October 1979*
>
> *Misha, privet!*
>
> *What's going on in your life these days? We haven't heard from you. Please write. Zhenya asks about you all the time. He still remembers how much fun he had playing with you on the train. And I am still recovering from finding bruises on his arms from "playing" with you. What did you do to my child, you crazy uncle?*
>
> *Rumor has it, you disappeared for three days after you took us to the train station. I won't tell you who told me so don't ask—it wasn't Mama so don't give her a hard time—but I will tell you that you gave our parents the fright of their lives. Not that before this you never did anything insane but this was a bit extreme, given the timing. They thought you threw yourself under the train or got killed by Kiev hooligans roaming the streets. I am happy you came home in one piece but don't do this again because I can't calm them down from here.*
>
> *They don't say that to me but they must be so vulnerable after the denial and so torn. If they are allowed to leave, they would leave you behind (and Mama would rather die!), and if they stay—they would live without us. What an impossible choice I left them with! I am sorry.*
>
> *All right, enough whining! Don't disappear. Don't be a jerk—take care of Mama and Papa.*
>
> *We all love you. Yan says hi. Zhenya drew you a picture of your white truck.*
>
> *Be good. G.*

19

Rabbi and the Christmas Tree

December 27, 1956—Stalingrad

"Galya, Galya, wake up…wake up…"

What's happening? Am I hearing Misha's voice or dreaming it?

My almost four-year-old brain was fast asleep but Misha persisted: "Wake up…I have a surprise for you…wake up, Galya." Misha firmly shook my shoulder until I responded. I sat up in bed, eyes closed, head leaning toward my right shoulder.

"What surprise?" I asked, trying to open my eyes.

"Do you want to see *Ded Moroz* decorate our *Novogodnyaya Elka*?"

What? What a silly question! Who wouldn't? Every child knows Grandpa Frost comes to their house a few nights before the New Year to decorate their New Year fir tree and comes back on New Year's Eve to leave presents for the children, but no one has ever seen him do that. Papa explained he comes in the middle of the night so kids will have a surprise in the morning. I can't believe I'm going to be the first one to see a real Ded Moroz!

Still half asleep, I climbed out of bed and followed Misha to the door into the dining room, which also served as my parents' bedroom. He gave me a signal to be quiet by pressing his index finger to his lips. I was quiet and a little scared. It was pitch dark in the room—no light came through the window curtains like it would in the morning. There were voices outside the closed door. *Who is* Ded Moroz *talking to?* I wondered. Grabbing Misha's hand, I whispered, "I am scared."

"Don't be scared. Here is your surprise!" He pushed the door wide open, yelling, "Surprise!" Blinded by the bright light, I closed my eyes for a few seconds, and when I opened them again, I saw Mama and Papa standing next to half-decorated *Elka*.

"Where is *Ded Moroz*?" I asked.

"Well…," Papa began, "he…he had to leave before he finished decorating your *Elka* because he still has many children to visit before the New Year, so Mama and I are helping him out," Papa concluded. He gave Misha a stern look, the look Papa gave when we were in trouble, but he would give us a pass, just this once.

Papa's explanation made sense, and I believed our parents were *Ded Moroz's* helpers and were now responsible for tree decorating and all the other aspects of the beloved holiday.

The New Year was undoubtedly the biggest holiday of the year for the Soviet people. Besides putting up *Elkas*, holiday preparations included hunting for special-occasion produce items like canned *shproti*, the same sprats we brought with us when we left for Chop; gastronomical meat delicacies like salami and Canadian bacon; canned green peas and mayonnaise for an Olivier salad; any fresh vegetables available, and all the basics: eggs, potatoes, herring, and any type of meat or chicken. Year after year, New Year celebration preparations swept the land. People talked about what produce they'd hunted down, where they were celebrating, and with whom. Children attended holiday events, singing and dancing around beautifully decorated trees. Of course, there were special appearances by *Ded Moroz* and his granddaughter, *Snegurochka* (Snow girl), who brought holiday treats for the children: a bag of goodies filled with candy, cookies, whole walnuts, and if you were lucky, a *mandarin* (a small citrus fruit resembling an orange but much sweeter and easier to peel).

Kids talked about their *Elkas*, bragging to friends about having their tree up earlier than others or having fancier decorations. It wasn't difficult to find a New Year's tree. There were *Elka* bazaars in every major area of the city, but finding a tree that was symmetrical and more or less full was a cause for major bragging. Over the years, it seemed harder and harder to buy *Elka* that was nicely shaped and had enough sturdy branches to hold decorations. More often than not, we bought two lopsided, bare trees and tied them together to make one that looked somewhat decent. If we weren't successful in this effort, Mama would say, "It looks more natural this way."

As Misha and I got older, decorating Elka became a family affair. Misha helped Papa to secure the tree on a wooden stand and place it just right for the "best" side to be in the front. Misha usually spent the rest of the night complaining that we didn't have tree lights "like everyone else." He always got the same response from Mama: "Be grateful for what you have." Besides a few store-bought decorations, Papa made some out of eggshells. First, he emptied the egg. He used a needle to poke two small holes, one on each end of the egg, carefully blowing out the raw egg into a bowl.

Every year, I watched him do his magic with my mouth open as if for the first time. An empty eggshell became his canvas. He usually turned the eggshell into a head and made the rest of the "person" out of colored paper, newspaper, or whatever else we had around. My favorite eggshell decoration of all time was the clown with a brightly painted face that looked a lot like mine with a red and white striped cone-shaped hat. My job in the *Elka* decorating process was to throw tiny pieces of cotton all over the tree to make it look like snow had fallen on its branches. Mama usually ended up with final cleanup, and afterward, she made scrambled eggs and fried potatoes for dinner.

Why did we enjoy the New Year so much? I didn't question it, but in retrospect, this was the only holiday with no government-imposed activities. No army parades, no patriotic slogans. Just people enjoying each other and their families. It never occurred to me that *Elka, Ded Moroz*, and the surrounding celebration had a history to which I didn't belong, dating back to the times before the October Revolution of 1917 and the birth of the Soviet Union, the world's first Communist state with Atheism as its "religious" philosophy.

Prior to the establishment of the USSR in 1917, Russian Christians celebrated Christmas, *Rozhdestvo*, on January 7 per the "Julian" calendar still used today by the Russian Orthodox Church. Among the key attributes of *Rozhdestvo* were *Rozhdestvenskaya Elka*, essentially a Christmas tree, and *Ded Moroz*, the Russian equivalent of Santa Claus. So, just like in America and the rest of the Christian world, in the years prior to the revolution, Russians had celebrated Christmas with a Christmas tree and Santa Claus. But once the Soviets banned all religious attributes of life, they also banned Christmas, Christmas trees, and *Ded Moroz*. Until, in 1936, Stalin "gave" the Soviet children a New Year tree, which happened to look exactly like a Christmas tree of the past. And so it was then *Ded Moroz* and *Snegurochka* turned the New Year celebration into the biggest holiday of the year, while further separating Christians from their religion. The timing of this new holiday was peculiar; Stalin must have tried to show people he cared about them and their children while committing his atrocities during that period.

The love for New Year celebrations and the New Year tree grew from generation to generation. Soviet children, Jews and Gentiles alike, sang about their beautiful *Elka,* brought from the woods into the joyous New Year celebration.

For the first couple of years in America, we picked up our Elka from the sidewalk a few days before the New Year. We couldn't afford to buy one, but it thrilled us to give Zhenya the familiarity of a holiday he knew and loved, and the one Yan and I had celebrated since childhood. We ignored rumblings from other immigrants that "Jews aren't allowed to put up *Elkas,*" because no one explained why, and it made no sense to our Soviet brain.

While taking swimming lessons at the Jewish Community Center on Olympic Boulevard, Zhenya became aware that he "looked different" from other boys, who were all circumcised. He probably wouldn't have noticed, but the boys asked him questions that confused him. I worried about how this might affect him in the future. He had just turned five, but I imagined him wanting to marry a Jewish girl for whom this might be an issue. A Jewish mother has to think ahead! Yan didn't share my concern and was hesitant to even discuss the topic.

The more I kept thinking about it, the more obsessed I grew. I lay awake at night contemplating different scenarios. *What if someday Zhenya has a son and needs to explain to him why they look different? What if we have another son and follow the tradition with him, or would we not do that, either? Would Zhenya resent us when he is older for not making the "right" decision now?* I tossed and turned. *How can I put a healthy little boy under a knife? Would he even understand? Would he be traumatized for the rest of his life?* I had doubts, questions, and more doubts until one night, it became clear. *The Nazis killed my grandfather because he was a Jew; they found out he was a Jew from the physical evidence. I want his great-grandson to know he is a Jew and to know he is safe in America.*

Reluctantly, Yan agreed to discuss this with Zhenya. Many Russian immigrant boys and men of all ages were getting circumcised, but we decided we would only do this if Zhenechka understood and agreed. And he did. Zhenya said he wanted to be like all the other Jewish boys, and we scheduled the procedure for the 28th of December at Cedars Sinai Medical Center.

Yan and I were nervous beyond words but faked calmness in front of Zhenya, who, too, seemed undeterred. He had a chat with the doctor, who explained the procedure to him and reassured it would only take a minute before Zhenya would be back in his room. A rabbi came by and gave Zhenya a pat on the shoulder, said something in Hebrew, shook Yan's hand, and told us not to worry. My nervousness being in the presence of the rabbi came right back from the visit to the synagogue with Mama all those years ago, even though it was now my son who was five and not me.

Before too long, the nurse wheeled Zhenya back into the room on the same bed she took him into surgery. Watching him, I remembered my barbaric childbirth experience in the Soviet hospital and the horror of having my tonsils taken out at fourteen. No rolling beds. No blankets and clean sheets. But our son was fine. We were ready to take our Jewish boy home.

Not a word of this to my parents, I told myself. *They will kill me.*

On the way home from the hospital, we spotted an *Elka* on the sidewalk next to our apartment. A beautiful, fresh, perfectly symmetrical fir tree just laid there helplessly. Still baffled that people threw away their fir trees before New Year, we decided that *Elka* was coming home with us. Perfect timing! The *Elka* would cheer Zhenya up and bring a sense of holiday to the house. We put the tree up in the corner of the living room, and I decorated it with pieces of cotton for snow. It looked lovely and smelled of fragrant spice, sweet pine, and childhood. To make Zhenya more comfortable, we settled him in the living room on the foldout couch Yan and I usually slept on, anticipating he would be cozy there.

I was in the kitchen when the doorbell rang: "Hello, Rabbi," Yan said.

"I stopped by to check on your son. How is he doing?" the rabbi said.

"He is doing well. Thank you. Please come in." Yan opened the door wider to let him inside. The rabbi made one step forward and paused at the door. His face flushed. His smile vanished and his body froze. Not understanding what caused such a reaction and still remembering the discomfort from the mere presence of a rabbi, I stood staring at him for a few seconds before offering him a chair next to the couch facing our lovely *Elka*. He thanked me and reluctantly walked toward the chair, turning it around to have his back to the tree.

The rabbi asked Zhenya if he was in much pain and said something like this: "Jewish boys get circumcised on the eighth day of their lives, and you fulfilled this very important ritual at five years of age. You are very brave. And you should remember this ritual is the everlasting sign of the Jewish people's connection to G-d." He got up and walked to the door, moving sideways, turning his head away from Elka. "Mazel Tov," he said, shaking Yan's hand once again. We thanked him for stopping by and wished him a Happy New Year.

"There was something about *Elka* the rabbi didn't like. What do you think it was?" I was perplexed.

"I have no idea." Yan was just as puzzled.

Unbeknownst to us, the rabbi's reaction was quite natural. Imagine if a priest walked into a Christian home and found a lit Chanukah menorah instead of a Christmas tree. He would most likely think "these people are a little strange," and try to get away as quickly as possible. We, the Soviet Jews with our *Elka*, seemed a little strange to the rabbi.

20

Not "That" Magazine!

January 1980—Los Angeles

Nina and I met in English class, finding ourselves much more interested in learning the language than our comrades' versions of their "Roman Holiday." We didn't live far from one another and took the same two buses to Glendale. The trip to school and back gave us a perfect opportunity to get to know each other.

Our families had arrived in Los Angeles around the same time. Nina came with her husband, Yakov, their fourteen-year-old daughter, and Yakov's mother. At forty-two, Nina was someone I looked up to like an older sister. Let me correct that; she was my sister, my mother, and a trusted friend all rolled into one.

Their apartment in West Hollywood was a warm and inviting refuge for the three of us. Zhenya loved checking the kitchen as soon as we walked through the doorway, where familiar dishes seemed to always be waiting for him. We drank tea with delicious pastries baked by Nina. They had four cups, two of them chipped at the top, so we took turns under Nina's watchful eye: "*Ostorozhno*, please be careful."

A few times, Yakov picked us up from school in his "new" car. He'd just gotten a driver's license but had no experience driving, didn't understand driving signs, and didn't realize the driveway was there for the cars to get onto the road. He once drove over the curb without slowing down, while Nina and I slid across the back seat from left to right and left again, no matter how much we tried to hold on to each other. In retrospect, the madness of driving with Yakov was well worth the fright—without exception, it was accompanied by his dry, witty sense of humor pouring through the stories he told us on the way.

"I've never worked in a store before," Nina said as we walked down Sunset Boulevard toward a tall building on the north side of the street. She had asked me to accompany her to her first job interview at *Cashbox* magazine in the West Hollywood area.

"What do you think the job might be?" she asked and continued without waiting for my answer. "I've never worked in a *magazeen*.... Selling is just not me.... But, of course, I'll take the job, whatever it might be. Hope they'll hire me."

We walked slowly, looking around, rattled because we were walking on the beautiful and famous boulevard, lined with tall glass buildings that reflected the warm January sun—and because we were in America, and we were looking for a job. Who would've thought?! We both graduated from our English course at the end of last year, and between the two of us, the administration offered Nina a job interview first. Frankly, I was secretly relieved it wasn't me—my hesitancy to speak English hadn't disappeared. The only difference was that by now, I would ignore the dread and pursue getting a job anyway. In the meantime, I welcomed the delay.

Nina checked a written note with the address provided by the school. "Yes. That's the building," she said, opening a large glass door. We were both quiet going up the elevator and easily found the correct entrance, which led into a small waiting room with two plush armchairs and a coffee table between them. The sign on the door read "Cashbox." The walls were decorated with framed pictures of music-related memorabilia.

"I wonder what they sell here," said Nina. I was just as puzzled—not seeing any sign of a *magazeen*. A woman appeared in the doorway, taken aback by the sight of two people sitting in the waiting room. "Which one of you is Nina Tregub?" she asked. Nina got up to follow her and asked me to wait. I sat in a comfortable armchair and looked around. I saw a large fresh-flower arrangement on a stand in the corner of the room, as well as stacks of journals neatly laid out on top of the coffee table. I glanced toward the closed door in front of me. *What questions are they asking? Hope she gets the job. She might enjoy working here. The place looks nice, and the woman who greeted us seemed friendly.*

Nina returned thirty minutes later, smiling. "Wait here," she said and disappeared inside again. A few minutes later, she came back, followed by a man. He introduced himself and shook my hand.

"George Albert. Your friend is very smart, and I hired her," he said, "but unfortunately, I don't have another position for you. Nina told me you are very talented, and I wanted to meet you and wish you luck."

Over the years, Nina and I told this story many times, remembering different nuances and making each other—and those listening—laugh time and time again, recounting how we mistook a "magazine" for a "store," *magazeen* in Russian. After working there for a couple of days, Nina realized she didn't work at a store. Instead, she worked for one of America's most prominent music-industry trade publications, established in 1942. Nina found a home at *Cashbox*. She worked there until the magazine dissolved in 1996 and remained friends with her boss, President and Publisher George Albert, and his entire family.

17 February 1980

Our dearest Mama and Papa,

Thank you for the birthday card and a parcel with choc-olate—both arrived on Friday. As much as I love chocolate, I need to ask you to please stop sending it to us, because we need to stop eating it. I can't keep Zhenya away from your packages—he knows what's in them. Just send us greeting cards. That's all we need.

I am celebrating my birthday in summer-like weather for the first time in my life. Imagine, in the middle of February, the sun is glowing in a clear blue sky without a cloud in sight, the temperature a balmy sixteen degrees as I write. It's beach weather all the time here, except for a few rainy days here and there, and yet the stores carry winter clothes. Coats, hats, scarves, gloves, jackets, sweaters, and boots. Who wears boots in this kind of weather?! I am definitely not used to having my birthday in the summer.

Papa, your birthday is just four days away. Hope you receive our present on time. We mailed the parcel five weeks ago. A pair of sweatpants and a sweatshirt with a zipper. I remember how you always complain about being cold; these should keep you warm and make you look like an Olympic champion! Mama, we bought you a red wool cardigan— please wear it yourself and don't give it as a gift to someone else. I also threw in four small sets of cosmetics—those you can give as presents to your doctors and nurses but not the cardigan. Papa, make sure she doesn't give it away.

And now my big news: I started a job last Monday at a company called "Equitable Title and Escrow." I wanted to work there for a week before sharing with you, just in case something went wrong, but when at the end of the week they told me to come back on Monday, I figured it was time to tell you.

To be honest, I don't understand what they do. It has something to do with the logistics of home purchasing—that's all I surmised during the interview. What it is I'll be doing there is just as much of a mystery. Don't laugh…it's all very different here. You can buy or rent an apartment or a house anywhere without the government's permission. We didn't have to worry about any of this in the USSR. You are born and you die in the same apartment, right?

Back to my job. The company has several areas, assuming each manages a part of the logistics process. I am in the Accounting Department, which includes my boss, whose name is Beth, and two other women. All three of them seem friendly. My title is "clerk." After offering me the job, the man who interviewed me (must be the head of the organization) said something that astonished me. He said, "I am certain this is not the job you should be doing. You are much smarter than this job, and I can tell you now, you will go far. Just don't be afraid." Surprised to understand him, I didn't know what to say, and even if I did, I wouldn't be able to express myself, so I thanked him and left. Now I need to figure out how to do the job "I shouldn't be doing." If he only knew!

On Thursday, the phone rang in the office while no one was around to answer it but me. When I picked it up, a thousand drops of sweat formed at the top of my head and one by one rolled down my neck onto my back, leaving me shivering with sweat and dread. To my complete and utter shock, I understood the person on the other side and scribbled a message for Beth, but I was shaken for a while afterward. In retrospect, I am glad

I had no choice but to answer the phone—next time I won't be as scared.

Last Friday, a co-worker took me to the bank to show me how to "deposit checks," meaning add checks to the company's bank account. Once I learn, this will be part of my task every week. I understand the process is like the one we use with Yan's checks, but until now, he was the one stopping at the bank every week to deposit his check from work so we can pay with our personal checks for rent and utilities. So confusing! I will be paid seven hundred and fifty dollars each month. I am rich! We have enough for everything we need. Glad we refused the state support (welfare) because as it is, Yan and I are making the same amount of money the government would've given us—maybe even a little more. Yan insisted we didn't take the handout. That's not why we came here.

Papa, you want me to be careful driving, but I am not driving yet. Yan drives to work and from there to school four nights a week. And I am being very careful taking two buses to work, so don't worry about me. Yan thinks I should learn, but for now, I am fine.

Uncle Vova and Aunt Lillia called to wish me a Happy Birthday. I was so happy to talk to both of them and Sonia. They said they sent you a letter a couple of days ago. They are doing well. Uncle Vova got a job as a civil engineer...by chance, really. The manager who interviewed him called another Russian who worked there to help translate because Vova's English was so bad. The manager wanted to establish if Vova was, in fact, a talented engineer. By some crazy coincidence, the man who came in to translate turned out to be Vova's former co-worker. Mama, your favorite cousin must've had some reputation in Kiev because they hired him on the spot based on the man's recommendation. And they pay him ten dollars an hour. Can you imagine?

That's all our news. Hope you are both healthy. Papa, we haven't received a letter from you in a while. Zhenya wants more drawings! Write about everything and everyone. Give our love to the family.

Obnimayem. Tseluyem.

Vashi, Galya, Yan, Zhenechka.

21

Becoming Los Angelenos

December 1981—Los Angeles

"Papa, and 'what Russian doesn't love a fast ride!'" Yan wrote in the letter to my father, citing a famous quote from Nikolai Gogol's *Mertvye Dushi, Dead Souls.* Well, Papa didn't find this tongue-in-cheek response to his guidance on safe driving humorous—his next letter was clear about that. He provided guidance from over six thousand miles away, having never driven a car himself. Yan wrote back, reminding him that a "fast ride" in the quote referred to nineteenth-century transportation, which didn't exceed the speed of twenty kilometers an hour; he reassured his father-in-law that he followed the rules of the road at all times. He did, indeed; however, the quote absolutely applied to Yan then, and it still does.

Yan found his first American indulgence in driving a car. "I especially loved driving from my day job in Santa Monica to the computer school in downtown Los Angeles when it rained." He remembers. He felt safe in his castle-of-a-car, driving thirty miles in traffic caused by the usual end-of-day commute, amplified by the known inability of Los Angelenos to drive in the rain. He listened to raindrops bouncing off the roof of the car and watched the windshield wipers rhythmically sliding across the glass, clearing his view of the road. He was finally far away from the years of schlepping all over Kiev—in the rain, snow, or both—for work, school, and life.

Over the years, Yan taught countless people to drive a car, including our boys, but I wasn't one of them. He tried. We made several attempts in an empty parking lot and those weren't too bad—I followed instructions and was relatively comfortable not sharing the road with another human. But when he took me onto the busy streets of West Hollywood's residential area with cars parked on both sides of a somewhat narrow road, I panicked, begging him to stop the lesson.

What do you think my husband—who wrote to his father-in-law "what Russian doesn't love a fast ride!"—did? He took me to the busiest corner in all of West Hollywood (Santa Monica Boulevard and La Brea Avenue) to teach me how to make a left turn. I made it as far as "the pocket" and put on a left signal, hands gripping the steering wheel, body frozen from the neck down, right foot pressing on the brake with all the strength in my body. I believe the streetlight on this corner now has a left turn arrow, which wasn't there back then. So, I inched forward on the green light, as my "driving instructor" directed, but when the light turned yellow and he said "go," I didn't move; instead I put the brake on (thank goodness for that!) and got out of the car, abandoning it and my husband. That's what I did.

By then, the light had turned red, and the car was blocking the street. Even though Yan reacted quickly by jumping out of the passenger seat and sliding into the driver's side to complete my unfinished left turn, we created a major disruption on the busiest corner in all of West Hollywood on a Saturday afternoon. It would take me over a year to get over my driving lessons with Yan and learn how to drive. And it would take me months after that to begin driving. If it hadn't been for an urgent need to take Zhenya to the doctor one day when I was alone with the boys, I might not have ever driven a car. But one must not underestimate the mama bear—there is no fear large enough to stop a mother from protecting her child.

But that was later. At the beginning of 1981, Yan graduated from a computer programming school called Advanced Computer Studies and had recently begun working at Magnavox, an electronics company in Torrance, his second computer programming job with a whopping salary of twenty-four thousand dollars a year—his first job had lasted only three months.

An unusually rainy winter and a busy Christmas season caused Yan to worry about me getting home from work by bus. I was six months pregnant—grateful that he tried to give me a ride twice a week. This was one of those days. The two of us picked up Zhenya from Yan's mother's, and drove to our apartment around the block. Once close to the front door, we noticed it was ajar. Yan signaled for Zhenya and me to wait and slowly pushed the door open. Two men wearing dark hoodies and holding our recently purchased stereo equipment were inside. They saw us and ran out through the wide-open patio door on the opposite wall, disappearing in the back entrance to the garage.

Yan chased after them, but they jumped into a car waiting for them with the engine running, and sped off. The inside of the apartment looked as if a tornado had come through it. A few decorations we had on the Elka were on the floor, smashed into tiny pieces, likely from someone stepping on them. The bookshelves were empty, and the books scattered on the floor. *What were they looking for?* The three of us walked around the apartment, pointing out things that were missing or thrown around.

"TV. The TV is gone," said Yan. I gasped, holding my stomach with both hands as I looked at the empty TV stand by the wall. The linen closet was turned upside down—sheets and pillowcases hung out, preventing the door from closing. Zhenya's toys and books were tossed on the floor in his room. I found a box of See's Candies chocolate we had bought for the holidays on the kitchen floor, torn and empty.

"*Kopilka!* Mama, my piggybank! It's empty!" Zhenya stood in the middle of his bedroom, holding an empty glass jar that was his piggy bank. His face flushed, eyebrows drawn together in a frown. "*Kopilka!*" He shook the empty jar and threw it on the carpeted floor. Then he ran to his toy chest and grabbed a toy watergun. "I'll show you! *Ya tebe pokazhu!*" he yelled, shaking the toy in his hand.

"Come here, Zhenechka. Come here." I sat down in a chair by the door, rocking him in my arms while Yan called the police. "Everything we need is right here, my love. You, Papa, and me. And your little baby brother or sister. The rest we can replace..."

All in all, it was quite a year. I got pregnant, six months after a miscarriage. I lost that pregnancy at fourteen weeks with heavy bleeding and an emergency medical procedure. When I came to work the next morning my boss and several coworkers asked if I was all right. I said "yes." For two reasons, I suppose. First, this was not the topic I was comfortable discussing, and second, I couldn't explain what had happened even if I wanted...I didn't know the word "miscarriage."

"You have a healthy pregnancy," the doctor said during my last office visit. But what if she was wrong? She hadn't foreseen any issues last time. For months I'd been walking around thinking I must've done something to cause the miscarriage. This time I resolved to be more careful and not stress about anything. So, for the first three months at least, I walked slowly so as to not "spook" the pregnancy; I had my hand on my stomach at all times. At night I would lie in bed listening to every movement in my body, analyzing what it might mean for the baby growing inside me. And, of course, I followed the old Russian superstition of keeping my pregnancy "a secret" until the second trimester.

I tried not to stress when Yan lost his first programming job, which left us without medical insurance and money to pay rent. We were beyond grateful to our landlords, Wolf and Sonia, two Polish immigrants themselves, who offered to wait for the rent payment until Yan began working again. *We were fine then and we will be fine now*, I told myself that night of the burglary. *We can replace everything they took.*

22

Our First American

April 21, 1982—Los Angeles

A nurse entered the hospital room once again, asking if we needed anything or had questions. I had a wild question, not related to anything going on at that moment.

"Thank you, nurse. Can I ask you something?"

"Of course." She walked closer to the bed.

"Do you think it might be possible to make an international call from this phone?" Yan chuckled, but he said nothing.

"I am not sure," the nurse answered with a faint frown. "No one has made such a request before. Try. Dial nine for an outside line and zero for an operator. Hope it works." She smiled and walked out of the room.

"Operator, I need to dial a number in Kiev, USSR."

"USSR?"

"Yes."

"How do you spell Kiev?" she asked. I answered this question every time

I called my parents.

"It's eleven o'clock on Thursday morning, April 22nd, in Kiev. Do you want to place the call?"

"Yes. Thank you." I looked at Yan. "They should be home."

"Please dial area code 044 and the number in Kiev...," I said back into the phone. "Alo-alo! Mama! *Eto ya*. It's me! Can you hear me?" I got through on the first try—that was a first. Even less believable was the fact that I was calling from a hospital bed.

"*Galochka-dochenka!* Yes. Yes, I can hear you. How are you feeling?"

"I am fine. The baby came a couple of hours ago! It's a boy!"

"What?"

"*Ya rodila.* I had the baby. He was born at six in the evening; it's still the 21st here. Can you hear me? It's a boy! *Malchik!* It's a boy... like I knew it would be!" I was used to speaking quickly and loudly when talking to them out of fear—not unfounded—that the call might be interrupted.

"What do you mean, you had the baby a couple of hours ago? Where are you calling from?"

"The hospital. Yes, Mama—a baby boy!"

"*Osya, Osya*—come here! It's *Galochka*. She just had the baby... *malchick... Dochenka*, how is it possible to call from a hospital? Are you on a payphone? What is that sound? How many people are in the room with you?"

"Ma, I am not on a payphone. I am in bed, in my room. I have the room all to myself. And the baby is right here. Crying. I probably scared him with all the yelling. Can you hear him? Yan is here too."

"What? The baby is in the room with you and Yan? No one else? Why is the baby crying?"

"Really? Can't believe you are asking that! 'Babies cry!' You told me that yourself when Zhenya was born, remember?"

"I remember... I remember everything..."

"I know, Ma... I know. Don't cry. Everything is fine. The nurse is coming in all the time to check on us, so don't worry...we are all fine." I was so fine that I wanted to jump out of bed and twirl around the room in some crazy joyous dance. I did it! My beautiful eight-pound baby boy was right here, next to me. I was fine.

"I hope you are telling the truth. I know how you are…. How is the baby?"

"He is healthy. Big. Weighs four kilos. Fifty-five-and-a-half centimeters long. He is loud. He is perfect, Ma…. We named him after your brother, Abrasha."

"You did?"

"Mama, are you there?"

"Yes, *dochenka*…yes…thank you."

"His Jewish name will be Abraham and his American name, Alexander—Alex for short."

"*Dochenka…dochenka….* We love him already. Osya, they named the baby after Abrashenka…. Alexander is a good name. Strong." She paused. "Can we call him Alik for his Russian family?"

I closed the receiver with one hand and looked at Yan. "The woman thinks quickly on her feet…. She asks if we could call him Alik. I like it. What do you think?"

"Yes. I heard her. Alik is great," said Yan. He put his hand on the baby's tummy.

"Alik."

"Alusha," I said. "Mama, are you there? Yes. We'll call him Alik. Yan and I love the idea, and the name suits him. Alik likes it, too. He just gave his papa the biggest smile."

"*Dochenka*, you made us so happy, but how are you going to take care of Zhenechka and the baby, not to mention Yan and the house, with no help? We are so far, far away…"

"You'll be here soon…*ne volnuysya*…don't worry." I swallowed a lump in my throat, waiting for her to say something. She was silent. "Ma, I'll be home tomorrow and call you again. I want to talk to Papa, and the two of you can talk to Zhenechka and Yan."

"What? You are going home tomorrow?"

My mother wasn't happy, not at all.

"Osya, did you hear that? She is going home tomorrow! Here, you would be in the hospital for seven days…resting…. What kind of crazy country do you live in?"

"Ma, we have to hang up now. The nurse is here. *Ya tebya lyublyu.* I love you. *Poka.*"

"Bye, *dochenka*…kisses to Zhenechka, Yan, and Alichek."

I hung up the phone and looked at Yan. "Mama calling America crazy! At least she didn't say we were crazy, although she may think that, too. It's a good thing I don't tell her half of what's going on—she would start World War III if she knew."

"She is just worried."

"I know…. Why don't you go home? Zhenechka might still be up waiting for you. It's late. Kiss him for me and his baby brother. Alusha and I will be fine here."

"Okay. I'll assemble the crib in the morning after dropping Zhenya off at school, and come here as soon as I can. I love you." Yan gave me a kiss and walked toward the door. "Don't be too hard on your mother. She means well…." He stopped at the door. "You may be underestimating how much of what you don't tell her she knows. Good night. I love you."

"You are right, as always. Congratulations, Papa. *Ya tebya lyublyu.*"

Alik made a loud sound (his voice reminded me of Zhenya's when he was a baby) as if saying "good night" to his father and settled back in his hospital bassinet. The bassinet was next to my bed, and the clear plastic sides made it easy for me to see his every move; the two open shelves below the cradle were packed with everything I needed to take care of him during the night: a stack of receiving blankets, onesies, disposable diapers, and wipes. The last three items I had never seen before. The diapers alone seemed like a gift from heaven.

How different this is from the time I had Zhenya, I mused. I might as well have lived on a different planet, not just in a different country. If this was "crazy," I'd take the crazy. The "rest" I had experienced in the Soviet hospital was something to remember. Nine other women were "resting" in the same room, and two of them had lost their babies during childbirth. They weren't allowed to say goodbye to their babies or bury them. They wept, watching the rest of us feed our newborns, and we cried with them, guilty for our happiness while sharing their sorrow. Zhenya was born in one of the best hospitals in Kiev, if not the best (miraculously, Mama found a connection and I was accepted there) and yet the place was filthy. Nothing was sanitized. Sheets were not changed in the week I was there. No visitors were allowed. I snuck out of the room in the middle of the night after giving birth to call home—that wasn't allowed either. I wouldn't call that "resting" ...more like "imprisonment." *Yes,* I thought, watching Alik sleep peacefully in the bassinet, *it's good to be here.*

23

Finding My Next

July 1982—Los Angeles

As my maternity leave was ending, I became more and more apprehensive about going back to work when Alik was only two months old. From a practical sense, it would take my entire salary to pay for a nanny, a completely foreign concept that I wasn't ready to embrace. Soviet babies didn't have nannies—women stayed home with their newborns for one year, after which time kids started *sadik*—a heavily government-subsidized daycare center—or they stayed home with a *babushka,* if they were lucky to have one.

A few words about the *sadiks.* Caregivers' salaries at *sadiks*—like in most places of employment—didn't justify the effort required to take care of these children like their own, so they didn't. In a typical Russian survival manner, *sadiks'* staff rebalanced their insufficient compensation and large workload. The staff (higher ranks took the most) stole the produce delivered by a government-operated warehouse to prepare meals for the children. The little kids didn't notice a cook made their *kasha* with water instead of milk; they didn't know their *kotletas* were a mix of bread with some ground chicken and not the other way around.

As far as a large caregiver-child ratio, that was often "resolved" by keeping windows open during naps, especially on cold, rainy, or wintry days. Little kids would pee through their clothes and sheets while they slept—no disposable diapers, remember—and the ones more susceptible to getting sick would easily catch a cold, time and time again, leaving their parents wondering why. I was one of those parents. In the two and a half years Zhenya attended *sadik*, he spent more time at home with me, recovering from colds, than he did at *sadik*. Unlimited sick days made "calling in sick" a simple choice every time. *Were there exceptions to my encounter with* sadik? *Not likely. Maybe.*

With that kind of childcare experience, I didn't want to leave Alik with anyone else and be away from him all day while he was so little.

I indulged in a memory of the Soviet policies of a twelve-month maternity leave and unlimited sick days, and called Beth to tell her I wasn't coming back to work. But first, I cried. And worried. And cried some more. "Galina, I understand completely. We will miss you, but I understand, and I wish you the best of luck. Please know, you are always welcome to come back should you change your mind," Beth said.

What? I thought, wondering if I'd heard wrong. *She's not shaming or chastising me? Not saying, "We did so much for you and this is how you pay us back? You are ungrateful!"* Tears of gratitude to the people I barely knew and apprehension for the future swept over my entire body. "Thank you for everything, Beth," I told her sincerely. "Goodbye."

When I said "Thank you for everything" to Beth, I meant to thank everyone I encountered at the Equitable Title and Escrow company for simply being friendly. From the day the word of my pregnancy leaked out to my coworkers, people stopped by to congratulate me; they asked how I was, sometimes surprising me by touching my belly as if to check on the baby. "Pregnancy suits you. You are glowing," were the comments. With time, I believed these sweet compliments less and less, steadily making my way to a whopping fifty-four pounds of pregnancy weight. But as I got bigger and clumsier, I was treated with more tenderness and warmth.

At first, this public manifestation came as both a shock and an embarrassment, but I soon appreciated the intention—it was nothing like what I had experienced when I was pregnant with Zhenya in Kiev. There, some colleagues stopped talking to me as if I had offended them. Come to think of it, maybe it was because they knew I would be gone for over a year (an additional two months of maternity leave was given before birth), and they would have to do my job? I will never know, but there were no accolades, presents, or baby showers—those were not the Russian traditions.

The doom-and-gloom Soviet culture prohibited preparing for the baby's arrival in advance. Everything had to be purchased after the birth. I suppose it was a blessing that a mother and her newborn stayed in the hospital for seven days—the rest of the family had a little time to hunt for baby apparatus.

When the time came to decide how to handle this unwritten Russian law in America, I was torn. On one hand, I had this "tradition" ingrained in me so strongly that I was fearing "bad luck" should I not follow the rules. On the other hand, I knew I would be home with the baby twenty-four hours after his or her birth. (There were no ultrasounds to determine the sex of the baby with an HMO in 1981-82. I didn't even know such a test existed.) And Yan would not have enough time to buy the things we needed. Plus, I didn't want to give up the pleasure of looking at, touching, and selecting the baby gear. I wanted the joy of that experience so badly!

Once again, Yan and I plotted. We bought what we needed at

Toys "R" Us and Kmart. The amount of choices and price ranges made my head spin, but our criterion was simple: everything had to be the lowest possible price. At home, I touched every item a hundred times, revering a pack of yellow receiving blankets, gauze burp cloths, green pacifiers, and a tiny outfit to bring the baby home in, before we hid it all in the living room closet, not telling a soul—except Zhenya, our partner in crime. If we shared this joy openly, Mama Rita would be the first to remind us of the "bad luck" associated with the premature shopping for the baby, and my parents (should they have known) would gladly join her warning. In the end, our plan worked; the night Alik was born, Yan and Zhenechka put the crib together and made everything ready for Alusha and me to come home the following day.

> *21 October 1982—Los Angeles*
> *Dearest Mama and Papa,*
> *Today our Alusha is six months old. Some people call it "half-birthday." I know you remember the day he was born every month like you did with Zhenya, even though we are far away from each other and you can't get us a cake. I hope we will be together soon and you will continue the tradition of celebrating the boys' birthdays monthly (although it may be too much for Zhenya at seven). In the meantime, I will buy a small cake to mark Alusha's milestone.*
> *We are doing well. Everyone is healthy. The boys love each other very much, and Zhenechka is the best older brother anyone could've asked for. The other day I asked Zhenya if Alik disturbs him at night when he wakes up for feedings—hard to believe otherwise—but Zhenya said he doesn't wake up when his brother does. I just remembered how he used to say: "Mama, open your mouth so I can talk to the baby," all through my pregnancy. The boys must've*

bonded then. Your older grandson is a wonderful little man. We are so lucky!

Alik had another big milestone earlier this week—he sat up by himself, and now he is trying to pull himself up in the crib. It's amazing to watch! He seems to be in a hurry to move. Given how determined he is, I wouldn't be surprised if he is an early walker! Alik wants to do everything his brother does and doesn't want to wait.

Zhenya is doing well in school. The teacher wants him to test for the "gifted and talented" program; if he passes, he would transfer to a different school with a more advanced curriculum. I am not sure what I think about the test. I don't want Zhenya to think he is "not gifted" if he doesn't pass the test. I don't need a test to tell me that my son is extraordinary—most of the time, that is. Papa determined that the day he was born. Yesterday may have been an exception. This is what happened. I walked outside after Zhenya left for school with the neighbor—whose daughter goes to the same school—and found his backpack sitting on the stairs in front of the building. Can you imagine? I threw Alik in the stroller and rushed to school, worried that Zhenechka would be upset and crying, looking for his backpack. But he wasn't crying; instead he looked at me and said: "Mama, what are you doing here?" It was ten o'clock in the morning and my "gifted and talented" son didn't even notice the absence of his backpack. So, who needs a test? I am joking. Of course, we'll figure out what to do when the time comes. You know how important his education is for us.

Speaking of education, I have some news to share. I've been thinking about going back to work six months to a year from now. Yan says it's up to me—of course, he would say that—but I don't want him to have all the pressure of providing for the family. Even though he has a great job now, loss of a job is pretty common in America, and I want to share the responsibility with him. Plus, I need to be around people if I ever want to speak English well and be more at home living here. So, as we discussed different possibilities, Yan kept coming back to the same suggestion—a computer school—similar to the one he attended. At first, his idea surprised me—I have no interest in data centers and huge computer machines. But Yan insisted I would love being a computer programmer and be good at it, because it's all about logical thinking and analysis, not just the technology. He also thinks that computers are the future, and soon this profession will be golden. In the end, he talked me into doing some research with him, and we found a six-month evening computer training program operated by two Russian guys from Kiev, which I plan to start in December.

What do you think about that? And I have an answer to your question which I know you'd ask: Who will take care of the kids while you are in school? The timing works perfectly. Yan will be home from work by the time I have to leave, and a neighbor, who also enrolled in this program, will give me a ride. We will buy a second car soon, and I will learn how to drive, eventually.

That's all about us. At least for now.

How are you two feeling? Any response to the latest appeal? When you know something, please call us "collect" right away. I don't want to wait a month for the letter with the news to get here, so don't worry about "how expensive a collect call is" and call. Please.

Thank you for sending us photos of you with Misha. I noticed Mama and Misha have dirt on their hands from working in the little garden outside your windows, but Papa is looking sharp in his Olympic jogging suit—no signs of working in dirt there! That's exactly how I would've imagined gardening with the two of you. Glad Misha was helping. How is he? Ask him to write us a note for you to include in your letter—otherwise, he will never do it on his own.

I have to run. Alik woke up from his nap, demanding my attention. He and I will leave soon to pick up his "gifted and talented" brother from school.

Sending you hugs and kisses from me, Yan, and the kids.
Say hello to the family and write soon.
With love, Galya, Yan, Zhenechka, i Alik
Poka! Bye!

My communication with Misha during the nine years apart was sporadic. I quickly realized he wouldn't be writing long letters or even short ones, and settled on occasional postcards for our birthdays. Sometimes he sent photographs: him with our parents; him with our cousin Zoya when she visited from Moscow; him behind the wheel of the truck he drove for work. The infamous truck! The same truck he once took a two-year-old Zhenya for a ride in, picking him up from *sadik* without asking me first. Of course he didn't ask! I would've said "no" and called him "crazy" for even suggesting such a thing. The thought of Zhenya sitting on his lap as he drove wasn't something I would've entertained, even for a second. There were no car seats, so that would've been the only way.

In any event, he didn't ask my permission and took his nephew on an adventure while I ran around the neighborhood, looking for a stranger who picked up my son from daycare (yes, they let Zhenya go with someone they'd never seen before). I was about to go to the police and report a missing child when the two showed up at the door, looking cheerful. Relieved and furious, I yelled at Misha: "*Idiot!* You are a total idiot!" Zhenya looked up at his uncle and said smiling, "Misha, you are an idiot!" My mouth dropped open in shock. I froze for a second, then I smacked Zhenya across the face. "You can't say that—it's a bad word!" Zhenechka began to cry, rubbing his cheek and looking at me in disbelief. I grabbed him in a tight hug, now crying myself. *I hit my perfect little boy, whom I thought just a minute ago was kidnapped.* I kissed his salty cheeks. Apologized. Explained. I couldn't stop apologizing. Finally, when we settled down and Zhenya was happily playing on the floor next to us, Misha whispered in my ear, with a smirk: "So, which one of us is a bigger idiot?" *Fair enough.*

I study the photograph of Misha in his truck. It's inscribed on the back: "To my nephew Zhenechka from Misha." In the photo, he is leaning out of the driver's window, hand stretched out in a wave. He wears sunglasses, the ones we sent him as a gift. He smiles through his mustache—when did that happen? He never had a mustache before. His hair is thinner. I smile at the "idiot" incident, feeling a connection to my brother through that memory.

Back to my computer school story. The six months of studying came and went—or that's how it seems almost forty years later. I remember pictures and snapshots of that period, but not day-to-day details: me running out the door as Yan was walking in, handing Alex to him and giving him instructions on what to feed the kids for dinner. Most of the time, Zhenya would finish his homework by then, and if he didn't, it would be because he dragged his feet all afternoon, and Alex was fussy, and I was too tired to push. It happened.

The short drive to computer school with my neighbor was the time to catch my breath from a busy day. She was my age, also from Kiev, and had a young son, so we never ran out of things to talk about. In school, however, there was no chatting or reminiscing; I focused until my brain became mush, which usually happened by nine-thirty, about an hour before the end of class. At home, I tried to study when Alik took naps, which were notoriously short and inconsistent. A huge English-Russian dictionary Yan used for his studies found a permanent place on the dining room table once again, just in case I had a minute to open the books during the day.

Did I learn anything at the Russian computer school? Did I at least understand the basics? I think barely, because when I received my completion certificate at the end of the program, I felt nothing but dread and fear. That I remember with certainty.

Now what?

24

The "Now or Never" Choice

August 1983—Los Angeles

After the agonizing exercise of writing my resume, I had been send-ing it out for the last month to any and all computer-programmer openings posted in the Sunday issues of the *Los Angeles Times*. My one-page resume stretched my "experience" in all ways possible. At the advice of the computer school instructors, I substituted a lack of actual work experience with the focus—admittedly, a bit too much of it—on my hard working habits, my strong work ethic, and my "superior" Soviet education. The names of the two instructors as references at the bottom of the page gave the resume some legitimacy.

The dining room table in our two-bedroom apartment on Spaulding Avenue in West Hollywood—which we began renting at the end of April when Alik turned one—served as my office. It was furnished with a borrowed typewriter, a dozen hand-addressed enve-lopes, stamps, a stack of my resumes typed by hand on "special resume paper" (the expensive kind), and the latest Jobs section of the *LA Times*.

Poring over the newspaper ads, I ignored the phone ringing just a few feet away from me. "This is for you," said Yan. He looked serious, even stern. *I better take this one.* My face flushed as I realized Yan suspected I didn't pick up the phone when he wasn't home, fearing a call I was so desperately waiting for. But Yan was home that day, and he would not let me flee this time. I grabbed a copy of my resume, took the phone and its long cord from him, and stepped into the bathroom for some privacy, closing the door behind me.

"Hello. This is Galina."

"Hello, Galina. This is Andrea Sobel from Andrea Sobel and Associates. Is this a good time?"

"Yes, of course."

"Are you still looking for a job in Information Systems?"

"Yes."

"Great. I may have an opportunity for you. Can I ask you a few questions?"

With my resume as my cheat sheet, I answered Andrea's questions about my background and my "experience," mentally squashing out with my entire body weight the fear, the doubt, and the dread.

"Would you be able to come for an interview at my office in Century City next Tuesday at eleven?"

Would I? Century City! What kind of company is "Andrea Sobel and Associates?" Who cares?! Yes, I would!

"Yes, Ms. Sobel. I am available. What is your address?" With my hand shaking, I wrote the address she gave me.

Avenue of the Stars! This place is in Century City on the Avenue of the Stars!

"Great. See you then, Galina. And please, call me Andrea."

I hung up, my head spinning. *I have nothing to wear!*

I spent the next several days studying my resume. By the end of the week, I knew it by heart and could explain every bullet point, date, and detail. After the boys were in bed, I studied my notes and textbooks from the computer school. I bought my first interview suit on final sale at JCPenney: a black skirt, a red collarless jacket with large black buttons, and my first pair of black high heels. The days of my waist-length hair were long gone (I'd cut it short before we left Kiev), and now I wore my hair pixie-style. A woman who worked out of her apartment while waiting for her hairdresser license had charged 10 dollars to cut my hair. I painted my nails. And I studied some more. I picked up the bus schedule and became familiar with the route to Century City and back, finally getting some use of the *Thomas Guide*. My car, a ten-year-old Plymouth Volare, would remain parked in the garage that day. I still avoided driving as much as I could.

The Tuesday of my appointment with Andrea must have been a hot day—Los Angeles in August never disappointed. Yet I don't recall the burning sun on my skin while I walked five blocks to the bus stop on the corner of Fairfax Avenue and Santa Monica Boulevard, wearing a synthetic wool suit, pantyhose, and three-inch heels. I wore no makeup—I didn't wear makeup then—just a sheer lip gloss. And I don't remember being hot walking down the Avenue of the Stars in the shade of several high-rises. In one of those high-rises was the office of Andrea Sobel and Associates.

> *15 August 1983—Los Angeles*
> *Privet, our dearest Mama and Papa,*
> *I hope you are well and healthy. We worry about you. Vera wrote about the food shortage in Kiev—it sounded more serious than ever before—but you said nothing in your letters. Vera told us she can't find basic things like eggs, flour, and milk, not to mention meat products and other*

241

necessities. We sent her a parcel yesterday with packages of dry soups, cake mixes, and rice that only require water to prepare. A couple of packages of noodles and a box of buckwheat. You keep telling us you have everything, but I don't see how, if others don't. I'll send a parcel to you next week with some items we sent to Vera. Ask Misha to pick it up from the post office when it arrives—it might be too heavy for you to carry home. Please don't keep things from us—it makes us worry even more. I'll stop the "lecturing" before you get mad and tell you about the latest in my job search.

Turns out my interview in Century City, which I told you about in my last letter—hope you received it—wasn't with the hiring company; it was with a recruiting agency, a place that helps companies find workers. The recruiting agency gets paid by the company if their person is hired. Think of the agency as a posrednik, a middleman between the company and the person who is looking for work—a matchmaker!

I spoke with the owner, Andrea, and now she is arranging for me to speak with the employer. I don't know who that is, but it doesn't matter; she must've thought I am employable. Honestly, I can't imagine why, but I didn't protest.

Yan suggested driving me, as I knew he would, but I wanted to do this by myself. I needed to do this on my own. I left almost two hours ahead of the interview, arriving with plenty of time to find my bearings and walk around. In the past, we drove by Century City a few times, admiring the tall glass buildings and imagining what it might be like to work in one of them. And here I was, standing in front of one.

Andrea offered me a chair across from her desk, settling in hers. The entire wall behind her was made of glass from top to bottom, and the unobstructed view of the other high-rises and mountains in the distance made my head spin every time my gaze fell over her shoulder. I tried not to look, but I was in Century City in a building with an all-glass wall!

What do you think she said first? "Galina—what an unusual name. I also detected a slight accent when we spoke on the phone.... Do you mind me asking where you are from?" You know how much I hate being asked that! And the "slight accent" comment seemed disingenuous. My accent is not "slight"—far from it. Don't worry, I didn't tell her that. Instead, I thanked her for the compliment and explained where I was from. I hope one day these questions will stop, but for now, I'll answer them with as much dignity as I can muster in each situation.

The rest of the interview went smoother. She asked a lot of questions about my prior work experience and my education, and at the end, we chatted about our families. She is a young mother of twins, and this is her company, "Andrea Sobel and Associates." Anyone can have their own business here. I am still not understanding how and what it all entails.... Imagine, a woman with small children is in a business for herself! Surprisingly, she shared a lot of personal information but I noticed it made it easy for me to share, as well. In the end, I forgave her for the "slight accent" comment.

Let's see what happens next. I'll write all about it. I doubt I will get a job right away—I don't expect miracles—but learning the process will be very helpful. And Andrea said if this place doesn't work out, she'll keep looking. I like her.

Everything is good on the home front here. The boys are doing well. We started looking for a daycare for Alik, and Yan's mama offered to help with Zhenya after school, which is an enormous relief. One way or another, I'll be working soon, and we need to make sure your grandchildren are in loving hands during the day. Alla has a friend who takes care of three children in her apartment near us. That would be ideal, but so far, the woman doesn't want to take another child, so we'll see. Alla wants us to stop by her house with Alik, maybe tonight, and see if we can change her mind. I'll let you know.

I am including a few pictures of us at the park with the boys, and a drawing Zhenya made for you. Fingers crossed, they won't get "lost."

Give our love to everyone. We miss you and hope you will be with us soon. Don't give up hope!

Sending you hugs and kisses,

Galya, Yan, Zhenya, i Alik.

The question "Where are you from?" that I mentioned in the letter to my parents, which Americans ask all the time, was by far the worst question anyone could have asked me. If I am completely honest with myself, it may still be true today, but during those early years it was crushing to hear and embarrassing to respond to. Yan agreed. Why? I think because we were "lost in space," without a real home. We were forced—there is no other way to say it—to leave the only home we knew, permanently cutting ties with people and places we loved, parting forever with the music, the movies, the sights and smells. We trekked through foreign countries and unfamiliar places to find shelter in America, but we didn't really belong anywhere. A white work-permit slip allowed us to work in the US, but we didn't belong.

We didn't understand the culture, the language, or the way of life. We didn't understand how people dressed, what they ate, or what they watched. The movies, the music, the sights and smells were all strange and foreign. We were lost in the supermarket among dozens of choices of bread, cheese, and milk. The variety of fruit and vegetables available all year around made our heads spin.

Why do people dress up for work but wear shorts and T-shirts during the weekend? we wondered. *Who wears shorts anywhere else but the beach? Why are people walking on the streets in their tennis shoes and workout clothes? How could a salad with nothing but green leaves be a meal? Why do people go "out to eat"? Can't they prepare their meals at home with all these groceries available at their fingertips? What's a hamburger? A hot dog? Russian dressing—never heard of such a thing!*

America wasn't home, and the home we left wasn't home anymore. How does one live with that? I understand now, our only way to survive—mentally and physically—was to wake up every morning with a single mission: put one foot in front of the other and make it till tomorrow so we could do the same, again and again. And that we did.

Our reaction to the question "Where are you from?" emphasized us not understanding Americans just as much as they didn't understand us. We were from "another planet," and this question affirmed our inferiority to the people asking it.

I never told my parents what I just told you. In fact, this may be the first time I put my reaction to a simple question of curiosity into words. If you asked me "Where are you from?" today, I would say, "I am from a country that is no longer on the map," or "I am from Encino." Neither one of these is answering the question completely, but that's the best I can do.

Back to my job search story. A friendly chitchat with Andrea did not prepare me for a multi-phased interview process at Bullock's, with twenty-five other people going after the same job. Fortunately, I didn't know then, but the twenty-five people interviewing with me were only a fraction of the number of people who applied. To my complete and utter shock, I passed phase one—the written technical test—and they asked me to come back for a second round.

The fifty-person IS (Information Systems) department was located downtown, in the basement of an eight-story black-glass building on the corner of Hope and Eighth streets, the headquarters of Bullock's, a division of Federated Department Stores. If I were savvier, I would've prepared for the interview by not only memorizing my resume and studying textbooks (which I did), but also by learning the rich history of Bullock's. I would've known it was founded in 1907 by John G. Bullock, who came to California, after graduating high school in Paris, with 150 dollars his mother had given him as a graduation present and with an ambition to one day own a large department store in America. His dream materialized and Bullock's stores opened in California, Arizona, and Nevada.

If I had studied this history, I would've learned about Bullock's Wilshire—the upscale staple of the Bullock family. I would've learned everything I could about the company I was hoping to work for. But I didn't. It never occurred to me to find out, and frankly, I wouldn't have known how. I had never set foot in any of these elegant, expensive stores—they were far beyond my reach. And in the times before Google and laptops, supporting multiple languages, any research was a much more complicated endeavor than I could undertake.

The retail business itself was a mystery I didn't unravel until much later. The centralized government-operated Soviet economy had nothing in common with the free economy of capitalism. *Who is a buyer?* I wondered. *Isn't that a person who is purchasing merchandise at the store? What is point-of-sale? A barcode? A purchase order? An apron?* That last question haunted me for months. I knew nothing. Yet here I was, hired for the role of a programmer-analyst with a salary of twenty-four thousand dollars a year. Unimaginable. So in the end, it wasn't Nina who worked for a *magazeen*; it was me. The irony of that wasn't lost on the two of us.

My first day—an almost forty-year-old memory—began with introductions, another aspect of American culture I wasn't prepared for.

"Galina—what an unusual name!" said a woman in a cube across from mine. "Thank you."

"I detect a slight accent.... Do you mind me asking where you are from?"

"I am from the USSR." The country was still very much alive and well.

"Wow! How did you get out? I understand the government doesn't allow anyone to leave."

"They don't. My family was allowed to leave as Jewish refugees."

Blank stare. *I suppose she wanted to ask, "What are Jewish refugees?"*

Escorted by my boss's assistant, I continued the introduction ritual, which would become second nature eventually, but not that day. One after another, my new colleagues asked questions about me. They asked about my family, where I went to school, about my children. Some were surprised I had an eight-year-old and an eighteen-month-old—"Such age difference!" But "Where are you from?" remained the winning question.

We stopped by the office of the head of the IS last. Chief information officer (CIO)—a title that was as prestigious then as it is today. The door was open and my "guide" casually peeked in.

"Blake, do you have a minute for an introduction?" A man in his mid-thirties promptly got up and walked toward us, extending his hand to me. I would eventually embrace the casual way Americans interact with each other: showing up in a boss's office unannounced, addressing one another by first name (no Russian patronymic or comrade; American title like Mr. or Miss), regardless of age or rank. I would one day become one of those bosses whose door was always open—no appointments needed.

"Ga-lee-na? Is that how you pronounce your first name?"

"Yes." *Smile.*

"You are from the USSR?" Without a pause, Blake continued: "I know a lot about Russia. I watched *Doctor Zhivago* many times and visited Odessa once while on a cruise," he said with full seriousness, vigorously shaking my hand. "How do you pronounce your last name? Just say it slowly."

"CHER NEE AN SKEE."

"CHERNY-ANSKY?"

"Yes."

"That's a long name. You can always shorten or change it when you get your citizenship.... I loved Odessa! Have you been to Odessa?"

"No, I haven't."

"Beautiful city. Nice meeting you, Gale*nn*a. You are the first Russian among our ranks! Welcome aboard!" "It's Gale*ena*. Nice meeting you too, Blake."

I finally made it back to my cubicle and hid behind its three walls to wipe the drops of sweat dripping down my face and neck and find my bearings. I stared at my reflection in the black computer screen on top of my desk, afraid to press the "On" button. *What am I doing here? I will never survive more than a day! I am no programmer-analyst! And I am no Russian!*

An hour later, a young woman who sat two cubicles down from me appeared in the opening of my cube. "Galina, we want to take you out for lunch if you don't have any other plans." Immediately, my heart started to race. *What does it mean? Where are they "taking" me? Will I have to endure more questions about my name and how I got out of the USSR?*

At noon, six of us met outside and headed to a restaurant several blocks away. Downtown streets were busy with lunch hour office workers—men and women—in business suits; merchants selling hot dogs, snacks, toys, and T-shirts on the side of the street; and buses, cars, and taxis honking at pedestrians who ignored traffic rules and at each other. It was impossible to walk together, so our group separated into two, each having their own conversation. I desperately tried to understand what the women to my right were saying. I recognized individual words and some phrases, but I couldn't follow the conversation, nor could I take part in it.

English comprehension was still a multi-step process for me: First I translated a phrase or a question from English to Russian, then I formed a response in Russian, which I translated to English in my head before finally responding in English. Clearly, too many steps for a quick chat while walking on a busy street. I wanted them to stop so I could see their faces to help me understand what they were saying better, but no one stopped. The chat continued inside the restaurant while everyone was looking at their menus. *What are these dishes? Tandoori chicken…Chicken Masala… I have no idea what to order.* I buried my head in the menu.

"So, Galina, what city are you from?" a woman sitting across the table asked.

"Kiev."

"Oh…K-i-e-v…. Is it a big city?"

"Yes. Over two million people. Kiev is the capital of Ukraine."

"Ukraine…is that like a region or something?"

"Yes, you can say that. Ukraine is one of the fifteen republics in the Soviet Union."

"I am confused—are you Ukrainian or Russian?" another person chimed in.

Neither! Let's eat already! Tandoori chicken sounds great!

I wasn't fired the next day or the day after, but a week later, my manager—the one who hired me, the one whom I thought would be my protector, the one who knew all my limitations and hired me anyway—got a promotion and left the department. I found myself lost and alone once again.

"Yan, you don't understand! A new manager will not put up with my 'slight accent' and wait five minutes for me to answer a question because I have to translate everything in my head first. You don't understand..."

He smiled. "I understand." *Of course, you do! I can do this.* I was thirty years old and at the start of another journey.

Even though I would continue to understand only half of what people said around me, translate my responses in my head, and write long-winded technical specifications that sounded like Russian novels to my boss—I would eventually breathe again.

I would get used to colleagues chatting in the hallway about what they had for lunch like it was the most important event of their day, discussing the latest baseball game in excruciating detail, and bashing the current American president—all with the same enthusiasm. In addition, Monday topics also included the "What did you do over the weekend?" query, which I avoided at all costs.

I was the only one in my department who had children. Describing my weekends of cleaning, grocery shopping, cooking, taking the boys to the park, and visiting my mother-in-law wasn't exactly what people wanted to have a casual chat about. Especially after they shared about their weekends of bar-hopping, concerts and restaurants, Las Vegas, ski trips, and a plethora of other adventures I couldn't even contemplate.

My hesitation to take part in hallway chitchat didn't go unnoticed by my boss. In an annual review, he wrote something like this: "Galina is intelligent and hardworking. She is self-motivated. Galina quickly grasps technical and business concepts, and the quality of her work is outstanding. However, Galina could do a better job integrating with a larger organization and the leadership team. To do that, I encourage her to take a more active role in casual interactions with her peers and leaders." I listened intensely as he continued reading his assessment. "Galina is shy. More interaction with her colleagues would help her overcome her shyness."

He has no idea, does he? How is it possible that he has no idea I don't talk to people on casual topics because I don't understand what the heck they are saying?!

After reading the review to me and asking if I had any questions, Gary handed me a book on technical writing. "This might be helpful," he said. "It's yours to keep." This may have been the best gift of my professional career.

25

Lessons and Other Truth

The significance of Gary's annual review and his "gift" didn't resonate with me until much later. Much, much later. I suppose I was too preoccupied with the idea that "he didn't understand" to recognize the value of our interaction or his honesty. Much less could I have foreseen how much he would influence my career throughout, years after we parted ways.

During that conversation and the years to follow, Gary treated me the way I've always wanted to be treated—like everyone else. Not a Russian. Not a Jew. Not an immigrant. He "told me like it was" that day, as if saying: "Here is what I think. Here is how I can help [giving me the book]. Do what you want with this information. And please, keep your 'accent' excuse to yourself. I don't buy it anymore."

In the same way, my father "told me like it was" when he insisted that "people judge you by the way you speak." Or how my mother pushed me to stand up for myself when she said: "If you think you are old enough to make big decisions, you must be old enough to follow through." And Yan, when he literally "pushed" me out of the house to buy my own darn stamps!

I had shared the Gary event with a couple of friends when it happened, and they suggested he was a jerk for insulting me by handing me the book. Yan agreed: "How dare he?!" Despite everyone's good intentions, their outrage on my behalf didn't help: I felt even less competent and quite bitter until I finally stopped talking about it and forced myself to look at the other side of this proverbial coin. However constructive it may be, I don't handle criticism well, and I don't want to be told I am not perfect, even though I know full well that I am far from being perfect by hundreds of thousands of miles. I just don't want another human to tell it to me. And that's the truth.

In retrospect, I had the sense to look at the conversation from a different angle. I decided that even if I didn't have a "problem" (which I knew I had if I was honest with myself), Gary had a perception that I did—and I needed to fix it either way. So I kept the technical writing book on my desk at work in plain sight and read pertinent pages as I wrote my specification documents. *Write in plain language. Consider every word. Be brief and to the point (no Russian novels!). Be clear and logical. Break down your instructions into simple steps. Be brief.*

Next to the infamous book on my desk, another found its home: an enormous English-Russian/Russian-English dictionary. Both resources became my trusted partners for some time. Online tools of the early eighties would seem ancient to any school-age child in 2022. At Bullock's, we used a text editor called Wylbur, one of the first interactive text-manipulation systems developed for IBM computers. Wylbur was an avant-garde, state-of-the-art, never-seen-before tool (not by me, anyway), but Wylbur didn't have a spellcheck, which no one missed because there was no such thing yet. *What would I have given then for a computer program with a spellchecker!* Like everyone else, I didn't know what I was missing, yet unlike anyone else, I really could have used one. Instead, I spent hours looking up words—their meaning and spelling—in the dictionary and checking my writing against "the book."

Turned out, that wasn't enough. After coming back from my manager's office with red ink all over my documents, I decided I needed something else. I asked for help—imagine that! I asked a colleague to review my work once I thought I did the best I could and then some. She agreed. Over time, she spent less and less of her time reviewing my work for grammar and spelling errors, and we began discussing business dilemmas and ideas for technical solutions. Soon, I oversaw the work of other programmers and was often sought to help with complex coding issues. Slowly, I began to breathe again.

I was becoming almost comfortable in my programmer-analyst skin when Alexandra gave me another American lesson and the best career advice. The two of us still remember the conversation:

"You should be a project manager, too!" she said. "You are doing the work already. Don't you want to be promoted?" She herself had recently been promoted.

"Of course I do!" I said.

"So, have you talked to Gary?"

"What do you mean, 'talked to Gary'?"

"Does he know you want to be a project manager?"

"Well…I assume so…. It's a logical next step from where I am. If he thinks I deserve a promotion, he'll give it to me."

"Galina, you are insane! You will wait forever! Do you think that's how I got promoted?"

"Well…yes. How else?"

"I walked into Gary's office at the beginning of the year, reminded him of my accomplishments so far, and asked what I needed to do to become a project manager in six months."

"You did what? And he didn't kick you out?"

"Obviously not; here I am, promoted six months later. You have to do the same."

"I don't know, Alex…" Her idea sounded borderline audacious to me. "I don't know if I can be so bold," I admitted.

"Oh, really? YOU can't be bold! And getting on a train to flee the Soviet Union wasn't bold? This is America! You are in charge of your life, not the government, and not your boss. Do it!"

"This is worse than writing a resume…but I'll think about it. I really do want to be a project manager."

A week after our conversation where Alexandra declared me "insane," I walked into Gary's office and made my pitch. And just like that, before the year was over, I had the title of project manager.

There it was: career advice I would use time and time again.

The lesson I learned next became my leadership jump board. I wish I could say I recognized its value, but I didn't. Intuitively, however, I began mirroring the behavior right away.

Alik must've been three because he was still attending a small daycare run by a young woman out of her house. We placed Alik there when we moved to San Gabriel, and he quickly transitioned from the Russian-speaking home of our friends to the loving care of this American family.

One morning, Alik woke up with watery eyes and flushed cheeks. He refused to eat his breakfast, and he didn't fuss about which pair of sweatpants was to his liking that day. I ignored the nagging churn in my stomach that was there to tell me to stop and pay attention, and I dropped him off at the daycare on the way to work. He didn't have a fever, and I had so much work—making a different choice didn't seem possible.

At about eleven, I received a call from the sitter. "Alex is running a fever, and he is throwing up. He is crying and asking for you." I told her I was on my way and hung up the phone, guilt already churning in my stomach. *I have truly committed a crime. I must leave. But how? I don't even know how this works. Am I allowed to leave work in the middle of the day? What if I get fired? I don't care!*

I walked into Gary's office, prepared to quit my job if he told me not to leave. Remember, my "fresh off the boat" brain still operated on my former life's experience. Of course, Gary was completely fine with me leaving, but he didn't just say that! He began by telling me that in the future, if I needed to leave early for whatever reason, I didn't need to ask his permission—simply notifying him would be enough. He said I was a valuable employee, so offering me this flexibility was a small way in which he and the company could express their gratitude. Stunned, I mumbled a thank you and ran to my car. I cried all the way home, not understanding what had just happened. What happened was, without checking HR policies or giving me a raise or a bonus, Gary inspired me to work better than ever. And I did!

26

Thanksgiving

November 1984

Most American families have Thanksgiving traditions—from the menu (very traditional vs. semi-traditional with favorite family dishes vs. not-traditional-at-all) to the type of turkey purchased (fresh vs. frozen, self-basting vs. pre-brined, kosher, organic, or free-range) to the method of preparing the bird (roast vs. deep fry vs. bake in a bag or order already cooked) to which family member is hosting the holiday (parents, adult children, or family friends) to what time (brunch, lunch, or dinner) and on and on. Americans have their Thanksgiving traditions down.

Our past, a life of scarcity and long lines, heavily influenced our Thanksgiving customs. Even after living in the United States for over five years, I continued to be in awe of the abundance of the very items and produce that Americans needed to celebrate their holidays, exactly when they needed them. It was the opposite of what I was used to—things disappeared from the shelves precisely when they were most needed. And since you never knew what might disappear tomorrow, stashing whatever you could find was a norm.

With this burdensome mindset, I couldn't allow myself to put the entire turkey in the oven on Thanksgiving Day and have it be eaten in one sitting. *How wasteful!* Never mind that year after year, the bird came to us at nearly no cost. One year, I received it as a gift at work; another year, it was free with a fifty dollar purchase of groceries at a local supermarket; a couple of years in a row, Yan brought home a turkey that was gifted to him at work. Even though every year a turkey found its way to us with little effort, I continued to justify to myself why cooking the bird whole would be careless. I remembered the "Soviet wings" we lived on in Italy and all the dishes we created from them during our two-month stay there. *I could make enough meals for a month from a sixteen-seventeen pound turkey.* And I did. Grateful for a freezer, whose feature of self-cleaning and its enormous size proclaimed it to be "innovative and futuristic," year after year, I chopped the uncooked bird into pieces and planned dozens of meals for the weeks ahead.

Standing in the kitchen of our brand new San Gabriel townhouse on the Eastside of Los Angeles, I looked at the seventeen-pound frozen turkey I'd brought home from the market and decided: "1984 is the year we are having a real Thanksgiving—the whole bird is going into the oven!" I had two days to figure it all out. First, I invited Yan's mother and Sofia with her family to join us for Thanksgiving dinner at five and placed the bird in the freezer, priding myself that I "made it fit."

Then I delivered the news to Yan and the boys. Yan was thrilled we would finally have a "real" Thanksgiving. Zhenya, who had by then experienced the holiday at a friend's house, said: "Just don't make any weird stuff like red-colored potatoes with sugar and marshmallows—I think they are called 'yams' or something. They are gross." Alik launched into a "gobble-gobble" dance he'd learned at preschool, the minute he heard the word "Thanksgiving." And for one moment, I second-guessed my decision, remembering a phrase from a TV commercial: "It's her first turkey—it won't be juicy." Never mind. *I can do this.* What I couldn't have known was that roasting a perfectly juicy turkey would've been a welcome challenge in comparison to the one I was about to face.

24 November, 1984—Los Angeles

Hello dearest Mama and Papa, hope all is well, vse horosho.

We received your parcel at the beginning of the week. Zhenya loved another new set of colored pencils and the drafting set. He said, "The drafting set is a grown-up present." At nine, your older grandson wants to be treated as a "grown-up." I suppose that's not quite accurate—he always wanted to be treated as a grown-up.

The Chukosky book, Moydodyr ("Wash 'til Holes") was perfect for Alik. Honestly, I hope the story encourages him to wash his hands so his things and toys won't "run away" from him like they did from the boy in the poem. You should've seen Alik's face when I read: "A blanket ran away, a bedsheet flew away, and a pillow, like a frog, hopped away from me." He stopped blinking, his already large eyes got bigger, he clenched his favorite blanket (which is always next to him) with his knees, he covered his mouth with both hands, and he froze, staring at the picture in the book depicting what I read. Afraid to scar my child for life, I rushed to the part when the boy ran home and "washed with soap to no end," and all of his things came back to him. I will report back to you how much the story influenced Alik in keeping up with his hygiene; for now, all I know is that he understood a poem in Russian. I think his Russian may not last too much longer since he spends the day at preschool—where no one speaks Russian.

Last Thursday, we celebrated Thanksgiving. I've written to you about this holiday before, but this year, we celebrated it the "right way." I roasted the whole turkey in the oven and made several of the traditional side dishes: cranberry sauce, green beans, stuffing, and mashed potatoes. And we always thought mashed potatoes were a Russian dish—Americans love their mashed! If you saw the different brands of potatoes at the stores, your head would spin—mine does. I assume American potatoes grow in the dirt just like the Russian ones, but I have yet to see a dirty or rotten potato at a store, not once! I remember digging inside a dirt-filled meshok (cloth bag) to "fish" for potatoes, which were also covered in dirt. Not here. Looks like each potato is cleaned separately and proudly placed on display. Some are packed in different-sized plastic bags for easy pickup and some are sold individually. Who buys one potato at a time? Here is the thing—you can if you want to.

So, I decided this was the year to celebrate Thanksgiving as it was meant to be celebrated, with "all the trimmings," as Americans say. We bought our first home two months ago (glad you liked the pictures—your room is all set up for you two, and the boys are happy to share a bedroom). Yan and I celebrated our tenth wedding anniversary this month, so it was time for a real Thanksgiving! I ran into a few hiccups with the holiday meal preparation, which I hope will make you smile. Papa may not care about these details but Mama, you will.

First, I didn't realize it takes three to four days to thaw a turkey. I should've known because I had defrosted it in the past when I cut it up for multiple meals, but somehow the thawing time slipped my mind. I could've read the instructions on the packaging, but I didn't. By the way, there are instructions for everything! Every package, every item comes with instructions and recipes—you have to really try to mess things up. So, on Wednesday night, my turkey was still frozen. In a moment of panic, I was ready to cancel Thanksgiving dinner, but luckily I thought of our brand new bathtub and how it might help save the day. I spent the entire night running cold water over the turkey, turning it from side to side, and by seven on Thanksgiving morning, it was thawed and happy. I know what you are thinking... or do I? Don't tell me what you are thinking now, because this was not the end of my first Thanksgiving drama. I also didn't check ahead how long it would take to roast the bird, and when I called Alexandra—my friend and a go-to expert on all things American—at two in the afternoon to ask if it was time to put the bird in the oven for our five o'clock dinner, she got quiet on the other line and then yelled in a panic, "Put the bird in the oven...now!" This was an eight-kilo bird that required six hours to cook, and I only had three. In the end, I made it happen, Mama, but it was quite an event! Now you can tell me what you think of your daughter's "masterful" kitchen shenanigans. I told the story at dinner, and we laughed the entire night.

That's all I have for now. Yan and the boys are doing well. They send you hugs and kisses. Yan said he will write to you before the weekend is over, and I am sure Zhenya will have a picture to put in his letter.

You should hear from OVIR soon. Please call us "collect" as soon as you can. We hope it's a "yes" this time.

How is everyone? How is Misha? Aunt Katya? Write about everyone.

We love you.

Yours, Galya, Yan, deti

With that infamous turkey drama, we began our annual Thanksgiving celebration the American way, except for yams with marshmallows, for which we never acquired a taste. As the number of people at our Thanksgiving table grew year after year, so did the size of the turkey. A twenty-five-pounder became the norm. And a sit-down dinner—regardless of how many people were coming—was a must. Russians don't do well with buffets; we love our *zastol'ye*—sitting around the table for hours talking over each other, toasting those who are at the table, those who are away, and remembering those who have passed. That's just what we do. The "Happy Thanksgiving" toast would always come from Yan. Then, someone would toast me—the hostess—to praise my hospitality and tasty food, *za khozyayku*! Next would be a toast to the children (grown-up children not excluded)—*za detey*! To the parents—*za roditeley*! To the future generation of Americans, our grandchildren—*za vnukov*! We toast to health—*za zdorov'ye*! And never to be skipped, a toast of gratitude to America—"G-d bless America"—that one usually would come from me, accompanied by watery eyes with a few teardrops sliding down my face.

No matter what I said, I could never truly express my gratitude. I still can't. I cry standing up for the American national anthem with my right hand over my heart, holding it from jumping out. I cry when my grandchildren recite "The Pledge of Allegiance." And I cry listening to Neil Diamond's "Coming to America."

Our American friends and family embraced the Russian *zastol'ye*. Through the years, they added their own touches to the celebration with their favorite dishes. It took me a long time before I became less obsessed with everyone speaking English at the table. Since there were usually multiple conversations going on anyway, why not have them in two different languages?

When my mother finally joined us in America, she quickly became an integral part of Thanksgiving festivities, playing the role of a co-host—or maybe I became a co-host in her presence. It was hard to tell. Her contribution to the holiday table was her famous Russian *blinis* with red caviar and sour cream; no amount of my protesting her eagerness helped. She ignored me every time I told her that *blinis* are not for Thanksgiving and Americans hate caviar; she kept on bringing *blinis*. Mama also took it upon herself to make sure everyone ate as much as they could and then some. She would grab a serving dish, say with potatoes, and walk around the table, squeezing between the wall and the chairs to offer each person more. Not waiting for a "yes" or "no" answer, she enthusiastically deposited a spoonful on the "victim's" plate, asking "*escho?*" and added more, regardless of their answer. I tried to interfere with her "hospitality"—painfully familiar to me—embarrassed in front of the Americans at the table, but there was no use. It turned out there was no need. Everyone loved her, and they quickly learned to say "*da, escho, Babushka. Spasibo.*"

In the meantime, the year 1984 brought another denial to my parents, another disappointment we never discussed openly, expecting each other to "deal with it" and move forward. Shortly after we received the news, Aunt Katya, in her last letter to me, wrote:

> *My dear girl, derzhis, be strong and don't panic. Take care of your malchiki, your boys, and I will always be near your parents. They live for your letters and photographs. Osik spends hours every day looking at the pictures through his magnifying glass—every detail is important to him. He tells the stories you write about time and time again, to anyone who will listen. "My daughter is this...my daughter is that...." I wish he would tell you himself how proud of you he is, but you know him. He won't say it to you directly but he is very proud. Can you believe he stopped smoking?*

He must really want to see you. I pray it will happen soon. Thank you for the beautiful scarf. It keeps me warm and reminds me of you. Give my love to Yan and the boys. I love you all very much.

27

Never Looking Back Again —
We Came to America

October 25, 1987
Rome—Fiumicino International Airport ("Leonardo da Vinci")
New York—John F. Kennedy International Airport
Los Angeles—Los Angeles International Airport

A large group of friends and family gathered at the arrival gate of the Tom Bradley International Terminal to welcome my mother. She left Kiev in May 1987, one year after my father died, and eight years after we left. She carried a single suitcase when she took a train from Kiev to Moscow, spending a few days with Aunt Maya and Zoya, before flying to Vienna.

A three-hour flight from Moscow to Vienna was now available for Jews leaving the Soviet Union. The plane tickets were expensive, but using the black market, we made sure Mama had the money. "I can take a train through Chop and Bratislava to Vienna, like everyone else," she protested, but Yan and I insisted on her flying instead. Typical. Mama never wanted "privileged" treatment.

In Vienna, she felt like a fish in water: it had been forty-two years since my parents lived in Germany, but Mama's German came back as if no time had passed. She quickly put her language skills to good use by becoming a "translator" to those around her who needed help. She accompanied complete strangers to doctor's appointments, helped fellow émigrés purchase stamps and make phone calls at the post office, and chaperoned them to the market.

During the four months Mama spent in Ladispoli, she made friends with whom she kept in touch for the rest of her life. At sixty-six, she still attracted people like a magnet and didn't get intimidated by her surroundings. She managed her HIAS appointments with no help and took the train from Ladispoli to Rome by herself, while many others her age and younger were completely lost. "Italian was an easy language to learn," she told the boys when she arrived and confidently shared with them a few words and phrases that she remembered: "*Quanto costa? Ti amo; grazie; per favore.*"

Her talent for speaking new languages served her well in the US. I never admitted it to her, but I was in awe watching her communicate in English with anyone she came across. Before she had any vocabulary to speak of, she "spoke" to our American friends, as I listened in horror to all the mistakes she was making. She treated the boys' friends as if they were her own grandchildren, lecturing them on manners and feeding them every Russian child's favorite dish—chicken cutlets and mashed potatoes—while telling them tales from her homeland.

I had none of her confidence when we arrived in 1979. We lived in West Hollywood, a district in Los Angeles where most Soviet émigrés settled upon arrival. We rented a one-bedroom apartment for 260 dollars a month, on the first floor of a two-story motel-style structure owned by Wolf and Sonia, who also lived in the building. Like many apartment building owners, they didn't want to rent to a couple with a child. Often "for rent" signs, including theirs, said "adults only" and "no pets, no kids." But as they told us later, they liked us, and Zhenya seemed like a well-behaved child, so they risked it. Their risk, however, was much bigger than letting a child live in their apartment. They didn't know (and neither did we) if we could pay rent beyond the two-month allowance of four hundred dollars we received from the Jewish Family Service.

If our experience of renting an apartment in Italy taught us anything, it was to agree to the landlord's rules and demands, sign the rental agreement without questioning anything, and be the most low-maintenance renters they've ever had. Instead of expressing our dismay with the "no pets, no kids" sign, we profusely thanked Wolf and Sonia for their generosity and moved in.

From the outside, the structure looked like a rectangular cardboard box with a flat roof and large, metallic boxes sticking out of windows. We learned that those were air conditioning units, which, however loud and expensive in electrical costs, proved to be lifesavers during hot Los Angeles summers. The building was raised above ground with its second floor sitting on top of the car garage. The street, lined with beautiful purple orchid trees and large evergreens, looked painfully peculiar and unfamiliar.

The apartment was small by American standards, but to us, a home with two rooms, a bathroom, and a kitchen seemed like an unreal luxury. Never mind that the front door had a flimsy lock and opened directly into the living room, and the kitchen was in the middle of the apartment between the living room and the bedroom. Let's not forget the carpet, the color of which was a dirty mix of brown and green—it was impossible to tell which shade was the original. The cabinets in the kitchen and the wall closet in the bedroom needed some dusting, but I was excited for all the built-in storage and happy to clean off the dust to make the place my own.

Two months after we moved in, Wolf brought us a bucket of

paint and said we could paint the walls ourselves if we wanted to. He also offered to replace the carpet if we paid for it by adding thirty dollars to our rent. Before too long, we had freshly painted walls, clean closets and kitchen cabinets, and a brand new carpet. As a final touch, we embellished the small dining area with some wallpaper.

Zhenya slept in the bedroom, and Yan and I on the foldout couch in the living room. After sleeping and eating on the floor in an empty apartment for a month, we spent eight hundred dollars of our last bit of savings to furnish our home. We bought a bed for Zhenya, a dining room table with four chairs, a couch, and three tall bookcases that stood empty against the wall. I probably wouldn't have braved spending that kind of money all at once, but Yan insisted. He told me later that my sadness became too much for him to bear, and our empty apartment had a lot to do with it. I didn't realize I was sad; thinking of my feelings was a luxury I didn't have. But Yan turned out to be right: turning an unfurnished apartment at 934 N. Stanley Avenue into a cozy home gave us a glimpse of belonging and stability.

For the first three months, I didn't leave the house without Yan, afraid I would say something incorrectly every time I opened my mouth, which undoubtedly would've been the case. My father's warning, "people judge you by the way you speak," never rang louder than those first months in America. I hid behind Yan's back until he'd had enough.

"I ran out of stamps for the letters to my parents. Let's take a walk to the post office to get some," I said one day.

"Why don't you go, and I'll stay home with Zhenya?" he replied, gently "pushing" me to the door.

"No, no, no. You know, I can't go by myself…I don't know what to say," I lied.

He opened the door, handed me a five-dollar bill, and gave me a kiss on the cheek, smiling. Before I could protest again, the door behind me closed, and there I was, slightly irritated at Yan but mainly petrified to proceed with my task by myself. I considered turning back, but that would mean a complete defeat, so I began walking.

The post office on Fairfax Avenue, just north of Santa Monica Boulevard, was five blocks from our apartment. The familiar walk down the boulevard, lined with poorly kept single-story buildings with boarded windows and secondhand shops, seemed even more foreign that day. For the first time, I was outside without Yan on a mission I didn't think I could accomplish. To calm my nerves, I rehearsed what I would say: "Please, may I have thirty fifteen-cent stamps? Thank you." I repeated this phrase the entire way to the post office and while standing in line. My heart was pounding, my mouth was dry, and my palms got clammy as the woman behind the window said, "Next."

"Please...may I have thirty...," I began. Swiftly taking the five-dollar bill out of my hand, she asked, "Thirty fifteen-cent?" before I finished my well-rehearsed, properly structured request.

"Yes. Thank you," I said, barely opening my mouth as she handed the stamps and two quarters back to me. "Thank you. Next, please."

On my way home, instead of secondhand shops and boarded windows, I saw tall, elegant palm trees gracefully swaying in a warm October breeze and a cloudless, blue sky stretched out for infinity. Clusters of sun-kissed oranges hung playfully from tree branches, bringing exquisite indulgence to arm's reach.

Thanks to Yan and the clerk at the post office, I stopped waiting for my confidence to come to me and began moving toward it, however slowly. It was courage I needed, not confidence.

When Mama arrived at JFK for a three-hour layover, Uncle Vova and Aunt Lillia drove from New Jersey to see her. Their reunion was both happy and agonizing—grief and joy collided into one overwhelming cloud of emotions. They cried for the missed time they would never recover, for the loved ones they'd lost over the years apart, and the ones they would never see again. Uncle Vova was still crying when he called to tell me that Mama was on her way to Los Angeles. She was on the last leg of her journey. The same journey Yan, Zhenya, and I had taken eight years before.

I hadn't thought about our journey from Ladispoli to Los Angeles in a very long time. And now, waiting for my mother's arrival, these memories came to life as if it all had happened yesterday.

We were scheduled to fly out of Rome on July 24, 1979, and arrive in Los Angeles late evening of the same day. With the layover at JFK, the trek would take over eighteen hours. This would be my third time on an airplane; the other two times were two-hour flights that Yan and I took together, both on Aeroflot, the only Soviet Airline. We flew to Leningrad for our honeymoon in November 1974 and to Sokhumi, Caucasus region, in 1977, when I joined Yan on his trip for several big car-repair jobs. Both experiences left me with zero desire to get on an airplane again. Yet there we were—days after receiving the news about my parents being denied permission to emigrate—getting ready for the last leg of our three-month voyage to America.

We dreaded another goodbye with Alla and her family, who headed to Cleveland, Ohio. Like that day in Kiev, after we exchanged our money at the Central bank, we spent hours making plans to see each other and promising to stay in touch. This time we made our plans while sitting in a small kitchen in Ladispoli. Naively, we believed that once in America, we could travel easily. In reality, Yan and I never visited Alla in Cleveland, but Alla came to California several times before finally moving here for good.

Two days before our flight, Zhenya became sick; all the symptoms he had when we left Chop came back with a vengeance. High fever was the most worrisome. An Italian doctor came to see him at home. "I wouldn't travel with a child in this condition. Consider postponing your flight," he said, speaking Russian with a thick accent. We agonized over the decision. There was so much to consider. We had paid our rent through the end of July. If we stayed longer, but Alla and her family left by the end of the month, we would have to pay both our and their portion of the rent in full for the following month. We couldn't afford to pay the entire rent and cover our living expenses for however much longer we would stay.

As problematic as this decision was from a financial standpoint, we were scared to embark on a long journey with a sick child once again. In the end, we followed the advice of Alla's mother, Maria Vladimirovna. She told us, "You will not receive the treatment you were given in Chop on the flight to America. Just go. The sooner you get to America, the quicker Zhenya will recover." We trusted her, and we are forever grateful for her advice: as a doctor, a mother, and a grandmother.

Our first taste of America on the Pan American flight from Rome to New York seemed surreal. As soon as the flight attendant noticed we had a sick child, she moved us to an empty row with four seats. She then pushed up the handle, dividing the two seats in the center of the row, and placed a couple of folded blankets across them, making the space into a bed. A pillow and another blanket completed the transformation. Yan and I sat in the seats at the opposite sides of the row, and Zhenya lay comfortably between the two of us. We didn't know what to think and how to react to such kindness.

After making Zhenechka smile with goofy faces, the flight attendant disappeared for a few minutes, then came back with a cup of warm water and a chewable tablet of children's Tylenol. Gesticulating with all her limbs and speaking slowly, she explained what the tablet was for. We had never heard of Tylenol, and a "chewable tablet" seemed like something out of a science-fiction movie, but after a few minutes of debating, we gave it to Zhenya. The fever dropped within forty minutes, and Zhenya slept on his cozy bed all the way to New York. His miraculous recovery didn't stop there. In all the years that followed, Zhenya was never sick like this again. His three-year-old battle with ear infections and high fevers ended on that plane. This was our first American miracle.

Customs at JFK was nothing like what we'd experienced in Chop. No one threw our luggage around and berated us for the content of our belongings. There was no military presence, not in the way we saw at the Soviet border. And yet, I felt jittery. Everything was unfamiliar and frightening. *Where is the joy I wanted to feel? I* felt none. It occurred to me that people who helped us get to this point would no longer be there once we boarded the plane to Los Angeles, leaving us on our own in a foreign land. The gravity of the new reality was setting in: we had turned our lives upside down and we had no clue how to be now. *What does Los Angeles look like? How do we make a life there? Where are we going to live?*

"Ladies and gentlemen, as we start our descent, please make sure your seat backs and tray tables are in their full upright position. Make sure your seat belt is securely fastened and all carry-on luggage is stowed underneath the seat in front of you or in the overhead bins. Thank you." The captain's announcement sounded like gibberish, but we understood "thank you," and the flight attendant helped us figure out the rest.

As the Pan American aircraft carrying over two hundred people began its descent toward LAX, the view outside took my breath away. I remembered our first night view into the streets of Vienna from a bus, and just like then, the three of us froze, staring at the ocean of lights below us, stretching as far as the eye could see and beyond. "Flight attendants, prepare for landing."

Los Angeles, here we come.

Returning from my daydreaming of our flight from Rome to Los Angeles, I noticed that a few more people joined us at the gate. It would please Mama to be greeted by people closest to her and to us. Alla with her husband, Lenny (she had parted ways with Leo and married her true love). Sofia and her husband, Alex, who took the most memorable pictures of our reunion. Alex's brother, Rafail, with wife Nina, Mama's friend from Kiev. Yan's mother, and the boys.

The boys. The two of them were the reason my parents fought relentlessly to get out of the USSR and why Mama risked embarking on this journey on her own after my father died. *What will she think of the boys?*

At twelve, Zhenya was thoughtful, talented, and creative. He loathed any remedial tasks, most notably his homework and his chores. His love for the arts continued to grow, and he had been attending an art school for almost five years. He had no interest in sports but could lose himself for hours in front of a computer, in the world of ones and zeroes. Long gone were the heartbreaking days of him standing in a playground, watching other kids play and not understanding them or their games. During those early months, we kept bringing him back to the park, weekend after weekend, and over time, he behaved more like himself.

His bright voice and his "prior singing experience" on a chair in my parents' living room landed him a role in a school musical. Coincidentally, the play was about people coming to America from Eastern Europe in pursuit of freedom and opportunities. He played the role of a young boy making the journey with his parents. His solo was a song about seeing the Statue of Liberty for the first time as the ship with immigrant families entered New York Harbor.

I wept silently as his voice filled the school auditorium with a sound coming intensely from the depths of his soul: "Lady of Liberty standing there before me... What do you hold for me?" The song brought back the pain. The anguish. The agony of having to decide to leave my home, my parents; losing friends and family members; not being there to say goodbye to my father before he died. And the song brought on joy. The gratitude. The happiness. Even after all these years, I was shocked that a play with this topic would be on a school stage, especially in an area with almost no Jewish population.

"How can a young boy express such adult emotions?" a woman sitting next to me said to her husband. "He couldn't possibly understand!" She clapped vigorously and wiped her tears.

At the airport, I looked at my watch for the fifteenth time in ten minutes. Mama's plane was landing in one hour. I could've thought of a million things at that moment, but what came to mind was: *How do I explain to my mother Zhenya's funky, asymmetrical haircut? She won't like it. I know she won't like it, but what are the chances she'll say something right away?*

I'll jump ahead to tell you: As soon as we got into the car—our first new car, a red Subaru—Mama gave me an earful for allowing "such frivolousness to a twelve-year-old child." Mama hadn't changed in eight years, nor was she intimidated by her surroundings to tone it down for a minute.

"Eugene, wait for me!" Alik's voice came first, before I saw him running to catch up with his brother. Zhenya stopped, stretching his arm behind him for Alik to grab onto, and they ran to the window to watch the airplanes. At five, Alik was a free-spirited, fearless American boy. Unlike Zhenya—a daydreamer who measured and rationalized his decisions before taking action—Alik jumped right into things with a fierce grip. He seemed to have been in a rush for his independence since the day he was born: early to sit up, stand up, and walk—without fear or hesitation.

Alik adored his older brother and wanted to be around him all the time, mimicking Zhenya's behavior and his interests in art, music, and technology. Alik behaved as if there wasn't a seven-year age difference between them, and Zhenya graciously and patiently nurtured his little shadow of a brother.

"I am the only one in this *whole* family who could become president, because I was born in America," Alik announced proudly to anyone who would listen. Our first American. After a miscarriage I didn't mourn, because I didn't know how and didn't understand I should, Alusha's birth was a blessing, wiping away the tears and the pain I stored inside.

"Ladies and gentlemen, flight number…from New York's John Kennedy International Airport arrived at gate number…"

The doors of the gate swung open. I stared down the empty corridor for a few seconds before a stream of people began making their way toward the exit. I moved to the side of the exit door to avoid blocking it, but everyone else in our group clustered right in front of it, stepping aside to let passengers pass through and closing in again as soon as they did. I was about to ask them to move away from the entrance when I saw my mother walking toward us, surrounded by other passengers—most of whom towered over her—periodically blocking her from my view. *When did she get to be so short?* Her hair was now silver, with streaks of black, but it still framed her face with soft curls.

"Mama!" I yelled, waving an enormous bouquet of light pink and white gladiolus—her favorites—over everyone's heads. She looked up, searching for my voice as she continued walking. I tried to see her face, but it looked blurry behind a wall of tears blocking my vision. "Maama!" She stopped. Our eyes met and, for a few seconds, locked in an invisible embrace. Her face grimaced, as if in pain when she looked at me. "I hope it was all worth it," I read in the deep sadness of her eyes, red and puffy from years of crying.

I attempted to move toward her as she got closer to the exit, but then I noticed Yan's sister nudging Zhenya to go greet his *babushka*. Zhenya quickly spotted her in the approaching crowd, and a moment later, they stood in a long, gentle embrace—Zhenya's head resting on her shoulder. He was now as tall as she was. Tears flooded Mama's face, washing away the pain imprinted on it just a moment ago. The radiance and light replaced her pain, as the little boy we separated her from lovingly held her to never let her go.

Years later, Zhenya still remembers her arrival in vivid detail: "I remember the strange anticipation of waiting to see someone that I was so close to, for the first time in years. I had seen pictures of *Babushka* and spoken to her, but would I recognize her in three dimensions among the crowd of people streaming through the terminal gate? I recognized her right away, of course."

As he embraced his *babushka*, I noticed Yan watching the scene from the back, quietly wiping the corners of his eyes with the back of his hand. Alla nudged Alik to come closer to Zhenya. Shyly and reluctantly, he complied, and before he knew it, Mama enveloped him in her arms, gasping with joy.

Still holding her flowers, I waited for my turn as she moved from one person to another, hugging and saying hello. A few minutes of delay allowed me to regain my composure, and by the time she reached me, I hugged her with a cheerful smile instead of guilt-and-sadness-ridden tears. "*Dochenka!*" was all she said, burying her head on my shoulder for just a second, before noticing Yan, who was now standing behind me. "*Moe dorogoy!* My dear! I waited for this day for so long..." She leaned against his chest, wrapping one arm around his waist as he tenderly hugged her with both arms. She looked tiny next to him, but her body seemed relaxed...she must have felt safe.

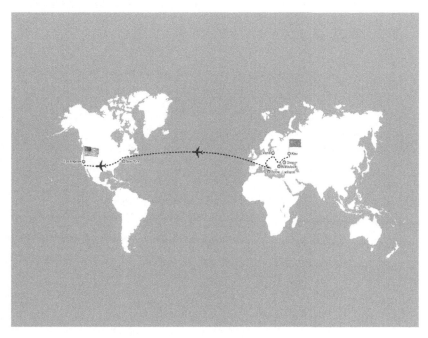

Journey Map

Epilogue

Misha

Autumn 1993—Los Angeles

I examined a small package that arrived with the afternoon mail. The handwriting on the label startled me—it resembled Papa's so much. The same tall, confident letters. I didn't recognize the return address—Kirovograd, Ukraine. The parcel was from Michail Kugel.

We hadn't heard from Misha in over a year. He left Los Angeles after a divorce, which began amicably until she threatened to claim half of his taxi business. The taxi was technically ours—we loaned Misha all our savings to purchase a White Taxi Cab license when he came to America in the spring of 1988, with his then wife. He was a natural and quickly began to make a decent living. He had regular clients who requested his services when they came into town for business. His friendliness and familiarity with the city drew customers to him. He knew Los Angeles like the back of his hand, almost like he knew Kiev.

And yet, I didn't think this was his life. I hoped to be wrong. In Kiev, he was a fish in water, in his habitat, so to speak. He was the giver and the getter. He was the one helping his friends. He was the one in charge. He lost all of that in America. He lost his emotional ground.

Why did he come, after all? Because of Mama, of course. She gets the credit and the blame. The minute she stepped foot in our house, she was on a mission to get Misha to come by any means possible. Her phone calls and letters to him described our life in the most glamorous way: our grand home, the two cars, the beautiful California weather, stores packed with everything you could possibly want, and with the things you didn't know you wanted. There was Las Vegas, Disneyland, and Palm Springs.

"Why are you telling him all this, Mama? Tell him the hard stuff!" She infuriated me. "No one starts their life in America with a trip to Las Vegas—you did, because we took you!"

"He will figure it out when he gets here. Everyone does."

"He will figure it out," Yan echoed his mother-in-law.

In the meantime, living in Kiev had become more difficult than ever. The residual effects of the Chernobyl catastrophe were still present. Fear of radiation lingering for decades to come was growing among citizens. Many tried to relocate if they had the means. And with the Jewish emigration opening again, the timing for Misha to leave seemed imminent—the window could have closed without warning, like it did in 1979.

In the end, Mama won.

Misha's arrival brought total chaos to what was beginning to feel like a steady life rhythm. Our American lifestyle disappeared the minute he walked through the door. There were seven of us in a two-thousand-square-foot, three-bedroom townhouse (not exactly cramped), but our privacy was no more. Misha walked into our bedroom to talk whenever he felt like it. Mama usually followed. He and Mama argued all the time, as if no time had passed. Misha's stuff was everywhere. Our brand-new kitchen was a greasy mess—my brother became an excellent cook but remained a terrible slob. I helped the newcomers with the logistics of applying for social security and getting their identification cards. Yan gave Misha a few driving lessons (automatic transmission was new to him) and helped him study for his driving exam (the Russian language version of the written test became available then).

The boys had just gotten used to having their grandmother living with us and learning her "Soviet" rules, which I still remembered well:

-finish everything on your plate (snacking your way to the next meal wasn't an option)

-eat each meal with bread and butter (to get your tummy full for longer)

-don't open the refrigerator or the cupboards without permission (the contents may be planned for another meal or intended for someone else)

-boys don't belong in the kitchen (mine did!)

And now Misha broke all of them in a single swoop and threw our lives up in the air. It was Alik he tumbled with now, like he did with Zhenya all those years ago. Zhenya became his ally. The two often played chess while Misha bombarded his nephew with questions about life in America, smiling through his mustache as Zhenya tried to find relevant Russian words, mispronouncing most of them.

During the two months Misha and his wife lived with us, we hosted frequent dinners with family and friends. Misha and I had never shared friends. We gravitated toward different people; his friends were rebels like him and mine were the "good" kids; I suspected it would be the same in America. But I gave it every chance and introduced him to "my people" anyway. At each gathering, we toasted his arrival and wished him success in his new homeland.

Welcome to America, Misha!

commotion caused by Misha's arrival wasn't enough,
preparations for Zhenya's bar mitzvah, a thir-
year-old Jewish boy's transition into adulthood. To a "real"
Jew, our version of the event would've seemed unorthodox. The
evening took place at Black Sea, a Russian restaurant in West
Hollywood. A Russian cantor/master-of-the-ceremony prepared
Zhenya for the big day by teaching him a few brief prayers. Yan
said a prayer over challah, reading it off a piece of paper (we didn't
even know that one!). In a touching ceremony, one by one, Zhenya
invited special guests onto the stage to light a candle with him on
a large menorah.

As unconventional as Zhenya's bar mitzvah was, to us it held
immense significance. The little boy who'd left Kiev at the age of
three, leaving behind everything he knew, was now surrounded by
both of his grandmothers, his aunts, his uncles, his friends, and our
friends. There were toasts—dozens of them! Mama spoke after Yan
and me. She began: "Usually, it would be my husband giving a toast
like this, but today I will speak for both of us." *Oh no! She will turn
Zhenya's* bar mitzvah *into a memorial for Papa!* I held my breath.
But I didn't need to worry. The words that followed expressed
nothing but her joy of being with her grandson on this special day,
and her hopes for his bright future. She concluded with something
to the effect of: "Even though Zhenya is now considered a man by
the Jewish tradition, he has a long journey ahead to become one."
Agreed, Mama.

Alik made a grand entrance carrying thirteen blue and white
balloons over his head across the room. He sang "Happy Bar
Mitzvah to you" into a microphone but ran off the stage when
everyone stood up, applauding.

Misha promised to help Zhenya with everything he could, and
always be there for him. He had been in the country for a little over
three months, so that was quite a promise.

Vodka was flowing like the Dnieper River. Russian hospitality was on display with a variety and quantity of food that shocked our American friends. Misha and I danced together for the first time since my wedding. At the end of the night, Zhenya stood in front of the adoring crowd—microphone in one hand, the other hand in the pocket of his brand new slacks—and spoke of what the day meant to him, the gratitude he felt for having his family together on a day like this. A little boy who climbed on a chair-stage at my parents' house for the last time ten years ago was on his way to becoming a man. I missed my father at that moment more than ever.

"Why did you do this?" Mama asked.

"Because I can, Mama. Because I can."

Zhenya's bar mitzvah breathed new energy into our lives. Misha threw himself into his business. He was up at four in the morning five days a week to catch early travelers at the airport, and he sub-leased his taxi on weekends. His wife got her hairdresser's license and worked out of the living room of their one-bedroom West Hollywood apartment—she was an excellent hairdresser and soon became popular with the Russian immigrants. By all accounts, theirs was the fastest adaptation to the new life I'd seen.

We soon bought a house with a beautiful backyard and a pool. Misha was proud, as if the house was his. He was proud of the boys. There were no formalities in our relationship, and he often drove up to the house in his taxi, unannounced.

"Misha is here!" Alik was the first one to greet his uncle.

"Who is washing my car today for fifteen dollars?"

"Misha, you are crazy! Fifteen dollars?" I protested.

But Alik was already outside with a bucket and a sponge. He never missed an opportunity to be grossly overpaid performing chores for Misha. Zhenya, on the other hand, didn't take his uncle up on his offers. His fifteen-year-old logic dictated these offers weren't good enough. Ironically, at sixteen, he began working for less and never looked back.

While Alik washed the car, Misha sat on a rocking-bench in the backyard, with a cigarette and a large cup of coffee. Sometimes we had lunch together, but often just chatted. He remembered how Papa had spent hours at the dining room table with our photographs spread around him, studying each photo through a magnifying glass, noting every little detail. He told us about Papa's last days—he, too, was convinced that Papa died from breathing the Chernobyl poison. He shared that his wife went through an IVF procedure, trying to get pregnant. It was painful, expensive, and worst of all—unsuccessful. This must've strained their relationship, but he never spoke about that part.

Life was settling down again, and before we knew it, Misha became an American citizen. He was beaming. A picture of him holding a small American flag said it all. He loved everything about America. The freeways. The freedoms. The ingenuity. The opportunities. California beaches, the desert, and the mountains. But he was missing something in his life, and I felt it.

After the divorce, he sold his taxi, paid us back the money we owed on our credit cards on his behalf, took the rest, and disappeared without saying goodbye. Mama made excuses for him; she was relieved he had the money wherever he went. Yan was convinced Misha would return soon. I was livid.

Hands shaking, I tore open the side of the parcel and dozens of photographs fell on the floor. *What is all this?* Inside the package I found a note:

> *Galochka, I am sorry I left the way I did. I will pay back the money I still owe you. Ne serdis. Don't be angry. I got married to a woman named Natasha. We live in Kirovograd.*

Natasha is thirty-two. She has a nine-year-old son, Denis, and we now have a six-month-old daughter, Katerina— named after Aunt Katya. I will come to LA soon. Natasha wants to live in America, so I will need to submit paperwork for her and the kids. Kiss the boys. Say hi to Yan. Tell Mama.

Tell Mama! Just like him, leaving me to deal with the fallouts of his craziness and make it all right for him! What's there to tell? He waited that long to tell us about the baby? So typical! What an idiot!

Suddenly, the fact that he was alive became trivial. The fact that he married a woman thirteen years his junior was only mildly amusing. She was a beautiful blonde, and if she wanted my brother, she was also brave. As for Misha, he finally got what he always wanted—an actual family. A baby.

Sitting on the kitchen floor, I pored over the photos. Some color, some black-and-white. Katya with her parents, about two months old, in front of a colorful wool rug as a backdrop; Katya with Misha on a park bench; on the couch at home; Katya with Denis; Katya in a stroller. I instantly fell in love with the little girl in these photos. Everything about her looked familiar and dear. The alluring half-smile, the piercing dark eyes—she was a spitting image of Misha... and someone else... Our mother! *I have to call Mama!*

Over the next five years, Misha lived with his family in Kirovograd, waiting for their green cards. He came to Los Angeles two or three times a year and stayed with us during those trips. To prepare for his visits, I bought bags and packages of gear and clothing for Katya that he would take with him. A baby walker, a toddler stroller, her first bike. And I couldn't stop buying her clothes. Just couldn't stop. A lot of Alik's clothes went to Denis. The boys were two years apart, so it worked. Misha brought photographs every time he came—that was his only luggage. Family outings. Katya on her new bike. Katya in Misha's duffle bag before he left for Los Angeles. Katya with their dog. Katya in her gymnastics uniform. Her hair had grown; she now had soft chocolate curls framing her face. It was painful to watch this little girl grow and not be able to hug her until she was five years old.

In the meantime, in Ukraine, Misha ran a small export business with big plans for the future. But soon he realized that, unless he was willing to "work" with the Ukrainian mob, his business wouldn't survive. Running an honest business wasn't possible. The very concept of a "business" was still very new in Ukraine and there were no rules. In the world of "free for all," mobs ruled. He wasn't willing to enter that world. So, his business died, the money ran out, and by the time he brought his family to America in 1998, he had nothing, once again.

Except that he had everything! As Natasha received her teaching credentials and began working as an adult ESL teacher, Misha gave all his attention to the kids. Katya was his life. A talented gymnast since an early age, she fulfilled her father's love for sports. He drove her to her practice across town three times a week in the worst of LA traffic. He bragged about his daughter's academic achievements. Her very presence elated him. We were all in awe of how quickly Katya began reading and communicating in English while speaking fluent Russian with her parents. She must've inherited *Babushka* Bella's talent for languages. My mother adored her only grand-daughter. And I kept buying her clothes and toys, taking care of her when Natasha took weekend classes and Misha worked. Sometimes they dropped her off early in the morning, when Yan and I were still in bed. We snuggled, laughed, watched TV, and played.

Misha made another unsuccessful attempt at running a business. Money was tight, but Natasha worked to support the family, and the kids were thriving.

In December 2005, he made plans to take Denis to visit his grandparents in Kirovograd, spending some time in Kiev first. Ukraine was now an independent country and travel became possible.

We had just lost my dear Alla. I was mourning her passing—we all were—and saying goodbye to our forty-year-old friendship. Misha's plan to travel to Ukraine scared me because of the timing and because I worried about his health. He had lost consciousness earlier that year, taking Katya to gymnastics, and had a few other occurrences of unexplained fatigue. After the last one, Yan took over driving Katya. As I made my plea, Misha promised to stop smoking, take his medications, but he was not willing to postpone the trip.

"You know how I miss Kiev. Everything is going to be fine," Misha told me days before he left.

The Ukrainian crisis and the violence around Kiev's Maidan Square were some years away, but turbulence was in the air already. Incidents with Chechnya's rebels became a regular part of the news cycle, and open violence became commonplace.

Misha and Denis flew to Kiev and stayed with Misha's friend who lived near Khreshchatyk Street, a few street blocks from the *Besarabsky bazaar*. On a crisp December morning, Misha walked to the market carrying an empty glass jar to buy pickles from his favorite local vendor. The city was awake, making last preparations to ring in the year 2006. Misha was happy to be in Kiev. I imagine, even in freezing cold, he walked with his coat unbuttoned, breezing the familiar air with his entire body, anticipating toasting the New Year in his beloved city.

Inside a grandiose structure that was the *Besarabsky bazaar*, he heard an unusual noise, much louder than the typical market buzz. He looked ahead and noticed a large presence of *militsiya*.

He turned around and headed toward the exit door, suspecting a disturbance he wanted to avoid. But it was too late. He was stopped with a violent strike to his head before he reached the door. He fell on the floor. The glass jar flew out of his hand and broke into small pieces, hitting the ground near him. Misha was caught in a Chechen *oblava*, a raid to catch illegal Chechens, which became routine in Kiev. He must've been mistaken for a Chechen because of his olive skin color.

"I am an American! Let me go! I am an American..."

They hit him again and again until he lost consciousness. He woke up in prison.

"I am an American! My friend can bring you my passport.... I am an American..."

He pleaded until he was finally allowed to call his friend. Misha was released from Kiev prison twenty-four hours later.

The night he returned to his friend's apartment, Denis was awakened by his stepfather's moans. Misha was burning up with fever; his body trembled. Cold sweat dripped down his almost white face. Denis sat next to him, wiping off the sweat.

"Misha, Misha, what's wrong?"

"Listen, Denis. I am sick...but...I don't want to die here. I want to go home.... Take me home."

"Okay, Misha."

"And promise me, not a word of this to anyone..."

"I promise."

The two returned to Los Angeles during the first week of 2006. Misha looked tired. He insisted jet lag was to blame. When I pestered him—one time too many—to see a doctor, irritated, he told me to worry about my husband and stop bugging him. Yan was scheduled for prostate cancer surgery on the 10th of January. As I said, there were no formalities in our relationship; we turned into little kids the minute we disagreed. Misha didn't have to tell me "to worry"; I had nightmares about the worst possible outcome. But I put on a brave face and kept telling Yan, "Everything is going to be fine." And it was. The surgery was successful, and I brought Yan home after spending four days at the hospital with him. He had a long recovery ahead but he was fine and that's all that mattered.

Misha came to visit his brother-in-law every day while I was at work. One day he brought red caviar, insisting it would help Yan heal faster. I yelled at him when I found out. Misha didn't have the money to buy caviar.

On Friday evening, January 20, Misha called and asked me to come get him—he didn't feel well and Natasha was working that evening. I jumped in the car and drove across the street where they lived. He climbed in the car looking pale and had difficulty walking up the stairs when we got to our house. I couldn't convince him to call 911 or go to the emergency room with me. We sat across from each other and I watched the color slowly return to his face.

"Do you have a cigarette?" he asked.

"Are you insane? I am not giving you a cigarette!"

"How about coffee?"

"No coffee. I can make you a cup of tea."

We went into the kitchen and I put on a tea kettle. It occurred to me that Papa, Misha, and I liked our tea the same way: strong, burning hot, in a large mug filled to the brim. Misha examined the cup, making sure the tea was strong enough, nodded in approval, and began pouring sugar into the cup. One teaspoon, two, three, four… Considering the sugar spilled on the way from the sugar bowl to the cup, by my estimate he ended up with two and a half teaspoons in his tea.

A familiar picture. And our last evening together.

The phone rang early Monday morning. I was getting ready for work. Yan was still in bed—he was less than two weeks after his surgery. It was Natasha.

"Misha collapsed.... The ambulance is taking him to Tarzana hospital. I am on my way there with the kids."

"I am leaving now..." The phone fell out of my hand.

"Yan, go get Mama.... It's Misha! Call the boys! I am going to the hospital..."

The sound of the ambulance sirens outside pierced through my body.

Misha was gone. He was sixty-four.

A Story That Wasn't Meant to Be

July 24, 2019—Los Angeles

On the fortieth anniversary of our arrival in America, it was just as hot in Los Angeles as it was on the day we landed in LAX in 1979 and each year since then. But unlike that first summer, today the scorching sun rays bathed my skin in a welcome warmth, and the cloudless blue sky stretched to infinity in its serene calmness. Turns out, it's true what they said about our summers: "It gets hot in Los Angeles, but the heat is dry, so it's really not bad."

Not bad? It's magnificent! And the ocean is minutes away!

Yan and I spent the morning strolling barefoot on the beach, soaking our feet in the freshness of the Pacific Ocean, watching dozens of seagulls soar over the waves, then stand still in almost perfect rows—like miniature soldiers—looking out toward the waves with graceful posture.

"Any regrets?" I asked, sliding my arm under Yan's as we walked in typical Russian fashion. *Pod-ruchki.*

"One. Wish your father would've made it here." He answered quicker than I expected. "You?"

"The same.... I often picture him watching the boys grow up... although he would've been disappointed that I still have an accent."

"You and your accent! Give it a rest, already. How do you think I feel? Mine is much worse."

We laughed.

"What's your biggest surprise?" I said.

"The fall of the Soviet Union. Never saw it coming.... Remember how we used to say 'this regime will not change in our lifetime'?"

"Still hard to believe. Remember when we stood in the middle of the street in Berlin where the wall used to be? I get goosebumps thinking about it. Chilling."

"What was your biggest surprise?" he asked.

"Mine? Everything.... How did we do it all? First, we survived. Really survived. We built careers. Bought a house, and another, and another. Raised the most amazing sons—they are good people, you know...solid men. All of it is a surprise.... I don't take anything for granted."

I didn't take for granted my mother's arrival in the US after eight years of separation. Just as I was beginning to lose hope, there she was coming back into our lives with a single piece of luggage and two Magen David necklaces for the boys. She said she'd bought them in Italy with the money she'd "saved" from her allowance. I wanted to ask how exactly she managed to save any money from that allowance but I didn't. Instead, I reminded her of the time, years ago, when she ran away from a woman who wanted to give me a Star of David necklace. What was the likelihood that Alik would be the exact age I was then, receiving one from her?

We stopped to watch a surfer catch that perfect wave, which carried him on a smooth and seemingly effortless ride toward us, gently sliding onto the white sand, then forcefully rolling back into the water with a roar to get ready for another spin.

This resembles life, I thought. *You glide through your days thinking your circumstances have predetermined your life's trajectory until a single event—an unexpected wave—puts you on a path so different it makes your head spin. And before you know it, another wave follows, and another one after that, giving you a choice to get back on your surfboard and face your next ride or let the moment pass.*

I thought of an unlikely wave that brought Yan and me together. The one that caused me to say "yes" to his marriage proposal and to his invitation to go to America. I leaped into those decisions, but after that, I froze and almost missed the next wave and my only chance of pursuing happiness and freedom. I sat tight, stalling—out of fear for the unknown ahead and out of fear of losing my parents' love. When my marriage became threatened, I finally risked catching another wave that moved our story forward. The waves kept coming. I seized some and missed others. The likelihood of our story to continue was challenged at every turn, but in the end, our little family boarded the last train to freedom.

What a wave that was!

"Do you feel at home in America?" Yan interrupted my rumination, as he gazed at the surfer who waited for the next perfect wave, sitting on his surfboard in a relaxed posture.

"Yes, and no," I answered with a sigh. "Sometimes I feel like I lived two lives: my childhood and youth on one planet, and my adulthood on another—and the two have no ties, no bridge or connection of any kind. If I am ever in a conversation where people my age talk about the movies they grew up with, books they read, high school homecomings, proms, and college experiences, I can't relate and they wouldn't be able to relate to mine. What about you?"

"I feel deeply grateful, but do I feel at home? I do, actually... I can't imagine living anywhere else."

We walked in silence for a while.

"Any regrets about retiring? Although technically you are still working..." He smiled, fixing my arm under his.

"No regrets. It was time. And I wanted to know what it was like to run my own business, however small—another American dream, right? I love the flexibility we have to spend time together. And I want to write about our journey. So, no regrets."

We walked hand-in-hand, each lost in our own thoughts. A scene from my last business trip to Paris popped into my head. I was there with a small group of colleagues to kick off a large project that was to be rolled out to the company's offices in twelve countries outside of the US, including Russia. General managers from each country traveled to Paris with their key staff for the two-day project-launch event. I had never interacted with our Moscow office before and was curious to meet the people who came to Paris. A man who was the general manager and the two women who accompanied him all appeared to be in their mid-thirties. They kept to themselves throughout the day, and I didn't introduce myself to them like I did to everyone else. A casual dinner gathering in one of the local restaurants seemed like a good opportunity to do so. The two women settled at the end of the table, and I sat down in a chair across from them. This was my first conversation in forty years with people from my former Motherland (excluding a tour guide during our brief visit to Saint Petersburg during our cruise).

"Hello. I am Galina. We didn't have a chance to meet earlier," I said, extending my hand to one of them.

"Svetlana..." She paused. "Galina...? That's a Russian name. Are you Russian?"

"Nice meeting you, Svetlana. I came to the US many years ago from the former Soviet Union. So in a way, yes, but I am mostly American."

Her colleague was quiet after we introduced ourselves. I made a few more attempts to start a conversation, asking them what they thought of the technology we would roll out, and if they came to Paris often. Svetlana answered for both women—I assumed she was in a superior role. She gave me brief answers until something I said—I can't remember what—sparked her interest, and she continued with the questioning, in lovely English that had a combination of a British and Russian accent.

"So, Galina, you live in Los Angeles?"

"Yes."

"And how long have you been with the company?"

"Fifteen years."

"You are a vice president?" I'd never said what my title was, so she must've noticed me earlier in the day and asked someone.

"Yes. I head up a technology group in LA."

"What about these men? Are you their boss?" She pointed toward the group.

"Yes, we work together. I also work with the team here in London." I was quickly becoming uncomfortable—*these questions won't end well.* She reminded me of the crazy women from Kiev with her interrogation.

"But you weren't born in America?"

"No. I was born in Kiev."

"Did you come to America as a child?"

"No. I came at twenty-six, with my husband and our young son."

"Really…" She looked at her colleague and back at me.

"So, how is it possible? You are an immigrant…a woman. And you made it to vice president, with all these men reporting to you? But technically you are not even an American…," she blurted in disbelief.

"It's a long story, Svetlana, and I would love to tell it to you some-day. But in short, I am an American—technically and in any other way. America is unique in this way. No one cares where I came from and what I did or didn't do before. I worked hard, like everyone else who wants to achieve professional and personal success. There are no guarantees for anyone, but the possibilities are endless. It's hard to explain.... You have to live it."

"This would not be possible in Russia.... We have our jobs because we had the connections—otherwise we would struggle like everyone else."

"I know." I can't be certain I said it out loud.

I also knew there and then that the Moscow office had no inten-tion of using the technology we were proposing, because it would expose too many details of their business to the American company that owned them. And in that respect, nothing had changed in Russia. But that's a story for another time.

A roaring sound of a wave crashing at my feet brought me back to Yan, who stood in front of me, soaked from head to toe with the mischievous look of a child. I knew what would come next—he would turn around and dive into the next gigantic wave, emerging on the other side of it with a triumphant smile. At seventy-three, he is as vibrant and handsome as he was the day we met. *The "crazy woman" did not disappoint.*

I watched Yan dive under another wave, thinking of the cel-ebration we were having with family and friends the following Saturday. Our first such event was on the twenty-fifth anniversary of our arrival to the US, and now, fifteen years later, the forty-year milestone warranted another festive gathering. The backyard in Alik's family home would be flooded with patriotic-themed deco-rations and flower arrangements. Five giant red and blue balloons would float in the swimming pool, making a sign: "40 USA." Even the food would follow the theme—barbequed chicken and ribs with all the trimmings. Apple pie with ice cream for dessert. Red, white, and blue popsicles for the kids, who would dress in red, white, and blue attire.

Zhenya would be responsible for the music, creating an excellent playlist with our favorite '80s tunes and surprising me with Neil Diamond's "Coming to America," which would bring on my usual reaction—a stream of warm, quiet tears and an awkward search for a tissue. My makeup would be ruined.

Our guests would make the event look like the United Nations, with the generational representation from South Africa, Israel, Morocco, Lithuania, Ukraine, Poland, Canada, Cuba, and the US.

At the end of the night, Ella and Nathan would ask, almost in unison, "*Babulya*, why do you and *Deda* always say, 'We are grateful to America, we are grateful to America.' You always say that…and you cry…. Why?" Their younger siblings, Simon and Liam, would come closer—ice cream dripping on their naked tummies.

"Because, my loves, without America, *Deda* and I wouldn't have our story, and you wouldn't have started yours."

Family Tree

Included in the Family Tree are the members of Godl's family mentioned throughout the book.

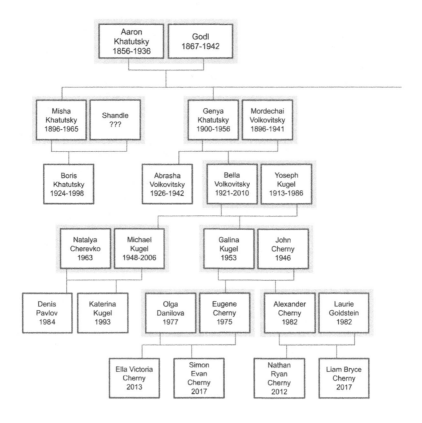

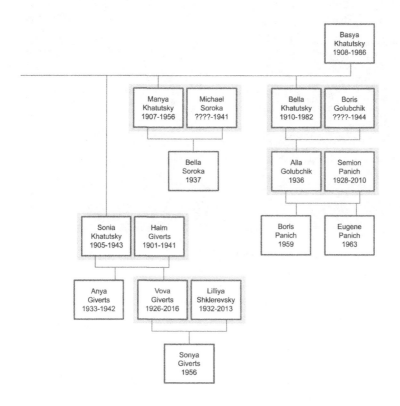

Family Album

Kiev. c. 1939.
My mother's parents.
Left: Genya Volkovitsky.
Right: Misha Khatutsky.

Kiev. 1934.
Left: Mama (thirteen) with brother Abrasha (eight).
Right: Inscription by Mama
In memory to dear parents from their daughter and son, Beba and Abrasha.
Keep this copy and don't forget us.

Kiev. c. 1936-1938.
Uncle Vova's and Anya's
parents, Sonia and Haim
Giverts.

Kiev. c. 1950. Vova Giverts.

Kiev. c. 1938. Anya Giverts.

Kiev, c. 1938.
Misha Khatutsky's children.
From left to right: Olya, Aaron, and Boris.

Babushka Fira with my father, the youngest of her thirteen children.
Papa had said he was two years old in this photo, which places it in 1915.

Mama. Kiev.
Inscription in her handwriting:
Be brave, be fearless in a cruel battle.
Fight for the Russian land.
Remember Moscow and your fiancé and come back to them soon.
In memory of your Birthday.
21 February, 1945.

Germany. 1946.
My parents, Bella Volkovitsky and Yoseph Kugel.
Mama referred to this photograph as their wedding photo.

Aunt Katya.
Inscribed on the back:
To dear Bebochka (one of many diminutives for Bella) from Katya.
27 March, 1946.
Kiev.

Kiev. Podol. 7 November 1953.
Left to right: Mama, Beba (Mama's cousin); Godl's daughters: Bella, Manya
(Beba's mother), Genya (my *babushka*).
In front: Misha (eight), and I am nearly ten months old.

Stalingrad c. 1955.
My parents.

Kiev. 1960.
Left: I am seven, a first-grader.
Oktyabryonok (Little Octobrist).
Below: Yan is fourteen.

Kiev, c. 1956.
Yan's Parents, Rita Chernyansky and Efim Roizsenblit.

Kiev. Summer 1974.
On one of our first dates. I am picking berries in the woods outside of Kiev.
Yan is relaxing at his sister's apartment afterward.

Kiev. 5 November 1974. Our wedding day.

Top left: Walking to the Marriage Palace surrounded by our family and by-standers. The car we came in dropped us off a block away.

Right: Family photo after the marriage registration. Such a photo has been a staple for Soviet newlyweds through the decades. My parents and Uncle Vova at the top of the stairs. Bella is in front of Mama. Behind Yan is my friend Vera; behind her is Misha. The little girl next to me is Yan's niece, Irina.

Yan's suit had to be custom made. He was 1.9 meter tall with long arms, and standard ready-to-wear suits didn't fit him.

My attire: Wedding dress: purchased for ninety rubles on a black market (smuggled from Poland). Veil: borrowed from a relative to be returned at the end of the wedding day. Shoes: after standing in line for hours, I possessed these patent leather platforms half-size smaller than I needed.

Bottom left: In front of the WWII Memorial of Unknown Soldiers in central Kiev. Placing flowers at the memorial on your wedding day has been a long-standing Soviet tradition.

313

Kiev. Podol. 1976. In our apartment on Shchekavytskaya
Street. Zhenya is a little over one.

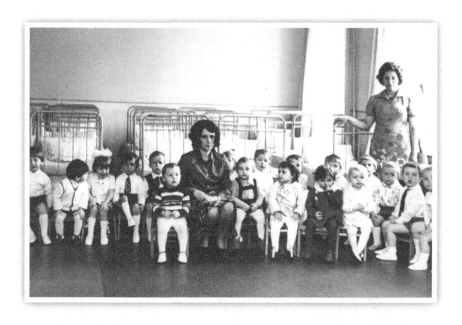

Above:
Kiev. Podol. 1976. *Sadik.*
Zhenya (in striped sweater) in
the first row to the left of the
teacher.

Left:
Kiev. Podol. 1977. *Sadik.*
New Year celebration.
Zhenya is first on the left.

Kiev. 1977.
With my parents and Zhenya in our apartment on Shchekavytskaya Street.
Yan is taking the photo. Zhenya is pointing at the camera in hopes to see a tiny
bird that Babulya promised would fly out if he sat still and looked straight into
the camera. I used this "trick" on my children, when they were small.

Kiev. Winter 1978.
National Circus of Ukraine on Victory Square.
Zhenya and Cheburashka.

Kiev. 12 May, 1979.
With Bella and Yan on the day of our farewell gathering with family and
friends at my parents' apartment on Ratmanskaya Street.

Los Angeles. August 1979.
Yan and I were invited to a casual Sunday brunch at the house of a woman who volunteered at UCLA as an ESL teacher.

Our impressions:
Who wants to live out in the boonies, away from civilization?
(The house was in the Hollywood Hills, one of the most affluent neighborhoods in Los Angeles.)
What is meatloaf? Seems like a large kotleta (meatball).
A salad with nothing but leaves? That's peculiar.
Everyone is wearing bathing suits in someone else's house! That's a little bizarre, even though she said, "Feel free to bring your bathing suit. The pool will be warm."

Other guests' and the hostess's impression (guessing):
Why are these two dressed for a swim party like they're going out to dinner?

Los Angeles. November 1979.
Our first car. Zhenya is sitting on the roof. Yan is to his right, and *Babushka* Rita is to his left. Inside the car is Yan's niece.

Los Angeles. December 1982. Alik is eight months old. I took this photo to reassure my parents (especially Mama) that Alik is well fed, as if it wasn't obvious from his appearance.

Kiev. October 1980.
Inscribed by Mama to Zhenya: *Look (at this photo) and remember. On your 5th Birthday. To our sunny grandson. Sending kisses. Your Babushka and Dedushka.*

Kiev. September 1983.
Inscribed by Misha: *To my love Zhenya in memory. From Uncle.*
This must be the truck in which Misha "stole" Zhenya from *sadik*.

Kiev. c. 1985.
The infamous gardening scene in front of my parents' windows.

Kiev. 1983.
Inscribed by Misha: *In memory to Zhenichka (Zhenya) and Alinka (Alik) from Babushka, Dedushka, and Uncle Misha.*

Kiev. 1987.
Mama bids final goodbye to her husband of forty years. Her journey to
America begins here.

Above: Los Angeles
International Airport.
3 October, 1987.
Mama's arrival in America.
In front, left to right: Alik and
Zhenya.
First row (from left): Me,
Mama, Yan's mother Rita, Sofia,
Alla.
Second row (from left): Yan,
with Sofia's brother-in-law and
his wife.

Right: Mama and Zhenya
reunited.

San Gabriel, Califormia.
1989. Hanukkah presenta-
tion at Alik's school.

San Gabriel, California. 1989. After Zhenya's performance in the musical about Eastern European
immigrants.

Los Angeles. 1990. Zhenya and Alik at Zhenya's art show.

Kirovograd, Ukraine. 1993.
Misha with his daughter Katya.

Los Angeles. 1995. Alik's bar mitzvah. Mama with the boys.

Above: Los Angeles.
October 2010.
Uncle Vova came to Mama's
funeral service and spent
a week with us in our new
house.

Left: Los Angeles. May 2012.
Uncle Vova meeting our first
grandson, Nathan.

Carpinteria, California. July 2014.
Celebrating thirty-five years in America with family.
Left to right: Alik's wife Laurie, Alik (holding son Nathan), me, Yan,
Zhenya's wife Olga (holding daughter Ella), Zhenya.

July 2019. Los Angeles.
Celebrating forty years since our arrival to the USA at Alik and
Laurie's home.

Ella and Nathan.

Yan with Nathan, Ella, and
Liam.

Zhenya and me.

Zhenya's family:
Olga, Simon, Ella.

Alik's family:
Laurie, Nathan, Liam.

Santa Monica Beach, California. 2021. Three generations of Chernys.
Celebrating Yan's milestone birthday.
Left to right: Simon, Yan, me, Olga, Ella, Zhenya, Laurie, Nathan, Liam,
Alik.

Afterword

"Never Again Is Now"

*"History repeats itself, but in such cunning disguise
that we never detect the resemblance until the
damage is done."* — *Sydney J. Harris*

November 2021—Los Angeles

When I wrote my memoir, I omitted current political and social events. After all, the story was not about that; my story was about a young couple's exodus, about their escape from the life of anti-Semitism under the Communist regime—hidden from the rest of the world behind the Iron Curtain—and about the life they built in the Land of the Free. But my story is also a part of a larger Jewish story. A story of almost fifteen million Jews around the world and their ancestors; those who didn't get a chance to live out their stories and build their legacies because they perished from those who took part in the persecution and extermination of the Jewish people since the beginning of their time on earth, almost four thousand years ago. Today a surge of anti-Semitism across Europe, alienation of the Jewish state worldwide, and an unsettling trajectory toward anti-Semitism in my beloved America are all painfully familiar to the Jews.

We've been here before.

"History repeats itself" is a recognizable expression for most people. For the Jews, these words are full of the heavy burden of the past. Our freedom is fragile; it always has been. History repeated itself throughout centuries with more violence, more pogroms, the Holocaust, and the continued desire of many around the globe to annihilate the only Jewish state in the world—a tiny sliver of land, the size of New Jersey—a single spot of freedom and democracy in the Middle East, on a little-over-eight-thousand-square-mile piece of land.

Generations of Jews are scattered around the world today because their parents, grandparents, or great-grandparents fled their homes to escape violence, persecution, and terror. Since the State of Israel was established in 1948, Jews knew they had a home whether or not they lived in Israel. Living in America, I've always believed that outside of Israel, America is the safest place for the Jews to call home. It became clear over the years with examples and experiences, many of which made it onto the pages above. I was touched, time and time again, by how comfortable the non-Jews I came across talked about Jewish traditions they may have been familiar with, and how much they knew about the Jewish holidays.

A colleague once told me that her young daughter came home from school with a question: "Can I be Jewish?" In response to her mother's "why," she said: "Sara gets presents every day for eight days on Hanukkah, and I only get them one day on Christmas." My colleague told me this story with laughter—not an ounce of discomfort—explaining that Sara was her daughter's best friend. If you guessed I teared up listening, you would be right. After the experiences of my life in the USSR, I could never take friendliness toward Jews for granted.

Over the years, non-Jewish friends wished me Happy Hanukkah and Merry Christmas in the same breath. I thanked them and shared my "Rabbi and the Christmas tree" story, and they wished me Merry Christmas again the following year. Some Jews get offended by the Merry Christmas greeting, but I never have. With the Jewish population in the US accounting for two and a half percent, the fact that people know anything about Jewish life is astonishing. I love this about America. It took years for me to stop cringing with embarrassment when asked about Jewish traditions and holidays and to finally see that there was nothing wrong with being Jewish. It also became natural to wish friends Merry Christmas and Happy Easter and take part in their celebrations as if they were my own.

As I watch with anguish the anti-Semitic events of today, a memory of one conversation with my mother fifteen years ago comes to mind. At eighty-five, she was still sharp and independent but for the occasional moments—later recognized as early signs of dementia—when she brought up stories and topics, seemingly out of place. "Don't display a mezuzah, put away your Magen David, and hide your menorah," she said one day. When I asked why, she explained, lowering her voice: "*They* will find out Jews live in this house. You don't want *them* to find out the Jews live in this house." I laughed. "Who is the 'they,' Mama? There is no 'they' in America."

Could I still declare: "There is no 'they' in America"? Yes. By and large, that is true today.

But "history repeats itself" is not just a slogan—it does so with a vengeance if we ignore the early signs. Hitler would have gone after the rest of the world in WWII if twenty million military personnel hadn't died stopping him. But because the world ignored the early signs, besides the military loss, fifty-five million civilians perished from genocide, massacres, mass bombings, disease, and starvation. Six million of them were Jews.

History repeats itself.

I hope most Americans would not stand by while their Jewish neighbors and friends are verbally and physically assaulted, whether it's in America or elsewhere in the world. I hope my grandchildren will be free to wear the Star of David, have a menorah on display in their homes, and hang a mezuzah at every door in their house if they choose to do so. They will freely celebrate Jewish holidays, eat matzah in the daylight, and have Jewish weddings under the chuppah. They will embrace their heritage and respect the heritage of others. They will rejoice, celebrating Christmas with their family and friends who are not Jewish and fill their homes with Jews and non-Jews to observe their beloved Holidays, retelling my story of the "Rabbi and the Christmas tree," and thanking America for all her blessings at Thanksgiving.

"If I am not for myself, who will be for me? If I am not for others, what am I? And if not now, when?"
— Rabbi Hillel

"Don't Call Me Russian"

April 2022—Los Angeles

Thursday, February 24, 2022, Russia invaded Ukraine.

News channels and social media reported that in the early hours of the morning, explosions were heard in Kyiv, Kharkiv, Odesa, and Donbas. Kyiv! I dialed my friend, hoping to find out this was all a big misunderstanding and she and her children were safe in their apartment in Obolon District, tucked away from the city center on the left bank of the Dnieper River. I was hoping to hear all was well, as another frigid winter day in Kyiv had begun.

But it wasn't a misunderstanding. Forty-four million people in Ukraine woke up to a nightmare resembling the old WWII movies

I watched growing up in the USSR. It wasn't a misunderstanding. And it wasn't a movie. Russian planes flew over the Ukrainian sky as Nazi Germany did in 1941, bombing and burning schools, hospitals, orphanages, residential buildings, and everything else in sight. Russian tanks, marked with signs resembling a half-swastika, rolled through a frosted land that wasn't theirs, murdering civilians, raping women and children. Destroying lives. Together with millions around the world, I watched in horror the devastation in Kyiv, Kharkiv, Mariupol, and Irpin. The bombings of several train stations as thousands were trying to flee to safety, the explosion at Babi Yar, which vandalized a sacred spot and killed a family of four as they walked nearby holding hands. Ukrainian cities, streets, and sites, once unknown to most outside of Ukraine and Russia, overnight became household names for the most gruesome of reasons.

This is not happening. I can't fathom it.

I began my memoir by revealing how difficult it was for me to explain my Soviet identity. Russian or Ukrainian? "I am neither," I said dozens of times. That was what I was told by my country. I was a Jew born in Kiev, then the capital of Soviet Ukraine. But I was no Ukrainian. Even after the fall of the Soviet Union, Americans I came across linked my origin to Russia, and often I didn't object. Russian. Ukrainian. Whatever was easier to agree to in the moment. Conveying the anti-Semitic logic of Stalin and his totalitarian cohort to free-thinking people was exhausting. And why? They certainly wouldn't think to identify a Jew differently.

In the USSR, the Russian-Ukrainian identification was the opposite of the Jewish one. Russians and Ukrainians were the same people. Nations-Brothers. *Narody-Brat'ya.* Most spoke Russian, ate the same food, drank the same vodka, and, above all, used the same profanities with identical, relentless passion. Those who have been following the war coverage probably noticed this sameness by now. Many Russians and Ukrainians had families in both states.

They intermarried with ease. There was no distinction when a Russian dated or married a Ukrainian or the other way around. Now, Russian or Ukrainian dating or marrying a Jew was always noted and often judged. I have never given a thought to which of my friends were Russians and which were Ukrainians. They all knew they were friends with a Jew, however. But that was then.

I have now lived in America for almost forty-three years. I stopped following the politics of Russia and Ukraine a long time ago—I was disconnected from their current events and cared very little about what was happening in the countries of the former USSR. I never believed they would steer toward democracy. Between the Soviet-like Russia's regime of brainwashing and information suppression, the events of Ukrainian corruption, and reports of increased anti-Semitism, in my mind, very little has changed in that part of the world. And I didn't care to take sides—I was an American, and those were foreign countries, each with its problems.

My concern grew with America when I noticed a tendency to shut down "unpopular" points of view in the press, on social media, and in the corporate world. When I watched people being attacked and fired from their jobs for expressing their take on policies, politics, and the social aspects of life. I feared we were on the verge of betraying the First Amendment, which guarantees all Americans freedom to speak their mind. It protects those whose opinions we disagree with. Otherwise, it would be pointless to have the First Amendment. I feel compelled to state this obvious point because, now that Russia's totalitarian policies of information and speech suppression are exposed to the entire world, we must take notice. We must protect America from falling anywhere near the vicinity of such life.

As I write this, it has now been forty-six days since the war began. The recount of atrocities is beyond human comprehension. We may not know the exact number of civilian deaths for a long time, if ever. Nine hundred dead and 1,500 thousand wounded are accounted for so far. Over four million Ukrainians, mostly women with children, have fled Ukraine to neighboring Poland through the only available escape corridor. The lucky ones caught a train that took them part of the way or drove a car until it ran out of gas, walking an additional two or three days to reach the border, with no food or water, under continuous air attacks by the Russian forces. In the thick of the fierce Ukrainian winter, people have run from their homes or what's left of them with little more than a suitcase and, often, a pet. Many seek refuge throughout Europe; some try to make their way to Canada, Australia, or the United States. Most want to return home someday soon.

In Russia, a twenty-first-century version of the Iron Curtain is coming down hard as those opposing Putin try to flee, while others hide in fear of retribution for thinking outside the party lines (few speak out), and the rest, who believe their *vozhd,* leader, of the last twenty-plus years, continue to pledge solidarity with Volodya, sing praises to him and Mother Russia, and blame the Ukrainians for provoking the war.

The world I am from is in crisis, the likes of which we have not seen since WWII, and the world at large will never be the same. Today, I have no choice but to reevaluate my position of not caring for either side, and I must choose. Today, when the Russian Army storms through Ukrainian cities and villages, killing innocent people, raping Ukrainian women, and burning their homes, I cry for my beloved Kyiv as if I were Ukrainian. I cry for the Ukrainians and the Russians, who wake up in terror each morning since February 24. I cry for the Jews of Ukraine and Russia. And I take sides.

Next time someone asks where I am from, my answer will be: "I am from Kyiv, Ukraine. Please don't call me Russian."

Acknowledgments

My first gratitude is to my husband, Yan. You've been telling me for years, "You have to write a book." When I finally began writing despite petrifying fear, you encouraged me daily to keep going. And when I saw tears in your eyes as you read the first clumsy draft of each chapter, I knew I wouldn't stop until the book was finished. As in many other aspects of my life, your encouragement and support meant everything. For that and a million other ways you show you believe in me, I love you.

Eugene, my Zhenechka! You inspired me to write our story long before I began writing. Over the years, you listened to me reminiscing of the life you were a part of as a little boy, asking me to tell you more. Thank you for editing parts of my writing with so much care. Your very presence in my life created a story I could've never imagined. I love you.

Alex, Alusha! My first American. My creative partner. Thank you for investing your time and your talent in my project. I cried when I saw the draft of the book cover you designed. You captured the essence of my emotions and of that moment, on the train station. You astonished me with your deep connection to our past of which you only heard and not lived. I love you.

Dearest Juliette Fechter. My very first writing coach. Thank you for encouraging me to begin. To keep going. Thank you for engaging so passionately in the story I was trying to tell. I would hesitate much more if it weren't for you. I am so very grateful to you.

My editors, Sara Kocek with Yellow Bird Editors and Flo Selfman with WordsalaMode.com, thank you for helping me transform a messy manuscript into an actual book. I am beholden to both of you.

My beta readers, friends, and family, I appreciate the time you invested in reading my manuscript, sharing your thoughts and insights, and listening to my endless recounts of the steps I took toward publishing my first memoir. I love you all.

Made in United States
North Haven, CT
01 October 2023

42226911R00196